STUDY GUIDE on SHAKESPEARE'S

HAMLET

MADE SUPER SUPER EASY

TEXT EXPLAINED IN GREAT DETAIL

ACHIEVE TOP GRADES
A MUST FOR ALL STUDENTS

EVELYN SAMUEL on Shakespeare

Shakespeare's Hamlet
Made Super Super Easy
First Edition Published by Evelyn Samuel

EveMadeSuperEasyBooks
www.EveSuperEasyBooks.com
evesupereasybooks@gmail.com

DEDICATED TO

My brother Vincent Samuel
Thanks for being a great role model to me

You've shared my joys and sorrows
My laughter and my tears
You've been my inspiration
As we grew up through the years

REVIEWS

★★★★★ **The Book to Buy on Hamlet**
Reviewed 19 December 2021
Everything you need to know about Shakespeare's play Hamlet to achieve top grade!

★★★★★ **Amazing!!**
Reviewed 20 February 2022
This book is amazing with all the information you need to understand Shakespeare's Hamlet.

PREFACE

To all students reading my study guide **HAMLET made super super easy**. I do hope that my wealth of information will assist you to achieve the highest possible grades. I have formulated a unique structure where detailed explanations are next to the text to make it super super easy for you to connect and understand the book, and to revise without the need to resort to more than one book.

Each ACT is defined by a Summary followed by in-depth explanations which are highlighted with relevant important quotes. Within the explanations, connotated meaning, imagery, symbolism, and linguistic devices are identified.

A detailed explanation of each main character in the book is provided so that the fabric of their relationships can be better understood. To further create understanding, the Structure, Form, Language, and Themes within the play are explored. Typical exam questions are included to give some idea of the scope sought by the Exam Boards. Further details can be found in the Specification published by each Exam Board on their websites.

Finally, sample essays are provided to give you some idea of the standard expected by the Exam Boards.

Good Luck with your studies and your exam results.

FOREWARD

What a super super easy way to study and understand Shakespeare's **HAMLET**. No need to match text with explanation when both are next to each other.

I really enjoyed looking left at the text and right at the explanation. The structure and content of this fantastic book is a solid base to get to grip with the revenge, the madness, the supernatural, and final demise of ALL involved, where Hamlet's encounter with the ghost of his dead father, the King of Denmark, makes him take revenge on the usurper Claudius, King Hamlet's younger brother. Tragically, Hamlet's mother Queen Gertrude, Hamlet's love Ophelia, Ophelia's father Polonius and brother Laertes are killed as well. Through sleight of hand, Hamlet's treacherous schoolfellows Rosencrantz and Guildenstern are executed instead of him.

I can definitely recommend this study guide to all students, and hope they gain as much insight, as I did, into Shakespeare's **HAMLET**.

Teacher of English

BOOKS PUBLISHED IN THE SERIES
MADE SUPER SUPER EASY

Shakespeare's
MACBETH
ROMEO AND JULIET
OTHELLO
HAMLET

Priestley's
AN INSPECTOR CALLS

Dickens'
A CHRISTMAS CAROL

SOON TO FOLLOW IN THE SERIES
MADE SUPER SUPER EASY

Shakespeare's
THE TEMPEST
TWELFTH NIGHT
A MIDSUMMER'S NIGHT DREAM
THE MERCHANT OF VENICE

www.EveSuperEasyBooks.com
EveSuperEasyBooks@gmail.com

CONTENT

INTRODUCTION

SHAKESPEARE

William Shakespeare was a renowned English playwright, poet, and actor born in 1564 in the town of Stratford-upon-Avon during the Elizabethan and Jacobean ages of British theatre. The play Hamlet was Shakespeare's fourth tragedy play written circa 1600. It is considered one of his most popular works where a prince seeks revenge for the death of his murdered father by his uncle, and the betrayal of his mother for wedding this uncle. Hamlet is alerted to the murder by a ghost. By feigning madness, Hamlet survives until his uncle is exposed as a murderer. Hamlet takes revenge and kills his uncle but is himself mortally wounded by a poisoned blade. Hence the tragedy together with other tragic and vengeful deaths in the play. Notable quotes include 'To be, or not to be, that is the question'. Shakespeare died circa 1616.

CONTEXT

England in circa 1600 was approaching the end of the Tudor age. Queen Elizabeth the First died in 1603. England was a Christian country where religion instructed the people in their duty to God and to themselves. Births, Baptisms, Marriage, and funerals were the fabric of society. Education was for the rich or those of scholarship calibre, progressing through Grammar schools, with few attending University. Latin was the Scholars' language. Drama was the great art form of the Elizabethan age where plays were performed by groups of male actors. In 1576, the first playhouse was established in London, followed in 1599 by the Globe playhouse located in Southwark on the south bank of London's River Thames, where most of Shakespeare's plays were performed, including Hamlet. Not all religious factions were in favour of theatres, considering them dens of iniquities. Not until 1642 were plays like Hamlet suppressed when England became a Republic under the Puritan Oliver Cromwell. With restoration of the monarchy in 1660 onwards, plays like Hamlet returned as theatres reopened. Although based on past events in history, Hamlet is a fictional play on a genre of much interest to Tudor audiences then as it is to audiences world-wide today – the genre of revenge.

THE PLAY

CHARACTERS

[VICTIMS of the TRAGEDY]

HAMLET	Prince of Denmark, son to the late King Hamlet
The GHOST	Deceased King of Denmark, murdered by his brother Claudius
CLAUDIUS	King of Denmark
GERTRUDE	Queen of Denmark, wife to Claudius, previous wife to King Hamlet
POLONIUS	Advisor to the King
OPHELIA	Daughter to Polonius
LAERTES	Son to Polonius
ROSENCRANTZ	Schoolfellow of Hamlet at Wittenberg
GUILDENSTERN	Schoolfellow of Hamlet at Wittenberg

[SURVIVORS of the TRAGEDY]

HORATIO	Trusted companion to Hamlet
REYNALDO	Servant to Polonius
OSRIC	Royal Courtier
VOLTEMAND	Danish Ambassador to Norway
CORNELIUS	Danish Ambassador to Norway
FORTINBRAS	Prince of Norway
The CAPTAIN	Norwegian soldier
FIRST PLAYER	acting the part of the king
SECOND PLAYER	acting the part of the queen
THIRD PLAYER	acting the part of the king's nephew Lucianus
FOURTH PLAYER	speaking the Prologue
MARCELLUS	Danish sentry
BARNARDO	Danish sentry
FRANCISCO	Danish sentry
GRAVEDIGGER	Digger of graves
OTHER	Companion to Gravedigger
PRIEST	Church official presiding over Ophelia's funeral

[EXTRAS]	Lords, Attendants, Servants, Sailors, English Ambassadors

SYNOPSIS

In Act I, the audience is introduced to an initial incident, termed **the Exposition**, where in five scenes the protagonist Hamlet learns through his trusted friend Horatio of a ghost stalking the castle battlements and later encounters the ghost on the castle battlements at midnight. Hamlet recognises the physical features of ghost as he father, who speaks to Hamlet seeking revenge on his murderous, incestuous brother Claudius who usurped the throne and married his widow, Gertrude. Meanwhile, Claudius dispatches his Ambassadors Voltemand and Cornelius to Norway to do their duty, but Hamlet agrees to not to return to his school in Wittenberg. Laertes is granted permission to return to France. He says goodbye to his sister Ophelia and father Polonius the trusted advisor to Claudius. Both warn Ophelia that Hamlet love may not be genuine, as he is above her social station.

In Act 2, the audience is introduced to a growth in tension, termed **the Rising Action**, where in two scene Polonius seeks to advance his position by spying on his son Laertes to ensure his behaviour is appropriate and not a hinderance to advancement, and bring to the attention of Claudius, Hamlet's wild infatuation towards his daughter Ophelia. In response, Claudius sends Rosencrantz and Guildenstern to discover Hamlet's true intent, but he begins to suspect that his two former school friends are agent provocateurs. The arrival of a troupe of players known to Hamlet gives him an idea to expose Claudius as a murderer and incestuous usurper by adapting a known play '*The Murder of Gonzago*'.

In Act 3, the audience is introduced to a climax, termed **the Climax**, where in four scenes Claudius is anxious to discover if Hamlet's madness is due to love or a threat to himself. He instructs Gertrude to arrange an interview with her son Hamlet while Polonius listens concealed behind an Arras. Meanwhile, Hamlet instructs the players on their forthcoming performance. The ruse works, and the adaptation causes Claudius to raise and remove himself from the performance, resulting in the Hamlet being summoned to his mother's chambers. On route Hamlet passes Claudius confessing his guilt in silent prayer. Hamlet is tempted to take revenge but reasons that this may send Claudius to heaven and leave his father in purgatory. Startled by a sudden noise in his mother's chamber, Hamlet stabs and kills Polonius hidden behind the Arras. He confronts he mother with accusations of lust and betrayal, but is interrupt by his father's ghost, the deceased husband of his mother, who rebukes him for his tirade against his mother. She is baffled because Hamlet seems to be talking to nobody.

In Act 4, the audience is introduced to an unravelling of the story, termed **the Falling Action**, where in seven scenes Gertrude tells Claudius about the murder of Polonius; Rosencrantz and Guildenstern are sent to find the body; Hamlet tells Claudius where to find the body; Claudius sends Hamlet to England with Rosencrantz and Guildenstern convinced that Hamlet is a threat to his throne sending sealed letters ordering Hamlet's immediate execution by the English King on his arrival; Hamlet encounters the Norwegian Prince Fortinbras on route to defeat the Poles with resolve, and questions his own resolve to not confronting Claudius direct and taking revenge as demanded by his father's ghost. Further, mad with grief, Ophelia roams the court singing and answering in riddles, and handing out flowers. Laertes her brother blames Hamlet for both his sister's madness and the death of his father Polonius. Claudius tells Laertes to be patience and together they will exact revenge. Meanwhile, Sailors deliver a letter to Horatio, where Hamlet relates his capture by pirates and escape. Rosencrantz and Guildenstern still hold their course for England. Hamlet instructs Horatio to delivery letters to Claudius and then to join him post haste. Finally, Claudius knows that Hamlet has returned to Denmark, and plots with Laertes to kill Hamlet in a duel with a bare tipped rapier dipped in poison, and if that should fail, get him to drink from a cup of poisoned wine. Enter Gertrude with the devastating news that Ophelia had drowned in a brook when a willow tree branch, she was sitting on broke.

In Act 5, the audience is introduced to resolution, termed **the Denouement**, where in two scenes Hamlet and Horatio philosophise about life and death; Hamlet picks up the skull of his father's court jester, Yorick and talks to it in a eulogy; Laertes leaps into Ophelia's grave onto her open coffin insisting to be buried with her, followed by Hamlet who grapples with him professing as much grief and love until separated by Attendants. Next day, Hamlet tells Horatio the full story of his sea crossing to England. How in the dark, the night before his capture by pirates, he entered Rosencrantz and Guildenstern cabin and discovered letters signed by Claudius ordering his immediate execution by the King of England. To placate this villainy, Hamlet wrote new letters, replacing his name with those of Rosencrantz and Guildenstern, authenticating it with his father's signet ring, so sealing their fate. Next day, Claudius sends Osric to invite Hamlet to a friendly duel with Laertes. At the end of the first bout, Claudius drops a poisoned coated pearl into a cup of wine to celebrate Hamlet's win inviting him to drink, but he declines. Instead at the end of the second bout, despite Claudius' warning to Gertrude not to drink, she drinks from the poisoned cup, to honour Hamlet's second win. At the start of the third bout, Laertes desperate to kill Hamlet, wounds him with his poisoned rapier, but in the scuffle, rapiers are exchanged, and Hamlet also wounds Laertes with the same poisoned rapier. Suddenly, Gertrude falls and declares she is poisoned by the drink. Gertrude dies. Mortally wounded, Laertes alerts Hamlet to Claudius' villainy. Hamlet then wounds Claudius with the poisoned rapier and forces him to drink the poisoned wine. Claudius dies, then Laertes dies. Mortally wounded, Hamlet dies telling Horatio the crown is to be passed to Prince Fortinbras, and make the events known to all. Fortinbras instructs four captains to bear Hamlet's body away in pomp and ceremony.

SETTING

The play is set in and around the remote royal residence at Elsinore castle, in Denmark, and on the road to England. It is set post 1502, the date when Hamlet's school at Wittenberg, was founded. Hamlet's initial scepticism about the Ghost's claim to be in purgatory fits in with the Protestant's believe of no such realm. This would seem to indicate the play is set post 1517, the date when Martin Luther founded Protestantism in Wittenberg. By Shakespeare's time, both England and Denmark were Protestant kingdoms.

Although the characters and events are fictional, they are based on murderous intent and intrigues exhibited during the 16th century.

FORM

Shakespeare's Hamlet takes the form of a play made up entirely of dialogue where the audience discover through words delivered by actors, the type of characters, their motives, their relationships together with the storyline.

Shakespeare's aim was to educate and entertain ordinary people in an age when few people could read - to draw out the emotions in people. In this case, to expose the dark side of human desire where jealousy, lust and ambition destroy people through connivance and deceit.

Shakespeare writes in prose and verse. Prose is normal speech without rhyme.
Verse always has a set rhyme and structure.

In Act 1 scene 1 line 26, the sentry **Marcellus** in **Prose** (normal speech)

> **Horatio say 'tis but our fantasy,**
> **And will not let belief take hold of him**

Blank verse is made up of roughly ten syllables of unrhymed iambic pentameter, organised into five groups of two, where an unstressed syllable is followed by a stressed syllable. This creates an air of authority and identifies higher status characters such as Hamlet from lower characters such as servants who speak in ordinary prose.

In Act 1 scene 2 line 1, Claudius in **Blank Verse** (iambic pentameter group 1, group 2):

> **Though yet of Ham-let our dear broth-er's death** (iambic syllables)

Rhyming verse is used by Shakespeare to end lines in a memorable way so that the audience recall it in later scenes; to make characters complete each other's rhymes to emphasise unity in thought, action, ideas, and moods between them. Hamlet frequently uses them in his monologues and soliloquies.

In Act 3 scene 3 line 95, **Hamlet** in **Rhyming Verse** (verse with homonym endings)

> **As hell, whereto it goes. My mother STAYS**
> **This physic but prolongs thy sickly DAYS**

STRUCTURE

The play *'Hamlet'* is edited into five Acts, each containing several scenes. The storyline is straightforward based on the classical five-part structure:

- an initial incident - termed **Exposition**
- a growth in tension - termed **Rising Action**
- a climax to the drama - termed **Climax**
- an unravelling of the plot - termed **Falling Action**
- a resolution to the drama - termed **Denouement**

There are no subplots and therefore the play conforms to the structure of place, action, and time. The action moves apace from the opening scene where Hamlet's father appears as a ghost to the watch manning the battlements of Elsinore castle, to the closing scene of carnage where first Hamlet's mother Gertrude is poisoned by wine, then Laertes mortally wounds Hamlet, who then mortally wounds him, and finally, in revenge, mortally wounds and poisons his uncle Claudius, The audience is spell-bound by the machinations which leads to this carnage of death, ending in Hamlet being borne away as a hero in ceremony and pomp and prince Fortinbras proclaimed the new king of Denmark.

The Soliloquy is a structure used by Shakespeare to present a deeper insight into the characters. The monologue informs others.

In Act 3 scene 1 line 56, **Hamlet** begins his **soliloquy** with:

"To be, or not to be, that is the question:"

In Act 1 scene 3 line 55, **Polonius** begins his **monologue** to his son Laertes:

"Yet here Laertes? Aboard, aboard for shame"

LANGUAGE

Shakespeare uses different language devices to create the atmosphere for revenge by the protagonist Hamlet and deceit by the antagonist Claudius.

The **device of Alliteration** is used in the play, to emphasise something important, in which a series of words begin with the same sound.

In Act 1 scene 5 line 43, the **Ghost** vilifies **Claudius**:

"With witchcraft of his wit, with traitorous gifts" (Alliteration)

The **device of Allusion** is used in the play to indirectly reflect and assess situations, to reveal feelings and emotions.

In Act 5 scene 1 line 237, **Laertes** reflect on the tragic death of his sister **Ophelia**:

"T'o'ertop old Pelion or the skyish head" (Allusion)
Of blue Olympus"

The **device of Anadiplosis** is used in the play to link phrases by ending one phrase with a word and starting the next with the same word.

In Act 3 scene 1 line 64, **Hamlet** in a soliloquy:

"To die, to sleep" (Anadiplosis)
To sleep, perchance to dream"

The **device of Anaphora and Repetition** is used in the play, to emphasise a particular aspect, in which a key idea is repeated more than once.

In Act 2 scene 2 line 115, **Polonius** reads **Hamlet's letter** to the **Claudius** and **Gertrude**.

"**Doubt** thou the stars are fire" (Anaphora & Repetition)
Doubt that the sun doth move
Doubt truth to be a liar
But never **doubt** I love"

The **device of Irony** is used in the play to create a contrast between the character's present situation and the action to come, thus creating audience anticipation and interest.

In Act 3 scene 1 line 14, **Rosencrantz** and **Guildenstern** report to **Claudius** and **Gertrude** nothing unexpected about **Hamlet's** motives

"Most free in his reply" (dramatic irony)

In Act 3 scene 2 line 120, **Hamlet** taunts **Ophelia**

"O God, your only jig-maker" (verbal irony)

In Act 3 scene 4 line 30, **Hamlet** thinks he has killed **Claudius** behind the Arras, but instead it is **Polonius**

"Is it the king?" (Situational irony)

The **device of Metaphor** is used in the play to compare one phrase by a similar phrase, thus creating a better understanding of the first phrase.

In Act 1 scene 5 line 39, the **Ghost** of Hamlet's father compares Claudius to a poisonous snake

"The serpent that did sting thy father's life (Metaphor irony)
Now wears his crown"

The **device of simile** is used in the play to make the attributes in one phrase equivalent to those in another phrase, thus creating a better understanding of the first phrase.

In Act 3 scene 3 line 16, **Rosencrantz** uses this simile to compare **Claudius** to a gulf of water where if he died others would die with him

"Dies not alone, but like a gulf doth draw (Simile irony)
What's near it with it."

The **device of imagery** is used in the play to create a visual picture of a character or event to enhance its impact.

In Act 4 scene 1 line 7, **Gertrude** describes the magnitude of **Hamlet's** madness

"Mad as the sea and wind when both contend (Simile irony)
Which is the mightier."

MONOLOGUE

The monologue is a literary device used by Shakespeare to express the inner thoughts and feelings of the characters in the play, so that the audience gains a better insight into the drama unfolding. The character speaks in the presence of one or more characters. Perhaps, the most famous soliloquy in Hamlet occurs in **Act 5 scene 1 line 169**. The Gravedigger hands Hamlet the skull of Yorick, his father's court jester. Hamlet laments his passing (Alas, poor Yorick) and state of preservation.

HAMLET

Monologue	ACT	scene	line	length	first line
1	1	4	14	22	Ay marry is't. But to my mind, I am native here
2	1	4	39	19	Angels and ministers of grace defend us!
3	2	2	291	15	*I have of late, but wherefore I know not,*
4	3	2	1	43	*Speak the speech, I pray you, I pronounced it to you,*
5	3	4	53	36	Look here upon this picture, and on this,
6	**5**	**1**	**169**	12	Alas, poor Yorick. I knew him, Horatio, a fellow of

CLAUDIUS

Monologue	ACT	scene	line	length	first line
1	1	2	87	31	*'Tis sweet and commendable in your nature, Hamlet,*

GERTRUDE

Monologue	ACT	scene	line	length	first line
1	4	7	166	18	*There is a willow grows aslant a brook,*

POLONIUS

Monologue	ACT	scene	line	length	first line
1	1	3	55	27	*Yet here, Laertes? Aboard, aboard for shame.*
2	1	3	115	21	*Ay, springes to catch woodcocks. I do know,*

LAERTES

Monologue	ACT	scene	line	length	first line
1	1	3	12	33	Think it no more. For nature crescent does not grow

HORATIO

Monologue	ACT	scene	line	length	first line
1	1	1	83	28	*That can I at least the whisper goes so: Our last king,*
2	1	1	115	14	*A mote it is to trouble the mind's eye*

GHOST

Monologue	ACT	scene	line	length	first line
1	1	5	9	14	*I am thy father's spirit,*
2	1	5	42	50	*Ay, that incestuous, that adulterate beast,*

SOLILOQUY

The Soliloquy is a literary device used by Shakespeare to express the inner thoughts and feelings of the characters in the play, so that the audience gains a better insight into the drama unfolding. Unlike the monologue, the character speaks to her or himself. Perhaps, the most famous soliloquy in Hamlet occurs in **Act 3 scene 1 line 56**. Hamlet is in turmoil questioning what he should do next. Should he persevere in his struggle for revenge and love (**to be**) or kill himself (**not to be**) and accept eternal sleep leaving the pain and agony of life behind.

HAMLET

Soliloquy	ACT	scene	line	length	first line
1	1	2	129	31	*O that this too too solid flesh would melt,*
2	1	5	91	21	*O all you host of heaven! O earth! what else?*
3	2	2	534	59	*Ay, so, God b' wi' ye!*
4	**3**	**1**	**56**	35	*To be, or not to be: that is the question:*
5	3	2	372	11	*'Tis now the very witching time of night,*
6	3	3	73	24	*Now might I do it pat now he is praying,*
7	4	4	33	34	*How all occasions do inform against me*

CLAUDIUS

Soliloquy	ACT	scene	line	length	first line
1	3	3	37	37	*O, my offence is rank, it smells to heaven;*

OPHELIA

Soliloquy	ACT	scene	line	length	first line
1	3	1	150	12	*O, what a noble mind is here o'erthrown!*

HORATIO

Soliloquy	ACT	scene	line	length	first line
1	5	2	352	2	*O Now cracks a noble heart. Good night, sweet prince,*

TEXT AND EXPLANATION

The Shakespearean text is written in the left column, and the explanation and interpretation, in the right column.

Important quotes and phrases in the text are highlighted and reproduced in the explanation column for discussion, on the same page. Consequently, there is no need to turn pages!

A summary of each Scene precedes the text and explanation to give an overall perspective of the events in the play.

In Act 1 scene 1, the setting is the battlements of Elsinore castle, on a bitter cold silent night around midnight. On sentry duty are Barnardo and Francisco.

Enter Marcellus to relieve Francisco. With him is Horatio whom he had invited to witness a supernatural event experienced by him and the two sentries on the previous night, a ghostly figure with the features of the dead King, Prince Hamlet's father.

As the castle bell beats one, from the direction of a star westward from the pole, enters the Ghost. Marcellus and Barnardo ask Horatio to mark its likeness to the dead King, and to challenge it but the Ghost exits.

Horatio confirms the likeness and armour the dead King had worn when he slayed Fortinbras, King of Norway, well ratified by law and heraldry.

They debate the timing and meaning of this ghostly apparition and wonder whether it is a harbinger of heaven and earth.

Without warning, the Ghost reappears, spreading its arms. Again, Horatio ask the Ghost to speak and made its intent known.

The cock, the trumpet to the morn, crows and it is gone. Marcellus thinks no spirit dare stir abroad once the cock crows, but Horatio is not so sure.

Superstition reigns. Horatio commands that they should impart what they had seen to Prince Hamlet, as the spirit is dumb to them.

TEXT ACT 1 scene 1

*The castle at **Elsinore**.*
A platform upon the battlements

*<Enter **BARNARDO** and **FRANCISCO**, and two sentinels>*

BARNARDO
Who's there?
FRANCISCO
Nay, answer me. Stand and unfold yourself.
BARNARDO
Long live the king!
FRANCISCO
Barnardo?
BARNARDO
He.
FRANCISCO
You come most carefully upon your hour.
BARNARDO
'Tis now struck twelve. Get thee to bed, Francisco.
FRANCISCO
For this relief much thanks. 'Tis bitter cold,And I am sick at heart.
BARNARDO
Have you had quiet guard?
FRANCISCO
Not a mouse stirring.
BARNARDO
Well, good night.
If you do meet Horatio and Marcellus,
The rivals of my watch, bid them make haste.
FRANCISCO
I think I hear them. — Stand, ho! Who's there?

*<Enter **HORATIO** and **MARCELLUS**>*

HORATIO
Friends to this ground.
MARCELLUS
And liegemen to the Dane.
FRANCISCO
Give you good night.
MARCELLUS
O, farewell, honest soldier.
Who hath reliev'd you?
FRANCISCO
Barnardo has my place.
Give you good night.

*<Exit **FRANCISCO**>*

EXPLANATION

*The castle at **Elsinore***

In this opening scene Shakespeare creates an ominous and eerie atmosphere. This sets the tone and the pace of the mysterious events to follow like the arrival of the King's ghost. Barnardo and Francisco are keeping watch at Elsinore Castle. Shakespeare also creates suspense and tension when Barnardo and Francisco nervously ask

"Who's there?"

This can foreshadow the arrival of the ghost and the mystery surrounding it. The use of the pathetic fallacy, " 'Tis bitter cold" also adds to the enigma of this scene. The guards' short and snappy speech is broken – it does not flow, and it lacks a certain rhythm. One can detect a nervousness and tension in their voices as though they are afraid of something. Their constant questioning,

"Stand, ho! Who's there?" Suggests this.

The striking of the clock at twelve is generally associated with ghosts and Francisco's very poignant utterance,

"And I am sick at heart."

Is important because it foreshadows the underlying theme of psychological, physical, and mental deterioration in the play.
Horatio and Marcellus swear their allegiance to king and country, "Friends to this ground.

Marcellus says, "O, farewell, honest soldier."

This can also foreshadow the underlying themes of 'Honesty' and 'deceit' that runs throughout the play.

MARCELLUS
Holla, Barnardo.
BARNARDO
Say what, is Horatio there?
HORATIO
A piece of him.
BARNARDO
Welcome, Horatio. —Welcome, good Marcellus.
MARCELLUS
What, has this thing appeared again tonight?
BARNARDO
I have seen nothing.
MARCELLUS
Horatio says 'tis but our fantasy
And will not let belief take hold of him,
Touching this dreaded sight twice seen of us.
Therefore I have entreated him along
With us to watch the minutes of this night,
That if again this apparition come,
He may approve our eyes and speak to it.
HORATIO
Tush, tush, 'twill not appear.
BARNARDO
Sit down a while,
And let us once again assail your ears,
That are so fortified against our story,
What we have two nights seen.
HORATIO
Well, sit we down,
And let us hear Barnardo speak of this.
BARNARDO
Last night of all,
When yond same star that's westward from the Pole
Had made his course t' illume that part of heaven
Where now it burns, Marcellus and myself,
The bell then beating one —

*<Enter the **GHOST** in armour>*

MARCELLUS
Peace, break thee off.
Look where it comes again!
BARNARDO
In the same figure like the king that's dead.
MARCELLUS (*to Horatio*)
Thou art a scholar. Speak to it, Horatio.
BARNARDO
Looks it not like the king? Mark it, Horatio.

The sense of tension is clearly heightened here when the men discuss the appearance of the ghost.

"What, has this thing appeared again tonight?"

Note that the guards treat the ghost as an inanimate object which has no value, calling it, 'this thing'. Yet we learn that it is the ghost of the dead king – old Hamlet.

Marcellus says that Horatio is sceptical of the ghost and says that it's just their imagination,

" 'tis but our fantasy."

He therefore decided to invite Horatio to come and keep watch with them. If he sees it then it will be a confirmation of its existence and he can speak to it,

"He may approve our eyes and speak to it."

Horatio is adamant that the ghost will not appear,

"Tush, tush, 'twill not appear."

Barnardo urges Horatio to sit down and listen to their encounter with the ghost.

"And let us once again assail your ears,"

Barnardo begins his tale about the ghost and reveals how they saw the ghost last night at one o'clock. As he was talking, he stopped his sentence in mid-air because the ghost enters.

"The bell then beating one —."

They all agree that the ghost looks like the dead king and Horatio says that it does, and it scares, 'harrows' him.

"In the same figure like the king that's dead."

Marcellus asks Horatio to speak to the ghost since he is educated and would know how to liaise with the ghost,

"Thou art a scholar."

HORATIO
Most like. It harrows me with fear and wonder.
BARNARDO
It would be spoke to.
MARCELLUS
Question it, Horatio.
HORATIO
What art thou that usurp'st this time of night,
Together with that fair and warlike form
In which the majesty of buried Denmark
Did sometimes march?
By heaven, I charge thee, speak.
MARCELLUS
It is offended.
BARNARDO
See, it stalks away.
HORATIO
Stay! Speak, speak! I charge thee, speak!

*<Exit **GHOST**>*

MARCELLUS
'Tis gone and will not answer.
BARNARDO
How now, Horatio? You tremble and look pale.
Is not this something more than fantasy?
What think you on 't?
HORATIO
Before my God, I might not this believe
Without the sensible and true avouch
Of mine own eyes.
MARCELLUS
Is it not like the king?
HORATIO
As thou art to thyself.
Such was the very armour he had on
When he the ambitious Norway combated.
So frowned he once when, in an angry parle,
He smote the sledded Polacks on the ice.
'Tis strange.
MARCELLUS
Thus twice before, and jump at this dead hour,With
martial stalk hath he gone by our watch.
HORATIO
In what particular thought to work I know not,
But in the gross and scope of mine opinion
This bodes some strange eruption to our state.

Bernardo says that it wants us to speak to it and Marcellus urges Horatio to question the ghost. Note the use of the repetition 'It' when referring to the ghost as though it has no value or credence.

Horatio very boldly addresses the ghost and enquires of who it is and why it walks about so late at night dressed in the old King's military uniform.

"What art thou that usurp'st this time of night."

The ghost, taking offence stalks away whilst Horatio commands it to speak, to no avail.

Barnardo notices a visual change in Horatio,

"You tremble and look pale."

Barnardo is now satisfied that Horatio is convinced that the ghost is not,

"something more than fantasy"

Shakespeare uses sensory imagery to describe Horatio's utter disbelief at actually witnessing the presence of the ghost.

"Without the sensible and true avouch
Of mine own eyes."

Horatio confirms that the ghost resembles the King wearing the same armour when he fought the King of Norway and wearing the same frown when he attacked the Poles. Marcellus confirms that the ghost comes at a specific time, and he stalks by them like a bold soldier,

"With martial stalk hath he gone by our watch."

Horatio is very intelligent and perceptive and says that he thinks that this won't bode well for the country and that something strange is going to happen. It's as though he had a premonition.

"This bodes some strange eruption to the state."

Note the tense atmosphere that Shakespeare creates with the arrival of the ghost.

MARCELLUS

Good now, sit down and tell me, he that knows,
Why this same strict and most observant watch
So nightly toils the subject of the land,
And why such daily cast of brazen cannon
And foreign mart for implements of war,
Why such impress of shipwrights, whose sore task?
Does not divide the Sunday from the week.
What might be toward, that this sweaty haste
Doth make the night joint laborer with the day?
Who is 't that can inform me?

HORATIO

That can I.
At least, the whisper goes so: our last king,
Whose image even but now appeared to us,
Was, as you know, by Fortinbras of Norway,
Thereto prick'd on by a most emulate pride,
Dared to the combat; in which our valiant Hamlet
(For so this side of our known world esteemed him)
Did slay this Fortinbras, who by a sealed compact
Well ratified by law and heraldry,
Did forfeit, with his life, all those his lands
Which he stood seiz'd of to the conqueror,
Against the which a moiety competent
Was gaged by our king, which had return'd
To the inheritance of Fortinbras
Had he been vanquisher, as, by the same cov'nant
And carriage of the article design'd,
His fell to Hamlet. Now, sir, young Fortinbras,
Of unimproved mettle, hot and full,
Hath in the skirts of Norway here and there
Shark'd up a list of lawless resolutes,
For food and diet, to some enterprise
That hath a stomach in 't, which is no other—
As it doth well appear unto our state—
But to recover of us, by strong hand
And terms compulsatory those foresaid lands
So by his father lost. And this, I take it,
Is the main motive of our preparations,
The source of this our watch, and the chief head
Of this posthaste and rummage in the land.

Marcellus is curious about all the activities surrounding him. He enquires why there are so many guards on patrol, why so many weapons are being bought and why shipbuilders are so busy working on a Sunday. Note the biblical imagery,

"Does not divide the Sunday from the week."

The Sabbath day in the Bible was meant to be holy according to the fourth commandment. The mere fact that the King is allowing his men to work on the Sabbath shows that he has no regard for religious rules. In Hamlet's country – Denmark, religious rules abounded yet the King flouted these rules and the "Divine rights of Kings," by killing the King and usurping the throne. Hamlet says, (Act 1 scene 5 line 196),

"O cursed spite,
That ever I was born to set it right."

One can connote that Hamlet is trying to restore the divine order of Majesty by avenging his father's death and hence restoring order in a chaotic Denmark.

We have two conflicting ideologies as Horatio explains that the late king was a rival of Fortinbras, who was the ruling monarch of Norway. Old Hamlet killed King Fortinbras in a battle and laid claim lawfully to all his land.

"Well ratified by law and heraldry,
Did forfeit, with his life all those his lands."

Now young Fortinbras,

"Of unimproved mettle, hot and full."

who is bold and erratic has now gathered up a bunch of lawless scoundrels to fight to regain the lands that his father had lost.

He is adopting a more unlawful and ferocious approach than his father did. Hence, Horatio explains, is the reason for all the unexplained activity around them – a preparation for war against young Fortinbras and his 'army.'

BARNARDO
I think it be no other but e'en so.
Well may it sort that this portentous figure
Comes armed through our watch so like the king
That was and is the question of these wars.
HORATIO
A mote it is to trouble the mind's eye.
In the most high and palmy state of Rome,
A little ere the mightiest Julius fell,
The graves stood tenantless and the sheeted dead
Did squeak and gibber in the Roman streets
As stars with trains of fire and dews of blood,
Disasters in the sun, and the moist star
Upon whose influence Neptune's empire stands
Was sick almost to doomsday with eclipse.
And even the like precurse of fear'd events
As harbingers preceding still the fates
And prologue to the omen coming on,
Have heaven and earth together demonstrated
Unto our climatures and countrymen.

<*Enter the **GHOST***>

But soft, behold! Lo, where it comes again.
I'll cross it though it blast me. —Stay, illusion!

<*GHOST* *spreads his arms*>

If thou hast any sound or use of voice,
Speak to me.
If there be any good thing to be done
That may to thee do ease and grace to me,
Speak to me.
If thou art privy to thy country's fate,
Which happily foreknowing may avoid,
Oh, speak!
Or if thou hast up hoarded in thy life
Extorted treasures in the womb of earth,
For which, they say, you spirits oft walk in death,
Speak of it. Stay and speak! —Stop it, Marcellus

<*The **COCK** crows*>
MARCELLUS
Shall I strike at it with my partisan?
HORATIO
Do, if it will not stand.

BARNARDO, MARCELLUS, HORATIO
On the Battlements

Barnardo acknowledges that the current situation warrants for the ghost's appearance since he was responsible for causing these wars.

Horatio is obviously a learned scholar, and he relays shocking events when Julius Caesar, the emperor of Rome was assassinated. He states that corpses rose out of the graves, shooting stars and blood mixed with dew. He also talks about how nature was at odds with itself because the moon which controls the tides went completely out. This phenomenon can also be associated with the Divine Right of Kings being hampered. He also uses biblical imagery,

"And prologue to the omen coming on,
Have heaven and earth together demonstrated"

*Enter the **GHOST***

The ghost appears again, and Horatio very bravely attempts to communicate with it to no avail. They desperately try to make the ghost stay but the cock crows and it disappears. The crowing of the cock is a religious imagery – Jesus told Peter that he will deny him three times when the cock crows. The theme of betrayal surfaces here because this can be associated to the betrayal of the late king by Claudius.

TEXT ACT 1 scene 1

BARNARDO
'Tis here.
HORATIO
'Tis here.
*<Exit **GHOST**>*

MARCELLUS
'Tis gone.
We do it wrong, being so majestical,
To offer it the show of violence,
For it is, as the air, invulnerable,
And our vain blows malicious mockery.
BARNARDO
It was about to speak when the cock crew.
HORATIO
And then it started like a guilty thing
Upon a fearful summons. I have heard
The cock, that is the trumpet to the morn,
Doth with his lofty and shrill-sounding throat
Awake the god of day, and, at his warning,
Whether in sea or fire, in earth or air,
Th' extravagant and erring spirit hies
To his confine, and of the truth herein
This present object made probation.
MARCELLUS
It faded on the crowing of the cock.
Some say that ever 'gainst that season comes
Wherein our Saviour's birth is celebrated,
This bird of dawning singeth all night long.
And then, they say, no spirit dare stir abroad.
The nights are wholesome. Then no planets strike,
No fairy takes, nor witch hath power to charm,
So hallowed and so gracious is that time.
HORATIO
So have I heard and do in part believe it.
But look, the morn, in russet mantle clad,
Walks o'er the dew of yon high eastward hill.
Break we our watch up, and by my advice,
Let us impart what we have seen tonight
Unto young Hamlet, for, upon my life,
This spirit, dumb to us, will speak to him.
Do you consent we shall acquaint him with it,
As needful in our loves, fitting our duty?
MARCELLUS
Let's do 't, I pray, and I this morning know
Where we shall find him most conveniently.
<Exeunt>

EXPLANATION

The guards tried desperately to delay the ghost, they even decided to strike it with their sword, but the ghost disappears.

They immediately regret their actions because the ghost resembles the King,

"We do it wrong being so majestical,
To offer it the show of violence."

Their attempt at stalling the ghost was futile,

"And our vain blows malicious mockery"

Horatio says that the cock crowed, and the ghost was about to speak but acted like,

"a guilty thing
Upon a fearful summons"

The simile suggests that the ghost, upon hearing the cock crow acted like a person who had flouted the law and disappeared.

The constant repetition of the crowing of the cock can be symbolic because it heralds a new dawn. And maybe the ghost's intention is for a new dawn for Denmark and to restore it from its chaotic situation.

Marcellus says that during Christmas the cock crows all night so that no ghosts are around. Once again, we see that Christmas – the birth of Christ reveals a new beginning, a new birth suggested for Denmark's woes.

A new day has heralded and the metaphor,

"In russet mantle clad,"

suggests this.

They all agree to be loyal and show their love to Hamlet and go and tell him about the ghost.
Maybe the ghost will speak to him.

"Let us impart what we have seen tonight
Unto young Hamlet"

In Act 1 scene 2, the setting is the Council Chamber inside the castle, later in the morning, where on a flourish of trumpets, enters Claudius, King of Denmark, Gertrude, the Queen, Prince Hamlet's mother, the Council, including Voltemand and Cornelius, the Danish Ambassadors to Norway, Polonius, advisor to Claudius, with his son Laertes, Prince Hamlet dressed in black, with others.

The King addresses the Danish Court recounting the importance of continuity: by his marriage to Gertrude, the widow of his deceased brother; by the achievements of his deceased brother who defeated King Fortinbras and pathed the way for a new beginning with the young Prince Fortinbras.

The King bides farewell to his Ambassadors Voltemand and Cornelius and commends them to their duty in Norway.

The King grants permission to Laertes to return to France but asks Polonius if he agrees which he does.

The King and Queen quiz Hamlet about his dark mood caused by the death of his father. They beseech him to stay in Denmark rather than return to his schooling in Witterburg.

Hamlet in a soliloquy riles against his mother's hasty marriage to his father's brother Claudius. Enter Horatio, Marcellus, and Barnardo to tells Hamlet of the Ghost, and its likeness to his father.

Hamlet is convinced, and they arrange to meet on the battlements twixt eleven and twelve.

TEXT ACT 1 scene 2

The Council Chamber in the castle
A flourish of trumpets

*<Enter **CLAUDIUS**, King of Denmark,*
GERTRUDE**, the Queen, Prince **HAMLET
*and **COUNCILLORS** including **POLONIUS***
*and his son **LAERTES**>*

CLAUDIUS
Though yet of Hamlet our dear brother's death
The memory be green, and that it us befitted
To bear our hearts in grief and our whole kingdom
To be contracted in one brow of woe,
Yet so far hath discretion fought with nature
That we with wisest sorrow think on him
Together with remembrance of ourselves.
Therefore our sometime sister, now our queen,
Th' imperial jointress to this warlike state,
Have we—as 'twere with a defeated joy,
With an auspicious and a dropping eye,
With mirth in funeral and with dirge in marriage,
In equal scale weighing delight and dole—
Taken to wife. Nor have we herein barred
Your better wisdoms, which have freely gone
With this affair along. For all, our thanks.
Now follows that you know. Young Fortinbras,
Holding a weak supposal of our worth
Or thinking by our late dear brother's death
Our state to be disjoint and out of frame,
Colleagued with the dream of his advantage,
He hath not failed to pester us with message
Importing the surrender of those lands
Lost by his father, with all bonds of law,
To our most valiant brother. So much for him.

*<Enter **VOLTEMAND** and **CORNELIUS**>*

Now for ourself, and for this time of meeting
Thus much the business is: we have here writ
To Norway, uncle of young Fortinbras—
Who, impotent and bedrid, scarcely hears
Of this his nephew's purpose — to suppress
His further gait herein, in that the levies,
The lists, and full proportions are all made
Out of his subject; and we here dispatch
You, good Cornelius, and you, Voltemand,

EXPLANATION

King CLAUDIUS and Queen GERTRUDE presiding

Claudius' smooth speech here reeks of hypocrisy. He tries to use the power of persuasion to convince the people that his actions are benevolent. Yet it's a well-known fact that he killed his brother, usurped the throne, and married his wife. He talks of the memory of his,

"dear brother's death"

And that it's only natural to mourn his death but in doing so it is also very natural that we think about ourselves and to allow life to go on as normal,

"Together with remembrance of ourselves."

He had married his brothers' widow, something that an Elizabethan audience will view as incestuous. He uses a juxtaposed statement,

"With mirth in funeral and with dirge in marriage, In equal scale weighing delight and dole –
Taken to wife."

He is trying to get the people to acknowledge his behaviour as proper because he says that he had mixed feelings of sadness and happiness when he married the queen, which the people sanctioned,

"Your better wisdoms, which have freely gone
With this affair along."

Young Fortinbras is thinking that because the king is dead, the country is now in turmoil, and he hopes to wage war to regain all the land that his father had lost to the late king, and he insists that Claudius surrender it.

CLAUDIUS (*continues*)
For bearers of this greeting to old Norway,
Giving to you no further personal power
To business with the king more than the scope
Of these dilated articles allow.
(*gives them a paper*)
Farewell, and let your haste commend your duty.
CORNELIUS, VOLTEMAND
In that and all things will we show our duty.
CLAUDIUS
We doubt it nothing. Heartily farewell.

<*Exit **VOLTEMAND** and **CORNELIUS***>

And now, Laertes, what's the news with you?
You told us of some suit. What is 't, Laertes?
You cannot speak of reason to the Dane
And lose your voice.
What wouldst thou beg, Laertes,
That shall not be my offer, not thy asking?
The head is not more native to the heart,
The hand more instrumental to the mouth,
Than is the throne of Denmark to thy father.
What wouldst thou have, Laertes?
LAERTES
My dread lord,
Your leave and favour to return to France,
From whence though willingly I came to Denmark
To show my duty in your coronation,
Yet now, I must confess, that duty done,
My thoughts and wishes bend again toward France
And bow them to your gracious leave and pardon.
CLAUDIUS
Have you your father's leave? What says Polonius?
POLONIUS
He hath, my lord, wrung from me my slow leave
By labour-some petition, and at last
Upon his will I sealed my hard consent.
I do beseech you, give him leave to go.
CLAUDIUS
Take thy fair hour, Laertes. Time be thine,
And thy best graces spend it at thy will. —
But now, my cousin Hamlet, and my son—
HAMLET (*aside*)
A little more than kin and less than kind.
CLAUDIUS
How is it that the clouds still hang on you?

CLAUDIUS talking to CORNELIUS & VOLTEMAND

Claudius is trying to stop young Fortinbras to wage war against Denmark by writing to his uncle who is old and bedridden and who does not know of his Nephew's plans to invade. He gives the task of delivering the message to Voltemand and Cornelius.

Laertes requests permission from the king to go back to France which he left for his coronation. The king, together with Polonius' blessing grants Laertes permission to leave,

"Take thy fair hour, Laertes"

The king then turns his attention to Hamlet and calls him,

"my cousin Hamlet, and my son"

Note Hamlets' bitter-toned utterance, in his first appearance,

"A little more than kin and less than kind"

This foreshadows Hamlets' disgruntled feelings towards Claudius.
Claudius asks him why he is still grieving for his father.

"How is it that clouds still hang on you"

The audience is, right at the very outset, given an indication of Hamlets' troubled state of mind.

HAMLET
Not so, my lord. I am too much i' the sun.
GERTRUDE
Good Hamlet, cast thy nighted colour off,
And let thine eye look like a friend on Denmark.
Do not forever with thy vailed lids
Seek for thy noble father in the dust.
Thou know'st 'tis common. All that lives must die,
Passing through nature to eternity.
HAMLET
Ay, madam, it is common.
GERTRUDE
If it be,
Why seems it so particular with thee?
HAMLET
"Seems," madam? Nay, it is. I know not "seems."
'Tis not alone my inky cloak, good mother,
Nor customary suits of solemn black,
Nor windy suspiration of forced breath,
No, nor the fruitful river in the eye,
Nor the dejected 'haviour of the visage,
Together with all forms, moods, shapes of grief,
That can denote me truly. These indeed "seem,"
For they are actions that a man might play.
But I have that within which passes show,
These but the trappings and the suits of woe.
CLAUDIUS
'Tis sweet and commendable in your nature, Hamlet,
To give these mourning duties to your father.
But you must know your father lost a father,
That father lost, lost his, and the survivor bound
In filial obligation for some term
To do obsequious sorrow. But to persever
In obstinate condolement is a course
Of impious stubbornness. 'Tis unmanly grief.
It shows a will most incorrect to heaven,
A heart unfortified, a mind impatient,
An understanding simple and unschool'd.
For what we know must be and is as common
As any the most vulgar thing to sense –
Why should we in our peevish opposition
Take it to heart? Fie! 'Tis a fault to heaven,
A fault against the dead, a fault to nature,
To reason most absurd, whose common theme
Is death of fathers, and who still hath cried,
From the first corse till he that died today,

Gertrude's demeanour for a grieving widow will be seen with disdain in an Elizabethan audience.
She does not observe the expected period of mourning following her husband's death, neither is she clad in black which represents the symbol of mourning. Only Hamlet is clad in black, mourning clothes. She also married her husband's brother-which is frowned upon and seen as a forbidden union, within a very short period. This very cold, indifferent speech suggests that she got over her husband's death very quickly and is urging her son to do the same.

"Do not forever with thy vailed lids,
Seek for thy noble father in the dust."

The biblical imagery 'dust' can be a reference to Gods' creation of man, "ashes to ashes, dust to dust."

God created man with dust and now the king has returned to dust. She thinks he is no more, and she is unaware of his appearance as a ghost. Her explanation that,

"Thou know'st 'tis common. All that lives must die,
Passing through nature to eternity."

Can reiterate this.
The use of the intransitive verb 'seems' by Gertrude infuriates Hamlet. It can suggest that Hamlet is pretending to grieve. He goes on to chastise his mother by saying that his black mourning gear, moods, his weeping nor his downcast eyes can portray his real grief that he feels for his father's death.

"Together with all forms, moods, shapes of grief, That can denote me truly."

Claudius also rebukes Hamlet for his lengthy period of grief insisting that it is a crime against heaven, against the dead and a 'fault to nature'.
He goes on to say that he is stubborn, 'obstinate condolement' and unmanly to grieve for so long and that it's only natural for fathers to die.

" 'Tis a fault to heaven,
A fault against the dead, a fault to nature."

TEXT ACT 1 scene 2

CLAUDIUS (*continues*)

"This must be so." We pray you, throw to earth
This unprevailing woe, and think of us
As of a father. For let the world take note,
You are the most immediate to our throne,
And with no less nobility of love
Than that which dearest father bears his son
Do I impart toward you? For your intent
In going back to school in Wittenberg,
It is most retrograde to our desire.
And we beseech you, bend you to remain
Here in the cheer and comfort of our eye,
Our chiefest courtier, cousin, and our son.

GERTRUDE

Let not thy mother lose her prayers, Hamlet.
I pray thee, stay with us. Go not to Wittenberg.

HAMLET

I shall in all my best obey you, madam.

CLAUDIUS

Why, 'tis a loving and a fair reply.
Be as ourself in Denmark. —Madam, come.
This gentle and unforc'd accord of Hamlet
Sits smiling to my heart, in grace whereof
No jocund health that Denmark drinks today
But the great cannon to the clouds shall tell,
And the king's rouse the heavens shall bruit again,
Respeaking earthly thunder. Come away.

HAMLET listening to CLAUDIUS

*<Flourish. Exeunt all but **HAMLET**>*

HAMLET

Oh, that this too, too sullied flesh would melt,
Thaw, and resolve itself into a dew,
Or that the Everlasting had not fix'd
His canon 'gainst self-slaughter! O God, God!
How weary, stale, flat, and unprofitable
Seem to me all the uses of this world!

EXPLANATION

Claudius further insists that Hamlet,

"throw to earth
This unprevailing woe, and think of us
As a father."

He is to inherit the throne after he dies.

"You are the most immediate to the throne."

He declares his 'love' for Hamlet like a father.

"with no less nobility of love
Than that which dearest father bears his son"

He urges Hamlet not to go to school in Wittenberg and to stay and be his

"chiefest courtier, cousin and our son."

Hamlet agrees to stay as a dutiful son to please his mother.

Claudius expresses his joy at Hamlet's decision, and he plans to toast to it.

"This gentle and unforc'd accord of Hamlet
Sits smiling to my heart"

Claudius speaks very calmly and with a forked tongue to try to entice Hamlet into thinking that he is fair in his duties and actions. His speech is very bold and forth right. He speaks in unrhyming blank verse in iambic pentameter. His words which have a
Measured beat is blank and pretentious. We see the theme of appearance versus reality here because Claudius is merely pretending to be good.

In this very emotive soliloquy, we see Hamlet's overwhelming pain as he tries to make sense of the terrible turn of events surrounding him.
His first utterance is a desperate plea to God,

"O God, God!
How weary, stale, flat and unprofitable
Seem to me all the uses of this world!"

He seems tired of life and is fighting his inner conflicts because he is suddenly plunged into a chaotic situation since his father's death.

HAMLET (*continues*)

Fie on 't, ah fie! 'Tis an unweeded garden
That grows to seed. Things rank and gross in nature
Possess it merely. That it should come to this.
But two months dead—nay, not so much, not two.
So excellent a king, that was to this
Hyperion to a satyr.
So loving to my mother
That he might not beteem the winds of heaven
Visit her face too roughly. —Heaven and earth,
Must I remember? Why, she would hang on him
As if increase of appetite had grown
By what it fed on, and yet, within a month—
Let me not think on't. Frailty, thy name is woman! -
A little month, or ere those shoes were old
With which she followed my poor father's body,
Like Niobe, all tears. Why she, even she—

HAMLET in Soliloquy

His dilemma can be detected in the structure of his speech, which is fragmented and disjointed, suggesting his confused state of mind, and allowing us to delve deep into it. There are many pauses and exclamation marks reflecting his pain and dilemma.

He also speaks in blank verse but his speech unlike Claudius' has a painful disjointed rhythm to it. It is genuine and emotional reflecting his inner conflict and pain. The repeated hyphens are pauses in his speech, as though he is too pained to continue. His speech is also fragmented and disjointed like his confused and tortured mind.

Hamlet uses the imagery of a garden and compares his flesh to it. He says that it is akin to a neglected garden growing with only nasty weeds in it. He is referring to his inner turmoil and we see that he is grappling with the betrayal and immorality of his mother's and uncle's disgusting behaviour.

"That it should come to this.
But two months dead—nay, not so much, not two"

He portrays his father in a very positive light and draws a juxtaposition to his uncle,

"So excellent a king, that was to this
Hyperion to a satyr."

He calls his uncle a beast and tells us of his father's devotional love towards his mother.

We can also juxtapose Claudius' smooth, flowing speech – so controlled, forced and business like to Hamlet's speech which is riddled with punctuation and imagery. He calls desperately to heaven and earth to ease his pain,

"Heaven and earth,
Must I remember?"

These painful utterances reflect his utter confusion and his desperation. He even loses faith in women after his mother's sordid behaviour.

"Frailty thy name is women!"

He accuses women of being weak and frail.

HAMLET (*continues*)
O God, a beast that wants discourse of reason
Would hav' mourn'd longer—married with my uncle
My father's brother, but no more like my father
Than I to Hercules. Within a month,
Ere yet the salt of most unrighteous tears
Had left the flushing in her galled eyes,
She married— O most wicked speed, to post
With such dexterity to incestuous sheets!
It is not nor it cannot come to good,
But break, my heart, for I must hold my tongue.

*<Enter **HORATIO, MARCELLUS,** and **BARNARDO**>*

HORATIO
Hail to your lordship.
HAMLET
I am glad to see you well. —
Horatio? Or I do forget myself?
HORATIO
The same, my lord, and your poor servant ever.
HAMLET
Sir, my good friend, I'll change that name with you.
And what make you from Wittenberg, Horatio? —
Marcellus!
MARCELLUS
My good lord.
HAMLET
(*to Marcellus*) I am very glad to see you. —
(*to Barnardo*) Good even, sir.
(*to Horatio*) —But what, in faith,
make you from Wittenberg?
HORATIO
A truant disposition, good my lord.
HAMLET
I would not hear your enemy say so,
Nor shall you do mine ear that violence,
To make it truster of your own report
Against yourself. I know you are no truant.
But what is your affair in Elsinore?
We'll teach you to drink deep ere you depart.
HORATIO
My lord, I came to see your father's funeral.

A beast would have mourned longer,

"A beast that wants discourse of reason
Would hav' mourn'd longer."

He is also enraged at the speed at which his mother married his uncle, calling it incestuous,

"O most wicked speed, to post
With such dexterity to incestuous sheets!"

Note the hissing alliterative devices used to show his disgust at his mother's sexual behaviour. He spits out these words with venom. We also witness his mental pain because he is afraid of speaking his mind and incur the wrath of the king.
"But break my heart for I must hold my tongue"

Enter BARNARDO with MARCELLUS

He also accuses his mother of pretending to cry for his father and compares her to Niobe – who was, in Greek Mythology mourning the loss of her children as punishment for her pride. Hamlet pours out his grief to Horatio,
"Horatio? Or I do forget myself?"

HAMLET talking to HORATIO

TEXT ACT 1 scene 2

HAMLET
I pray thee, do not mock me, fellow student.
I think it was to see my mother's wedding.
HORATIO
Indeed, my lord, it followed hard upon.
HAMLET
Thrift, thrift, Horatio! The funeral bak'd meats
Did coldly furnish forth the marriage tables.
Would I had met my dearest foe in heaven?
Or ever I had seen that day, Horatio.
My father—methinks I see my father.
HORATIO
Where, my lord?
HAMLET
In my mind's eye, Horatio.
HORATIO
I saw him once. He was a goodly king.
HAMLET
He was a man. Take him for all in all.
I shall not look upon his like again.
HORATIO
My lord, I think I saw him yesternight.
HAMLET
Saw who?
HORATIO
My lord, the king your father.
HAMLET
The king my father?!
HORATIO
Season your admiration for a while
With an attent ear, till I may deliver,
Upon the witness of these gentlemen,
This marvel to you.
HAMLET
For God's love, let me hear!

EXPLANATION

When Horatio told him that he came to see his father's funeral, Hamlet told him "do not mock me"
Because they have come,

"to see my mother's wedding"

Note Hamlet's bitter tone when he speaks of his mother's marriage. He uses a very poignant imagery to give vent to his feelings of disgust,

"The funeral bak'd meats
Did coldly furnish forth the marriage tables."

He very sarcastically says that his father had just died and the leftover food from the funeral was used at the wedding. That's how soon his mother forgot his father and married his scheming uncle.

BARNARDO, MARCELLUS, HORATIO revealing their encounter with the GHOST to HAMLET

HORATIO
Two nights together had these gentlemen,
Marcellus and Barnardo, on their watch,
In the dead waste and middle of the night,
Been thus encountered: a figure like your father,
Armed at point exactly, cap-à-pie,
Appears before them and with solemn march
Goes slow and stately by them. Thrice he walk'd
By their oppressed and fear-surprised eyes
Within his truncheon's length, whilst they, distilled
Almost to jelly with the act of fear,
Stand dumb and speak not to him. This to me
In dreadful secrecy impart they did,
And I with them the third night kept the watch,
Where—as they had delivered, both in time,
Form of the thing,
each word made true and good—
The apparition comes. I knew your father.
These hands are not more like.

HAMLET
But where was this?

MARCELLUS
My lord, upon the platform where we watch.

HAMLET
Did you not speak to it?

HORATIO
My lord, I did,
But answer made it none. Yet once methought
It lifted up its head and did address
Itself to motion, like as it would speak.
But even then the morning cock crew loud,
And at the sound it shrunk in haste away
And vanish'd from our sight.

HAMLET
'Tis very strange.

HORATIO
As I do live, my honour'd lord, 'tis true.
And we did think it writ down in our duty
To let you know of it.

HAMLET
Indeed, indeed, sirs, but this troubles me.
Hold you the watch tonight?

MARCELLUS, BARNARDO
We do, my lord.

MARCELLUS listens as HORATIO answers Hamlet's questions about the Ghost

When Hamlet learns of his father's ghostly apparition, he asks many short, snappy questions increasing the pace of his curiosity and his excitement.

We tend to empathise with him here because we get the feeling that he is excited and is longing to have some contact with his father because he enquires about his father's appearance, his moods etc. His anger at how wrongly his father was treated is quite evident and he is keen to take revenge.

"Did you not speak to it?"

HORATIO listens as HAMLET asks, "Did you not speak to it?"

HAMLET
Arm'd, say you?
MARCELLUS, BARNARDO
Arm'd, my lord.
HAMLET
From top to toe?
MARCELLUS, BARNARDO
My lord, from head to foot.
HAMLET
Then saw you not his face?
HORATIO
Oh yes, my lord. He wore his beaver up.
HAMLET
What, look'd he frowningly?
HORATIO
A countenance more in sorrow than in anger.
HAMLET
Pale or red?
HORATIO
Nay, very pale.
HAMLET
And fix'd his eyes upon you?
HORATIO
Most constantly.
HAMLET
I would I had been there.
HORATIO
It would have much amaz'd you.
HAMLET
Very like. Stayed it long?
HORATIO
While one with moderate haste
might tell a hundred.
MARCELLUS, BARNARDO
Longer, longer.
HORATIO
Not when I saw't.
HAMLET
His beard was grizzled, no?
HORATIO
It was, as I have seen it in his life,
A sable silvered.
HAMLET
I will watch tonight.
Perchance 'twill walk again.
HORATIO
I warr'nt it will.

Hamlet is quite shocked that his father's ghost is 'Arm'd'. He suspects some foul play and says that his father will reveal the treachery to him and that it cannot be hidden.

Hamlet is anxious to learn more details,

"Then saw you not his face?"

And

"What, look'd he frowningly?"

Horatio reveals that he saw his father's ghost and Hamlet says that it disturbs him, and he asks him whether his father was 'frowningly',' or if he was,

"Pale or red?"

Then Hamlet decides to stand guard with Horatio to see his father.

Hamlet's constant questioning of his father's ghost is very emotional because his detailed questioning gives an impression of a son who is missing his father terribly. After all he is left lonely, and he feels isolated, betrayed, and unloved after his father's death.

It's as though he is desperate to connect to his father and share his woes with him.

He says that he wished he had been there when his father fixed his eyes upon Horatio, shows us his longing to see his father.

"I would I had been there."

BARNARDO, MARCELLUS, and HORATIO about to depart

TEXT ACT 1 scene 2

HAMLET
If it assume my noble father's person,
I'll speak to it, though Hell itself should gape
And bid me hold my peace. I pray you all,
If you have hitherto concealed this sight,
Let it be tenable in your silence still.
And whatsoever else shall hap tonight,
Give it an understanding, but no tongue.
I will requite your loves. So fare you well.
Upon the platform, 'twixt eleven and twelve,
I'll visit you.

HORATIO, MARCELLUS, BARNARDO
Our duty to your honour.
HAMLET
Your loves, as mine to you. Farewell.

< *Exeunt all but* ***HAMLET***>

My father's spirit in arms!
All is not well.
I doubt some foul play.
Would the night were come!
Till then sit still, my soul.
Foul deeds will rise,
Though all the earth o'erwhelm them,
To men's eyes

<*Exit*>

EXPLANATION

He says that if the ghost looks like his father, then he will stand guard. He is determined to speak to it,

"I'll speak to it, though Hell itself should gape
And bid me hold my peace."

He asks the guards to keep what they saw a secret. Maybe he didn't want his mother and uncle to know about his father's ghost.

"If you have hitherto concealed this sight,
Let it be tenable in your silence still."

Hamlet is surprised that his father's ghost is armed.

"My father's spirit in arms!"

This suggests that the ghost is in a combative spirit and Hamlet suspects some foul play and he is impatient to see his father and learn what it is,

"I doubt some foul play.
Would the night were come!"

He says that 'foul deeds' will be revealed and that it cannot be hidden forever,

Foul deeds will rise,
Though all the earth o'erwhelm them,
To men's eyes."

HAMLET remarks to himself, "All is not well."

In Act 1 scene 3, the setting is a chamber inside the castle, during the day. Enter Laertes and his sister Ophelia who reminds her to write and warns her that love is fleeting, and that the love of a prince may not lead to marriage but lost of honour.

Enter Polonius to instruct his son Laertes in the ways of etiquette when in Paris.

Exit Laertes.

Polonius like Laertes instructs his daughter Ophelia to beware of love, and passion of youth, particularly when courting a prince who obligations are fixed by status in society.

Ophelia agrees to obey.

TEXT ACT 1 scene 3

*<Enter **LAERTES** and **OPHELIA**, his sister>*

LAERTES

My necessaries are embark'd. Farewell. And, sister,
As the winds give benefit and convey is assistant,
Do not sleep, but let me hear from you.

OPHELIA

Do you doubt that?

LAERTES

For Hamlet and the trifling of his favour,
Hold it a fashion and a toy in blood,
A violet in the youth of primy nature,
Forward, not permanent, sweet, not lasting,
The perfume and suppliance of a minute.
No more.

OPHELIA

No more but so?

LAERTES

Think it no more.
For nature, crescent, does not grow alone
In thews and bulk, but, as this temple waxes,
The inward service of the mind and soul
Grows wide withal. Perhaps he loves you now,
And now no soil nor cautel doth besmirch
The virtue of his will, but you must fear.
His greatness weigh'd, his will is not his own,
For he himself is subject to his birth.
He may not, as unvalued persons do,
Carve for himself, for on his choice depends
The safety and health of this whole state.
And therefore must his choice be circumscrib'd
Unto the voice and yielding of that body
Whereof he is the head. Then if he says he loves you,
It fits your wisdom so far to believe it
As he in his particular act and place
May give his saying deed, which is no further
Than the main voice of Denmark goes withal.
Then weigh what loss your honour may sustain
If with too credent ear you list his songs,
Or lose your heart, or your chaste treasure open
To his unmastered importunity.
Fear it, Ophelia. Fear it, my dear sister,
And keep you in the rear of your affection,
Out of the shot and danger of desire.
The chariest maid is prodigal enough
If she unmask her beauty to the moon.
Virtue itself scapes not calumnious strokes.
The canker galls the infants of the spring

EXPLANATION

Laertes bids a fond farewell to Ophelia.

He says that Hamlet is a hot-blooded youth, 'toy in blood'. And he warns that this relationship will not last.

"Forward, not permanent, sweet, not lasting"

He advises her not to pay too much attention to Hamlet and he wants her to remain pure and chaste,

"Then weigh what loss your honour may sustain."

He refers to her virginity as 'chaste treasure', and he urges her to remain pure. His reference to her virginity being 'treasure' is akin to that of an object. Something that can be traded.

He is very forthright in expressing his distaste in Ophelia becoming physically attracted to Hamlet.

"The chariest maid is prodigal enough if she unmask her beauty to the moon."

The imagery of the moon here can be seen as a threatening symbol and can represent Hamlet – if she has a physical union with Hamlet, it will be ready to cause destruction to her reputation and her purity.

He also uses the imagery of a flower in its 'infant' or 'budding' stage which can be destroyed by the diseased canker and hence killing its beauty and purity just like Ophelia's innocence and purity will be lost if she has a union with Hamlet.

"The canker galls the infants of the spring."

The mention of sexuality and promiscuity can be compared to Gertrude's disgusting affair with Claudius which revolted Hamlet. He scorns women and believes that their behaviour caused havoc in his life and ultimately contributed to the degradation of Denmark.

TEXT ACT 1 scene 3

LAERTES (*continues*)
Too oft before their buttons be disclos'd.
And in the morn and liquid dew of youth,
Contagious blastments are most imminent.
Be wary, then. Best safety lies in fear.
Youth to itself rebels, though none else near.

OPHELIA
I shall th' effect of this good lesson keep
As watchman to my heart. But, good my brother,
Do not, as some ungracious pastors do,
Show me the steep and thorny way to heaven,
Whiles, like a puffed and reckless libertine,
Himself the primrose path of dalliance treads,
And recks not his own rede.

LAERTES
O, fear me not.

< *Enter* ***POLONIUS***>

I stay too long.
But here my father comes.
A double blessing is a double grace.
Occasion smiles upon a second leave.

POLONIUS
Yet here, Laertes? Aboard, aboard, for shame!
The wind sits in the shoulder of your sail
And you are stay'd for. There, my blessing with thee
And these few precepts in thy memory
Look thou character. Give thy thoughts no tongue,
Nor any unproportioned thought his act.
Be thou familiar but by no means vulgar.
Those friends thou hast, and their adoption tried,
Grapple them unto thy soul with hoops of steel,
But do not dull thy palm with entertainment
Of each new hatched, unfledg'd comrade.
Beware of entrance to a quarrel, but being in,
Bear 't that th' oppos'd may beware of thee.
Give every man thy ear but few thy voice.
Take each man's censure but reserve thy judgment.
Costly thy habit as thy purse can buy,
But not express'd in fancy—rich, not gaudy,
For the apparel oft proclaims the man,
And they in France of the best rank and station
Are of a most select and generous chief in that.
Neither a borrower nor a lender be,

EXPLANATION

Ophelia gracefully heeds her brother's pleas and promises to keep this lesson close to her heart. Laertes speaks with a bitter tone and one can connote that this is a foreshadowing of Laertes' revenge of Hamlet later in the play.

"I shall th' effect of this good lesson keep
As watchman to my heart"

She tells her brother not to lecture her about life like an ungracious priest,

"Show me the steep and thorny way to heaven"

But to 'practice what he preaches' and to make sure that he too avoids the path of temptation and sin.

Polonius enters and very lovingly reprimands his son for delaying his trip.

"Yet here, Laertes? Aboard, aboard, for shame!"

We tend to pity Hamlet here when we witness the camaraderie between Polonius and Laertes. Polonius blesses his son and gives him some rich and wonderful advice on how to behave and survive in France yet Claudius' speech to Hamlet was all false and pretentious because he harboured a grudge against Hamlet.

It's strange how both Laertes and Polonius treats Ophelia like a child, and they control both her emotions and her sexuality. They both forbid her to have a relationship with Hamlet and they treat her sexuality like an inanimate object, (line 122)

"Set your entreatments at a higher rate"

Ophelia is very docile and subservient, and she perfectly fits the profile of the women in the Elizabethan era who were powerless in a male-dominated patriarchal society.

Polonius gives further advice here to Laertes on financial matters.

"Neither a borrower nor a lender be"

TEXT ACT 1 scene 3

POLONIUS (*continues*)
For loan oft loses both itself and friend,
And borrowing dulls the edge of husbandry.
This above all: to thine own self be true,
And it must follow, as the night the day,
Thou canst not then be false to any man.
Farewell. My blessing season this in thee.
LAERTES
Most humbly do I take my leave, my lord.
POLONIUS
The time invites you. Go. Your servants tend.
LAERTES
Farewell, Ophelia, and remember well
What I have said to you.
OPHELIA
'Tis in my memory lock'd,
And you yourself shall keep the key of it.
LAERTES
Farewell.

< *Exit* ***LAERTES***>

POLONIUS
What is 't, Ophelia, he hath said to you?
OPHELIA
So please you, something touching the Lord Hamlet.
POLONIUS
Marry, well be thought.
'Tis told me he hath very oft of late
Given private time to you, and you yourself
Have of your audience
been most free and bounteous.
If it be so as so 'tis put on me—
And that in way of caution—I must tell you,
You do not understand yourself so clearly
As it behooves my daughter and your honour.
What is between you? Give me up the truth.
OPHELIA
He hath, my lord, of late made many tenders
Of his affection to me.
POLONIUS
Affection! Pooh, you speak like a green girl,
Unsifted in such perilous circumstance.
Do you believe his "tenders," as you call them?
OPHELIA
I do not know, my lord, what I should think.

EXPLANATIO

He must not lend or borrow money because it can cause a friendship to fracture and break.

He says that Laertes must be true to himself and in doing so then he can't be false to any man -
which is the most important rule that he must follow.

"This above all: to thine own self be true"

They bid farewell to each other, and he tells Ophelia not to forget his advice. She says,

"Tis in my memory lock'd"

POLONIUS bids farewell to his son LAERTES with his daughter OPHELIA in tow

Polonius discusses the relationship of Hamlet and Ophelia. He is not impressed about this union and accuses her of being too generous with her time for Hamlet,

"And you yourself have of your audience been most free and bounteous."

He makes it clear that her flighty behaviour does not befit what is expected of a daughter of his.

"As it behooves my daughter and her honour."

He insists on knowing about their relationship and she admits that Hamlet has been giving her lots of affection,

"of late made many tenders
Of his affection to me"

Note Ophelia's submissive attitude to her fathers' angry response to her relationship with Hamlet.

"I do not know, my Lord, what I should think."

POLONIUS
Marry, I'll teach you. Think yourself a baby
That you have ta'en these tenders for true pay,
Which are not sterling. Tender yourself more dearly,
Or—not to crack the wind of the poor phrase,
Running it thus—you'll tender me a fool.

OPHELIA
My lord, he hath importuned me with love
In honourable fashion.

POLONIUS
Ay, "fashion" you may call it. Go to, go to.

OPHELIA
And hath given countenance to his speech, my lord,With
almost all the holy vows of heaven.

POLONIUS
Ay, springes to catch woodcocks. I do know,
When the blood burns, how prodigal the soul
Lends the tongue vows. These blazes, daughter,
Giving more light than heat, extinct in both
Even in their promise as it is a-making,
You must not take for fire. From this time
Be somewhat scanter of your maiden presence.
Set your entreatments at a higher rate
Than a command to parley. For Lord Hamlet,
Believe so much in him that he is young,
And with a larger tether may he walk
Than may be given you. In few, Ophelia,
Do not believe his vows, for they are brokers
Not of that dye which their investments show,
But mere implorators of unholy suits,
Breathing like sanctified and pious bawds,
The better to beguile. This is for all:
I would not, in plain terms, from this time forth,
Have you so slander any moment leisure
As to give words or talk with the Lord Hamlet.
Look to 't, I charge you. Come your ways.

OPHELIA
I shall obey, my lord.

<Exeunt>

He is furious and he warns her to ignore his affections and offer herself more self-respect or,

"you'll tender me a fool"

This suggests that she cannot think for herself. She portrays the typical Elizabethan woman who are dominated by their men and leave the decision to them. She is very docile and tells both her father and her brother that she will obey them. It's as though she is an inanimate object who doesn't have a mind of her own.

She is completely manipulated by them both and follows everything that they propose without any objections. It's like a list of orders that Polonius metes out to carve out his daughters' life and she is expected to follow that rigidly.

"From this time
Be somewhat scanter of your maiden presence.
Set your entreatments at a higher rate"

Polonius also treats his daughter as a commodity- something to be traded.

We can clearly see how she is trapped in a male – dominated society and we tend to empathise with her.

He very threateningly warns her not to spend time or communicate with Hamlet,

"Have you so slander any moment leisure
As to give words or talk with the Lord Hamlet"

Morality, respect, and honour were very important ingredients that shaped the Elizabethan society and when that is violated then one's reputation is sullied and frowned upon by society hence Polonius is worried about this and warns his daughter not to slander his name.

"I shall obey my Lord."

In Act 1 scene 4, the setting is the castle battlements, on a very cold night at around midnight. Enter Hamlet, Horatio, and Marcellus.

From the banqueting hall within the castle, they hear a flourish of trumpets, and two pieces of ordnance fired.

Hamlet remarks on his disdain for such revelry even though by custom he accepts it, he considers the practice Nature's livery or Fortune's star, the stamp of one defect.

Enter the Ghost.

Hamlet recognises the apparition as his father and demands of it why it has left its canonised bones, and what is its intent.

The Ghost beckons Hamlet to follow, but Horatio and Marcellus try to restrain Hamlet fearing he is being led to his death.

Hamlet is adamant, warning his companions that he will make ghosts of them if they do not unhand him.

Instead, they decide to follow Hamlet wherever the Ghost leads him.

The platform on the battlements

< *Enter* ***HAMLET, HORATIO,*** *and* ***MARCELLUS*** >

HAMLET
The air bites shrewdly. It is very cold.
HORATIO
It is a nipping and an eager air.
HAMLET
What hour now?
HORATIO
I think it lacks of twelve.
MARCELLUS
No, it is struck.
HORATIO
Indeed? I heard it not.
It then draws near the season
Wherein the spirit held his wont to walk.

< *A flourish of trumpets*
and two pieces of ordnance goes off >

What does this mean, my lord?
HAMLET
The king doth wake tonight and takes his rouse,
Keeps wassail and the swaggering upspring reels,
And, as he drains his draughts of Rhenish down,
The kettle-drum and trumpet thus bray out
The triumph of his pledge.
HORATIO
Is it a custom?
HAMLET
Ay, marry, is 't.
But to my mind, though I am native here
And to the manner born, it is a custom
More honour'd in the breach than the observance.
This heavy-headed revel east and west
Makes us traduced and taxed of other nations.
They clepe us drunkards and with swinish phrase
Soil our addition. And indeed it takes
From our achievements, though perform'd at height,
The pith and marrow of our attribute.
So oft it chances in particular men
That for some vicious mole of nature in them—
As in their birth wherein they are not guilty,
Since nature cannot choose his origin,
By the o'ergrowth of some complexion,
Oft breaking down the pales and forts of reason,

Shakespeare creates an atmosphere of eeriness and uncertainty. He also uses pathetic fallacy,

"It is a nipping and an eager air"

To express the mystery of the night. The ghost is expected to arrive at midnight, a typical time when ghosts visits. "I think it lacks of twelve"

The sound of trumpets is heard, and two cannons are fired. This is ironical because it coincides with the arrival of the ghost. Horatio is startled and Hamlet explains that the king is awake and is partaking in his heavy drinking party, highlighting Claudius' decadent lifestyle.

"As he drains his draughts of Rhenish down"

Hamlet says that the 'trumpets thus bray out'. Generally, donkeys bray but Hamlet attributes animalistic qualities of 'bray out' to the trumpets. This reference can be associated to Claudius' beast-like and animalistic character and actions.

It's obvious that this decadent lifestyle of the king foreshadows Denmark's downfall and decadence. Hamlet expresses his concern about how the other nations heaps scorn on Denmark for the king's flashy lifestyle and call them drunkards. He is distraught that all their achievements are now overlooked, and their reputation is sullied.

"Makes us traduced and taxed of other nations"

Hamlet goes on to say that a man with a birth defect which they are not responsible for, can become corrupt and is seen as vile because of that flaw of his.

"That for some vicious mole of nature in them"

CLAUDIUS and GERTRUDE revelling with guests

HAMLET (*continues*)
Or by some habit that too much o'er-leavens
The form of plausive manners—that these men,
Carrying, I say, the stamp of one defect,
Being nature's livery or fortune's star,
Their virtues else (be they as pure as grace,
As infinite as man may undergo)
Shall in the general censure take corruption
From that particular fault.
The dram of evil Doth all the noble substance of a doubt
To his own scandal.

<*Enter the* ***GHOST***>
HORATIO
Look, my lord, it comes!
HAMLET
Angels and ministers of grace defend us!
Be thou a spirit of health or goblin damn'd,
Bring with thee airs from heaven or blasts from hell,
Be thy intents wicked or charitable,
Thou comest in such a questionable shape
That I will speak to thee. I'll call thee"Hamlet,"
'King," "Father," "royal Dane." O, answer me!
Let me not burst in ignorance, but tell
Why thy canoniz'd bones, hearsed in death,
Have burst their cerements; why the sepulchre,
Wherein we saw thee quietly interr'd,
Hath op'd his ponderous and marble jaws
To cast thee up again. What may this mean,
That thou, dead corse, again in complete steel
Revisits thus the glimpses of the moon,
Making night hideous and we fools of nature,
So horridly to shake our disposition
With thoughts beyond the reaches of our souls?
Say why is this? Wherefore? What should we do?

This one flaw in their character,

"the stamp of one defect,
Being nature's livery or fortune's star"

Can make them fall from grace and they use that flaw to become corrupt and hence their reputation is ruined. This sense of reasoning by Hamlet can be associated with the corruption of Claudius and then to the corruption of Denmark because of a flaw in his personality and that was greed.

On seeing the ghost Hamlet is aghast and he calls,

"Angels and ministers of grace to defend us!"

Hamlet's speech is full of contradictions and juxtapositions because he asks the ghost if he is,

"a spirit of health or goblin damn'd"

He also uses biblical imagery to express both his surprise and confusion about the ghosts' presence,

"Bring thee airs from heaven or blasts from hell,
Be thy intents wicked or charitable"

Notice Hamlet's fast-paced speech and his wavy tone showing his uncertainty of dealing with a supernatural, cosmic being. There is a sense of urgency in his tone and a certain desperation in his voice and his questions to the apparition is ambiguous, intensifying his confusion about the living and the existence of the dead, God, the devil and the supernatural.

"Let me not burst in ignorance, but tell
Why thy canoniz'd bones, hearsed in death,
Have burst their cerements."

He uses a vivid imagery, 'marble jaws' referring to the grave that his father burst in from and is now terrifying us humans. He ends with several rhetorical questions to further exemplify his fear and confusion.

"Say why is this? Wherefore? What should we do?

TEXT ACT 1 scene 4

< ***GHOST*** *beckons* ***HAMLET***>

HORATIO
It beckons you to go away with it,
As if it some impartment did desire
To you alone.
MARCELLUS
Look, with what courteous action
It waves you to a more removed ground.
But do not go with it.
HORATIO
No, by no means.
HAMLET
It will not speak. Then I will follow it.
HORATIO
Do not, my lord.
HAMLET
Why, what should be the fear?
I do not set my life in a pin's fee,
And for my soul—what can it do to that,
Being a thing immortal as itself?
It waves me forth again. I'll follow it.
HORATIO
What if it tempt you toward the flood, my lord?
Or to the dreadful summit of the cliff
That beetles o'er his base into the sea,
And there assume some other horrible form,
Which might deprive your sovereignty of reason
And draw you into madness? Think of it.
The very place puts toys of desperation,
Without more motive, into every brain
That looks so many fathoms to the sea
And hears it roar beneath.
HAMLET
It waves me still.
—Go on. I'll follow thee.
MARCELLUS
You shall not go, my lord.

<***MARCELLUS*** *and* ***HORATIO***
try to hold ***HAMLET*** *back*>

EXPLANATION

Shakespeare employs rather dramatic techniques in this ghost scene. It's filled with suspense and tension as well. While the audience awaits with bated breath for the ghosts' response, the palpable tension between the guards and the atmosphere can be 'cut with a knife.'
They are visibly shaken, and the guards try to persuade Hamlet not to go with the ghost.

"But do not go with it."
"No by no means."

Hamlet insists on going and says that his life is worthless and there's nothing for him to be afraid of,

"I do not set my life in a pin's fee"

Horatio is adamant that Hamlet should not go, and he conjures up some imaginative excuses saying that the ghost might take him to the sea and tempt him to jump or it may take on some terrible form that will drive him insane.

"What if it tempt you toward the flood, my Lord?
Or to the dreadful summit of the cliff"

Hamlet is headstrong and insists that he will follow the ghost. We tend to pity Hamlet here. He is already a mentally and psychologically confused character and he is currently trying to deal with his mother's and uncle's betrayal.

MARCELLUS *and* ***HORATIO***
try to hold ***HAMLET*** *back*

HAMLET
Hold off your hands.
HORATIO
Be ruled. You shall not go.
HAMLET
My fate cries out
And makes each petty artery in this body
As hardy as the Nemean lion's nerve.
Still am I called. —Unhand me, gentlemen.

*<**HAMLET** breaks free and draws his sword>*

By heaven, I'll make a ghost of him that lets me
I say, away! —Go on. I'll follow thee.

*<Exeunt **GHOST** and **HAMLET**>*

HORATIO
He waxes desperate with imagination.
MARCELLUS
Let's follow. 'Tis not fit thus to obey him.
HORATIO
Have after. To what issue will this come?
MARCELLUS
Something is rotten in the state of Denmark.
HORATIO
Heaven will direct it.
MARCELLUS
Nay, let's follow him.

< Exeunt >

He feels alienated and lonely and now he is desperate to connect with the father that he idolised and misses so much.

He becomes furious when the guards try to hold him back and insists that his nerves are as hard as steel and that he is prepared to face what is to come,

"As hardy as the Nemean lion's nerve"

Hamlet is determined to go, and he threatens that if anyone stops him, then he will kill them,

"Unhand me, gentlemen.
By heaven, I'll make a ghost of him that lets me"

***HAMLET** breaks free and draws his sword*

Horatio and Marcellus remain faithful to Hamlet, and they are worried about his welfare, so they ignore his commands and follow him.

Marcellus is very perceptive, and he says that,

"Something is rotten in the state of Denmark"

This utterance foreshadows the events to follow. It spells disaster for Denmark and the verb, 'rotten' suggests the degradation of morals, rules and decency that is the current order of the day in Denmark. The indulgence of the king will bring the country into disrepute.

In Act 1 scene 5, the setting is a secluded part of the battlements.

Hamlet tells the Ghost he will go no further.

The Ghost tells Hamlet his hour is almost come to return to the tormenting flames, and that he must not pity him, but lend his serious hearing to what he will unfold and must take revenge on what he about to hear.

The Ghost tells Hamlet that he is his father's spirit, doomed for a term to walk the night, and for the day confined to fast in fires, till the foul crimes done in his day are burnt and purged away.

The serpent that did sting thy father's life, now wears his crown. An incestuous, adulterate beast, with traitorous gifts.

The Ghost continues its tirade against the Gertrude and Claudius the incestuous pair.

Exit the Ghost.

Hamlet in a soliloquy, vows to administer justice.

Enter Horatio and Marcellus calling for Hamlet and discover him by himself.

Hamlet makes both take an oath not to reveal what he is about to tell them.

The Ghost reappears and tell them to swear by his sword.

They swear.

TEXT ACT 1 scene 5

*< Enter **GHOST** and **HAMLET**>*

HAMLET
Where wilt thou lead me? Speak, I'll go no further.
GHOST
Mark me.
HAMLET
I will.
GHOST
My hour is almost come
When I to sulfurous and tormenting flames
Must render up myself.
HAMLET
Alas, poor ghost!
GHOST
Pity me not, but lend thy serious hearing
To what I shall unfold.
HAMLET
Speak. I am bound to hear.
GHOST
So art thou to revenge when thou shalt hear.
HAMLET
What?
GHOST
I am thy father's spirit,
Doomed for a certain term to walk the night
And for the day confined to fast in fires,
Till the foul crimes done in my days of nature
Are burnt and purged away. But that I am forbid
To tell the secrets of my prison house,
I could a tale unfold whose lightest word
Would harrow up thy soul, freeze thy young blood,
Make thy two eyes, like stars, start from theirspheres,
Thy knotted and combined locks to part
And each particular hair to stand on end,
Like quills upon the fearful porpentine.
But this eternal blazon must not be
To ears of flesh and blood. List, list, O, list!
If thou didst ever thy dear father love—
HAMLET
O God!
GHOST
Revenge his foul and most unnatural murder.
HAMLET
Murder?
GHOST
Murder most foul, as in the best it is.
But this most foul, strange and unnatural.

EXPLANATION

The ghost tells Hamlet that he must listen to what he has to say. He reveals that he is 'thy father's spirit'. It says that it is doomed in damnation until its sins are purged away,

"Doomed for a certain term to walk the night"

The ghost asks Hamlet to take revenge for his foul murder. Hamlet is shocked,

"Murder most foul, as in the best it is"

We must consider whether the ghosts' request for Hamlet to take revenge is morally and religiously ethical. Hamlet's disposition at present is grave and he is grappling with a moral dilemma concerning his mother and uncle.

One may ask the question, Is it fair for the ghost of his father to add a further burden on the already overloaded shoulder of a young man.

We had already seen that Hamlet just revealed to us that his life has no worth or meaning, (Act 1 scene 4 line 65)

"I do not set my life in a pins fee."

We must consider whether Hamlet is strong enough to manage this huge task.

THE GHOST recites his woes "thy father's spirit, Doomed for a certain term to walk the night"

TEXT ACT 1 scene 5

HAMLET
Haste me to know 't, that I, with wings as swift
As meditation or the thoughts of love,
May sweep to my revenge.
GHOST
I find thee apt,
And duller shouldst thou be than the fat weed
That roots itself in ease on Lethe wharf,
Wouldst thou not stir in this. Now, Hamlet, hear.
'Tis given out that, sleeping in my orchard,
A serpent stung me. So the whole ear of Denmark
Is by a forged process of my death
Rankly abus'd. But know, thou noble youth,
The serpent that did sting thy father's life
Now wears his crown.
HAMLET
O my prophetic soul! My uncle?
GHOST
Ay, that incestuous, that adulterate beast,
With witchcraft of his wit, with traitorous gifts—
O wicked wit and gifts, that have the power
So to seduce!—won to his shameful lust
The will of my most seeming-virtuous queen.
O Hamlet, what a falling off was there!
From me, whose love was of that dignity
That it went hand in hand even with the vow
I made to her in marriage, and to decline Upon a
wretch whose natural gifts were poor
To those of mine.
But virtue, as it never will be moved,
Though lewdness court it in a shape of heaven,
So lust, though to a radiant angel link'd,
Will sate itself in a celestial bedAnd prey
on garbage.
But soft! Methinks I scent the morning air.
Brief let me be. Sleeping within my orchard,
My custom always of the afternoon,
Upon my secure hour thy uncle stole
With juice of cursed hebenon in a vial,
And in the porches of my ears did pour
The leperous distilment, whose effect
Holds such an enmity with blood of man
That swift as quicksilver it courses through
The natural gates and alleys of the body,
And with a sudden vigor doth posset
And curd, like eager droppings into milk,

EXPLANATION

Hamlet is perplexed at this new information. He is very eager to adhere very swiftly to the ghosts' request. The use of the simile,

"Haste me to know 't, that I, with wings as swift
As meditation or the thoughts of love,
May sweep to my revenge"

One may wonder if this impulsive action can lead to both Hamlet's and Denmark's demise.

The ghost gives Hamlet a vivid imagery of how he was so brutally killed when Claudius poured poison into his ear,

"With juice of cursed hebenon in a vial, and in the porches of my ears did pour"

The ghost speaks with a very bitter tone about his brother's treachery. He uses some harsh verbs to describe his revolting behaviour,

"Ay, that incestuous, that adulterate beast,
With witchcraft of his wit, with traitorous gifts"

Was able to seduce,

"The will of my most seeming-virtuous queen"

It's interesting to note that both Hamlet and his father's ghost use the term 'seems' laying bare the pretentious behaviour of Gertrude.

The theme of appearance versus reality surfaces here. Both men accuse her of pretending to be loving and loyal but in face she violated the sanctity of her marriage vows and had an incestuous affair with her brother-in-law,

"So lust, though to a radiant angel link'd,
Will sate itself in a celestial bed
And prey on garbage""

He explains how he was a loyal husband and he loved her with dignity unlike his brother whose natural gifts were poor compared to his.

TEXT ACT 1 scene 5

GHOST (*continues*)
The thin and wholesome blood. So did it mine.
And a most instant tetter barked about,
Most lazar-like, with vile and loathsome crust
All my smooth body.
Thus was I, sleeping, by a brother's hand
Of life, of crown, of queen at once dispatch'd,
Cut off even in the blossoms of my sin,
Unhousel'd, disappointed, unanel'd.
No reckoning made, but sent to my account
With all my imperfections on my head.
Oh, horrible, oh, horrible, most horrible!
If thou hast nature in thee, bear it not.
Let not the royal bed of Denmark be
A couch for luxury and damn'd incest.
But howsoever thou pursuest this act,
Taint not thy mind, nor let thy soul contrive
Against thy mother aught. Leave her to heaven
And to those thorns that in her bosom lodge
To prick and sting her. Fare thee well at once.
The glowworm shows the matin to be near,
And 'gins to pale his uneffectual fire.
Adieu, adieu, adieu. Remember me.

HAMLET
O all you host of heaven! O earth! What else?
And shall I couple hell? O fie! Hold, hold, my heart,
And you, my sinews, grow not instant old,
But bear me stiffly up. Remember thee!
Ay, thou poor ghost, whiles memory holds a seat
In this distracted globe. Remember thee!
Yea, from the table of my memory
I'll wipe away all trivial fond records,
All saws of books, all forms, all pressures past
That youth and observation copied there,
And thy commandment all alone shall live
Within the book and volume of my brain,
Unmixed with baser matter. Yes, by heaven!
O most pernicious woman!
O villain, villain, smiling, damn'd villain!
My tables! —Meet it is I set it down
That one may smile, and smile, and be a villain.
At least I'm sure it may be so in Denmark.
(*He writes*)
So, uncle, there you are. Now to my word.
It is "Adieu, adieu. Remember me."
I have sworn 't.

EXPLANATION

The ghost bemoans the fact that his wicked brother robbed him of his wife, kingship, and his life 'on one fell swoop'. He didn't even have time to repent for his sins before going to heaven,

"No reckoning made, but sent to my account
With all my imperfections in my head."

The repetition of the adjective by the ghost,

"Oh, horrible, oh horrible, most horrible!"

Highlights the ghosts' immeasurable and intense pain, so he urges Hamlet,

"Let not the royal bed of Denmark be
A couch for luxury and damn'd incest."

The ghost's request is controversial, unholy, and contradictory and opened to much debate. He asks his son to take revenge for his death which is a violation of the Ten Commandments in the bible – 'You shall not kill.' Yet he also upholds the Ten Commandments by telling Hamlet not to cause any harm to his mother because God will deal with her,
'Honour your father and your mother'.

Hamlet is horrified at the ghosts' revelation, and he uses many expletives to give vent to his frustrations. The use of the repeated exclamation marks and rhetorical questions can suggest this.

"O all you host of heaven! O earth! What else?"

He is obviously in the depths of despair, and he promises the ghost that he will do everything in his power to avenge his untimely death.

"And thy commandment all alone shall live
Within the book and volume of my brain."

He is filled with revulsion at his mother's deceit, and he is galled at her pretentious behaviour and her fake smile.

"O most pernicious woman!
O villain, villain, smiling, damn'd villain!"

< *Enter* ***HORATIO*** *and* ***MARCELLUS***>

HORATIO
My lord, my lord!
MARCELLUS
Lord Hamlet—
HORATIO
Heaven secure him!
HAMLET
So be it.
HORATIO
Hillo, ho, ho, my lord!
HAMLET
Hillo, ho, ho, boy. Come, bird, come.
MARCELLUS
How is't, my noble lord?
HORATIO
What news, my lord?
HAMLET
Oh, wonderful!
HORATIO
Good my lord, tell it.
HAMLET
No. You'll reveal it.
HORATIO
Not I, my lord, by heaven.
MARCELLUS
Nor I, my lord.
HAMLET
How say you, then?
Would heart of man once think it?
But you'll be secret?
HORATIO, MARCELLUS
Ay, by heaven, my lord.
HAMLET
There's ne'er a villain dwelling in all Denmark
But he's an arrant knave.
HORATIO
There needs no ghost, my lord, come from the grave
To tell us this.
HAMLET
Why, right, you are in the right.
And so, without more circumstance at all,
I hold it fit that we shake hands and part.
You as your business and desire shall point you
For every man has business and desire,
Such as it is—and for my own poor part,
Look you, I'll go pray.

Marcellus and Horatio are very concerned about Hamlet and enquire about his well-being after his encounter with the ghost.

MARCELLUS asks, "How is't my noble Lord?"

He asks them to promise him loyalty and to keep his meeting a secret. They nobly promise. He also asks them not to pay attention and remark on his strange behaviour that they witness in the future.

Horatio and Marcellus promise that they will remain loyal to Hamlet and will not breathe a word of the night's events.

They swear by 'heaven' that they will keep it a secret,

"Not I, my lord, by heaven"

"Nor I, my lord"

Hamlet tells them that

"There's ne'er a villain dwelling in all Denmark
But he's an arrant knave"

Horatio says that they don't need a ghost to tell them that.

"There needs no ghost, my lord, come from the grave
To tell us this."

Hamlet concurs,

"Why, right, you are in the right"

TEXT ACT 1 scene 5

HORATIO
These are but wild and whirling words, my lord.

HAMLET
I'm sorry they offend you, heartily –
Yes faith, heartily.

HORATIO
There's no offense, my lord.

HAMLET
Yes, by Saint Patrick, but there is, Horatio,
And much offense too.
Touching this vision here
It is an honest ghost, that let me tell you.
For your desire to know what is between us,
O'ermaster 't as you may.
And now, good friends,
As you are friends, scholars and soldiers,
Give me one poor request.

HORATIO
What is 't, my lord? We will.

HAMLET
Never make known what you have seen tonight.

HORATIO, MARCELLUS
My lord, we will not.

HAMLET
Nay, but swear 't.

HORATIO
In faith, my lord, not I.

MARCELLUS
Nor I, my lord, in faith.

HAMLET
Upon my sword.

MARCELLUS
We have sworn, my lord, already.

HAMLET
Indeed, upon my sword, indeed.

GHOST
(*cries under the stage*) Swear!

HAMLET
Ha, ha, boy! Sayst thou so?
Art thou there,truepenny?
Come on, you hear this fellow in the cellarage.
Consent to swear.

HORATIO
Propose the oath, my lord.

HAMLET
Never to speak of this that you have seen.Swear by my sword.

GHOST
(*beneath*) Swear

EXPLANATION

Horatio is startled at Hamlet's revelation. Hamlet apologises for offending him,

"I'm sorry they offend you, heartily"

Horatio reciprocates,

"There's no offense, my lord"

Hamlet concludes,

"It is an honest ghost, that let me tell you"

Once again, Hamlet asks them to grant him 'one poor request',

"Never make known what you have seen tonight"

They swear loyalty on their swords and depart.

HAMLET makes his companions swear upon the sword
"Never make known what you have seen tonight"

They promise their loyalty again to Hamlet and we see later that Horatio carries it to the very end until Hamlet's death.

The Ghost also asks them to swear.

"Swear!"

"Swear"

TEXT ACT 1 scene 5

HAMLET
Hic et ubique? Then we'll shift our ground.
Come hither, gentlemen,
And lay your hands again upon my sword.
Swear by my sword
Never to speak of this that you have heard.
GHOST
(*beneath*) Swear by his sword.
HAMLET
Well said, old mole!
Canst work i' th' earth so fast?
A worthy pioneer!
Once more remove, good friends.
HORATIO
O day and night, but this is wondrous strange!
HAMLET
And therefore as a stranger give it welcome.
There are more things in heaven and earth, Horatio,
Than are dreamt of in your philosophy.
But come,
Here, as before, never, so help you mercy,
How strange or odd some'er I bear myself
(As I perchance hereafter shall think meet
To put an antic disposition on),
That you, at such times seeing me, never shall—
With arms encumbered thus, or this headshake,
Or by pronouncing of some doubtful phrase,
As "Well, well, we know,"
or "We could an if we would,"
Or "If we list to speak,"
or "There be an if they might,"
Or such ambiguous giving out—to note
That you know aught of me. This not to do,
So grace and mercy at your most need help you,
GHOST
(*beneath*) Swear!
HAMLET
Rest, rest, perturbed spirit! —So, gentlemen,
With all my love I do commend me to you,
And what so poor a man as Hamlet is
May do, to express his love and friending to you,
God willing, shall not lack. Let us go in together,
And still your fingers on your lips, I pray.
The time is out of joint. O curs'd spite,
That ever I was born to set it right!
Nay, come, let's go together.
< *Exeunt* >

EXPLANATION

Hamlet asks them to

"lay your hands again upon my sword.
Swear by my sword
Never to speak of this that you have heard"

The Ghost asks them once more to,

"Swear by his sword"

Horatio is shocked and he exclaims,

"O day and night, but this is wondrous strange!"

So, now they have sworn not to reveal what they have heard as well as what they have seen.

Hamlet asks the Ghost to,

"Rest, rest, perturbed spirit!"

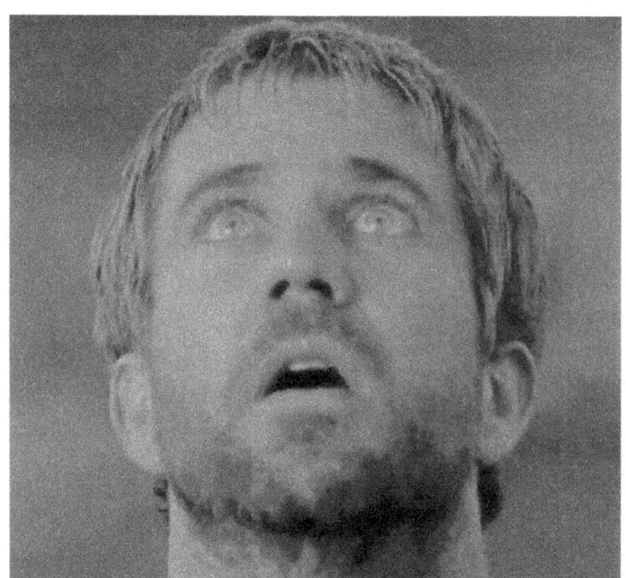

HAMLET proclaims "Rest, rest, perturbed spirit!"

Hamlet expresses his love to his companions and once again asks them to not to speak about what had occurred this night,

"And still your fingers on your lips, I pray"

In Act 2 scene 1, the setting is a chamber inside the castle, the next day.

Enter Polonius and his servant Reynaldo who is instructed to go to Paris and spy on Laertes to find out if he is adhering to the advice Polonius gave him before he left for Paris.

Enter Ophelia who tells Polonius about Hamlet's unwarranted physical behaviour towards her. Polonius thinks Hamlet is mad for Ophelia love, but she does not know.

She did repel his letters and denied him access.

Polonius thinks Hamlet is mad and decides to take Ophelia to see the King, so that Hamlet's actions are known.

TEXT ACT 2 scene 1

*<Enter **POLONIUS** with his man **REYNALDO**>*

POLONIUS
Give him this money and these notes, Reynaldo.
REYNALDO
I will, my lord.
POLONIUS
You shall do marvelous wisely, good Reynaldo,
Before you visit him, to make inquire
Of his behavior.
REYNALDO
My lord, I did intend it.
POLONIUS
Marry, well said, very well said. Look you, sir,
Inquire me first what Danskers are in Paris,
And how, and who, what means,
And where they keep
What company at what expense; and finding
By this encompassment and drift of question
That they do know my son, come you more nearer
Than your particular demands will touch it.
Take you, as 'twere, some distant knowledge of him,
As thus: "I know his father and his friends,
And, in part, him." –
Do you mark this, Reynaldo?
REYNALDO
Ay, very well, my lord.
POLONIUS
"And in part him, but" you may say, "not well.
But, if 't be he I mean, he's very wild.
Addicted so and so. —" And there put on him
What forgeries you please. Marry, none so rank
As may dishonour him. Take heed of that.
But, sir, such wanton, wild, and usual slips
As are companions noted and most known
To youth and liberty.
REYNALDO
As gaming, my lord?
POLONIUS
Ay, or drinking, fencing, swearing,
Quarreling, drabbing—you may go so far.
REYNALDO
My lord, that would dishonour him!

EXPLANATION

Polonius' actions in this scene can very well represent Denmark's state of degradation and decay. It is characterised by deceit, lies, greed, dishonesty and spying for information.

Shakespeare also gives us an insight into how the father's selfish behaviour is responsible for the breakdown of the family structures, values, and morality. – somethings Hamlet is trying to put right in Denmark.

The women are silent and subservient as is the expectation of Elizabethan women in that era. Hence, we see the dominant patriarchs wreaking havoc in their unsuspecting children's lives.

We will take a closer look at all the fathers' detrimental behaviour in the play which so cruelly and negatively impacts on their children's lives.

Here Polonius asks Renaldo to spy on his son and to find out if he is misbehaving or if he is upholding the family reputation. Polonius also ask Reynaldo to lie and pretend to elicit information about his son's behaviour.

"And there put on him
What forgeries you please"

Incidents of spying is prevalent in the play and here Polonius foreshadows his own death, and he becomes the victim of his own actions while spying.

Polonius insists that Renaldo find out about Laertes' behaviour without besmirching his name.

"Ay, or drinking, fencing, swearing,
Quarrelling, drabbing – you may go so far"

Reynaldo agrees with Polonius' idea.

Note that Reynaldo is used by Polonius to carry out some devious actions like spying on Laertes. In the same way, Polonius was used by Claudius to spy on Hamlet which resulted in his death.

POLONIUS
'Faith, no, as you may season it in the charge.
You must not put another scandal on him
That he is open to incontinency -
That's not my meaning.
But breathe his faults so quaintly
That they may seem the taints of liberty,
The flash and outbreak of a fiery mind,
A savageness in unreclaim'd blood,
Of general assault.
REYNALDO
But my good lord—
POLONIUS
Wherefore should you do this?
REYNALDO
Ay, my lord. I would know that.
POLONIUS
Marry, sir, here's my drift:
(And I believe it is a fetch of wit)
You, laying these slight sullies on my son
As 'twere a thing a little soiled i' th' working—
Mark you, your party in converse, him you would sound,
Having ever seen in the prenominate crimes
The youth you breathe of guilty, be assured
He closes with you in this consequence:
"Good sir" or so, or "Friend," or "Gentleman,"
According to the phrase or the addition
Of man and country.
REYNALDO
Very good, my lord.
POLONIUS
And then, sir, does he this, he does—
What was labout to say?
By the mass, I was about to say something.
Where did I leave?
REYNALDO
At "closes in the consequence," at "'friend,'Or so"
and "'gentleman.'"

"You must not put another scandal on him"

We may have to consider an argument on how the relationship and behaviour of fathers in the play affects the psychological and mental states of their children.

Polonius treats both Ophelia and Laertes like children. Not only does he control their mind, body, and soul, but he also controls their feelings. He insists that Ophelia break her relationship with Hamlet, and he does not consider her emotional feelings for him. She is very docile and adheres to his request and not once did she question his reasoning.

Polonius also treats Laertes' like a child. He invades his privacy by doing something so conniving so as to employ Reynaldo to spy on him. He is also unwittingly exposing his son's faults (if there are any) hence tainting his reputation because Reynaldo will learn of it.

Hamlet, after meeting the ghost of his father is on a psychological and emotional rollercoaster.
Let us consider Hamlet's father's demands on the very volatile, naïve, and already confused Hamlet.

The late king asks Hamlet to take revenge on Claudius and flouts the biblical rule, 'vengeance is mine,' says the Lord.

The Elizabethan audience upheld their religious faith and killing or taking revenge is scorned upon by the bible. Even Hamlet makes many references to heaven and hell. He too upholds his moral and religious values and later in the play we see that he refuses to kill Claudius whilst he was praying because he will be forgiven for his vile sins.

Yet we see that his father is very selective in his religious and moral judgements because he asks Hamlet to spare his mother and let God deal with her. This is obviously misleading Hamlet, and he is forced to go against his biblical beliefs, determined on keeping his promise to his father which ultimately leads to his destruction.

TEXT ACT 2 scene 1

POLONIUS
At "closes in the consequence." Ay, marry.
He closes thus: "I know the gentleman.
I saw him yesterday"—or "t' other day,"
Or then, or then, with such or such— "and, as you say
There was he gaming, there o'ertook in's rouse,
There falling out at tennis," or, perchance,
"I saw him enter such a house of sale"—
Videlicet a brothel, or so forth. See you now,
Your bait of falsehood takes this carp of truth.
And thus do we of wisdom and of reach,
With windlasses and with assays of bias,
By indirections find directions out.
So, by my former lecture and advice
Shall you, my son. You have me, have you not?
REYNALDO
My lord, I have.
POLONIUS
God be wi' you. Fare you well.
REYNALDO
Good my lord.
POLONIUS
Observe his inclination in yourself.
REYNALDO
I shall, my lord.
POLONIUS
And let him ply his music.
REYNALDO
Well, my lord.
POLONIUS
Farewell.

*<Exit **REYNALDO**>*

*<Enter **OPHELIA**>*

How now, Ophelia? What's the matter?
OPHELIA
O my lord, my lord, I have been so affrighted!
POLONIUS
With what, i' th' name of God?

EXPLANATION

Not only, one can argue, that Hamlet's father was responsible for his moral, religious, and psychological decay – something Hamlet was fighting against but became a victim of it because of his father's zest for revenge, when he too loses his life.

He also psychologically damaged Hamlet after his revelation about how Claudius killed him. This staggered Hamlet and not only did he show his revulsion for his uncle but also his mother. We must look at the fake, dangerous relationship between Hamlet and his stepfather Claudius.

Claudius speaks with a 'silver tongue' to Hamlet saying that he will take over kingship when he dies and pretending to have his interest at heart, but in reality, he is holding a 'dagger' for Hamlet because we learn that he is plotting to kill him later in the play.

The theme of appearance versus reality once again surfaces here.

Polonius' diseased mind and manipulative character is shocking. He took control of Reynaldo's mind and got him to do his bidding.

"So, by my former lecture and advice
Shall you, my son. You have me, have you not."

Ironically, he calls him his 'son' and manages to taint him as well.

Now Polonius is busy prodding into Ophelia's private affairs. Ophelia reveals to him her shocking encounter with the deranged and horrifying Hamlet.

HAMLET confronting Ophelia with wild eyes

OPHELIA
My lord, as I was sewing in my closet,
Lord Hamlet, with his doublet all unbraced,
No hat upon his head; his stockings fouled,
Ungarter'd, and down-gyv'd to his ankle,
Pale as his shirt; his knees knocking each other,
And with a look so piteous in purport
As if he had been loosed out of hell
To speak of horrors—he comes before me.
POLONIUS
Mad for thy love?
OPHELIA
My lord, I do not know.
But truly, I do fear it.
POLONIUS
What said he?
OPHELIA
He took me by the wrist and held me hard.
Then goes he to the length of all his arm,
And, with his other hand thus o'er his brow,
He falls to such perusal of my face
As he would draw it. Long stayed he so.
At last, a little shaking of mine arm
And thrice his head thus waving up and down,
He raised a sigh so piteous and profound
As it did seem to shatter all his bulk
And end his being. That done, he lets me go,
And, with his head over his shoulder turned,
He seemed to find his way without his eyes,
For out o' doors he went without their helps,
And to the last bended their light on me.

OPHELIA says, "He seemed to find his way without his eyes"

She gives a detailed visual picture of Hamlet's craziness,

"with his doublet all unbraced,
No hat upon his head; his stockings fouled, ungarter'd, and down-gyv'd to his ankle"

She describes how unkempt Hamlet is and his strange behaviour,

"And with a look so piteous in purport
As if he had been loosed out of hell"

Polonius immediately comes to a strange conclusion and asks Ophelia if Hamlet is,

"Mad for thy love?"

HAMLET grabs OPHELIA's wrist, "He took me by the wrist and held me hard"

He grabbed my wrist very roughly
He looked at my face with such intensity as though he was going to make a painting of it,

"He falls to such perusal of my face
As he would draw it"

He jerked his head up and down as though it was his last breath,

"He raised a sigh so piteous and profound
As it did seem to shatter all his bulk
And end his being"

He left without the help of his eyes because they were fixated on me.

TEXT ACT 2 scene 1

POLONIUS
Come, go with me. I will go seek the king.
This is the very ecstasy of love,
Whose violent property fordoes itself
And leads the will to desperate undertakings
As oft as any passion under heaven
That does afflict our natures. I am sorry.
What, have you given him any hard words of late?
OPHELIA
No, my good lord. But as you did command
I did repel his fetters and denied
His access to me.
POLONIUS
That hath made him mad.
I am sorry that with better heed and judgment
I had not quoted him. I feared he did but trifle
And meant to wreck thee. But beshrew my jealousy!
By heaven, it is as proper to our age
To cast beyond ourselves in our opinions
As it is common for the younger sort
To lack discretion. Come, go we to the king.
This must be known, which,
being kept close, might move
More grief to hide than hate to utter love.
Come.

< ***Exeunt*** >

EXPLANATION

Polonius thinks that this is love craziness,

"the very ecstasy of love"

He says that the strong emotions of love can distort our reasoning and behaviour.

"As oft as any passion under heaven
That does afflict our nature"

We note Ophelia's submissive behaviour because she tells her father that she obeyed his wishes and gave Hamlet his letters back and would not allow him to visit her.

Now Polonius regrets his domineering and overbearing attitude when he thought that Hamlet is merely toying with Ophelia's feelings. This is a classic example of how Polonius' empowering attitude harms his daughter's love life because Hamlet loved her, but her father doubted it. He wrongly advises her to ignore his advances. This has serious consequences leading to her death as we see later in the play.

Polonius acknowledges that he misunderstood the young people into believing that they are nothing but wild and irresponsible,

"proper to our age
To cast beyond ourselves in our opinions
As it is common for the younger sort
To lack discretion."

One may argue that now Hamlet is pretending to be mad just as Claudius is pretending to be kind.
Note the theme of deception and appearance versus reality surfacing here.

In Act 2 scene 2, the setting is the Council Chamber inside the castle, later in the day, where on a flourish of trumpets, enters King Claudius, Queen Gertrude, Rosencrantz and Guildenstern, school friends of Prince Hamlet, with Attendants.

The King welcomes Rosencrantz and Guildenstern and commands them to stay and elicit Hamlet's unknown afflictions so that the remedy may be corrected. They agree invoking heaven in their forthcoming endeavours.

Exit Rosencrantz and Guildenstern and Attendants.

Enter Polonius to announce the return of the Danish Norwegian Ambassadors.

Exit Polonius who re-enters with Ambassadors Voltemand and Cornelius with news how 'old Norway' has rebuked his nephew, Prince Fortinbras, sending him to fight against the Poles, but with the King's permission, requiring his Army to pass through Denmark, which the King grants.

Exit Voltemand and Cornelius.

Polonius now informs the King and Queen of Hamlet's bizarre love madness towards his daughter Ophelia, supporting his accusations by reading aloud a love letter written by Hamlet to her.

Polonius informs the King and Queen that he had no knowledge until his daughter told him, prescribing her to rebuff all contact with the prince as he is above her station, to which she concurred.

The King and Queen are not convinced this explains Hamlet's dark and sullen mood, so Polonius proposes to hide with the King behind an Arras, to observe an encounter between the two, to confirm the truth.

Enter Hamlet, reading a book, to which the Queen remarks the poor wretch comes reading. Polonius beseech their Majesties to retire so that he may speak to Hamlet alone.

Exit the King and Queen and Attendants.

Polonius finds it difficult to make sense of Hamlet's oblivious remarks, which he considers madness, yet exhibiting method.

Enter Rosencrantz and Guildenstern.

Exit Polonius.

Hamlet elicits from his school friends by deception that this is not a chance encounter. The King had requested their present at Elsinore to discover Hamlet's intent, as he suspected that Hamlet may be faking his madness.

A flourish of trumpets sound. Enter Polonius.

Enter the Players, a troupe known to Hamlet.

After much debate with Polonius and the First player, Hamlet asks the First Player if his troupe can perform the play *The Murder of Gonzago*, modified with an additional dozen lines, the next day in the presence of the King and Court.

It is agreed. Hamlet trusts that the additional lines will trap Claudius into admitting his guilt.

Exit Polonius.

Exit The Players.

Exit Rosencrantz and Guildenstern.

Hamlet in a soliloquy, casts doubt on his own forthcoming actions.

How will Claudius react? He questions why he is indecisive, cowardly not brave. Is the Ghost an evil spirit, leading to him to damnation?

Flourish of Trumpets

*<Enter King **CLAUDIUS** and Queen **GERTRUDE, ROSENCRANTZ** and **GUILDENSTERN** and attendants>*

CLAUDIUS

Welcome, dear Rosencrantz and Guildenstern.
Moreover that we much did long to see you,
The need we have to use you did provoke
Our hasty sending. Something have you heard
Of Hamlet's "transformation"—so call it
Since nor th' exterior nor the inward man
Resembles that it was. What it should be,
More than his father's death, that thus hath put him
So much from th' understanding of himself,
I cannot dream of. I entreat you both
That, being of so young days brought up with him
And since so neighbored to his youth and 'haviour,
That you vouchsafe your rest here in our court
Some little time so by your companies
To draw him on to pleasures and to gather,So
much as from occasion you may glean,
Whether aught, to us unknown, afflicts him thus
That, opened, lies within our remedy.

GERTRUDE

Good gentlemen, he hath much talked of you.
And sure I am two men there are not living
To whom he more adheres. If it will please you
To show us so much gentry and good will
As to expend your time with us awhile
For the supply and profit of our hope,
Your visitation shall receive such thanks
As fits a king's remembrance.

ROSENCRANTZ

Both your majesties
Might, by the sovereign power you have of us,
Put your dread pleasures more into command
Than to entreaty.

GUILDENSTERN

But we both obey
And here give up ourselves, in the full bent,
To lay our service freely at your feet
To be commanded.

CLAUDIUS

Thanks, Rosencrantz, and gentle Guildenstern.

Claudius is feigning kindness and pretends to have Hamlet's interest at heart. We already know that he is a cold, calculated and ruthless murderer.

He puts on a brave front and appears very diplomatic and pragmatic in his kingly dealings.

His cool exterior is somewhat unnerving but it's obvious that he is becoming nervous in case Hamlet suspect his evil deeds. Therefore, he ensures that he must act in any way possible to avoid Hamlet's wrath. He very quickly, on learning of Hamlet's ailment summoned Rosencrantz and Guildenstern – to help them to accompany Hamlet to have some fun,

"To draw him onto pleasures."

They are worried about his strange behaviour after his father's death and since they are his friends, they are best suited to help Hamlet. His mother is also worried about Hamlet's crazy, unsettling behaviour.

"you may glean,
Whether aught, to us unknown, afflicts him thus."

You'll can detect what's ailing him because we are puzzled and don't know the reason for this change in his behaviour says his concerned parents.

GUILDENSTERN and ROSENCRANTZ declare to Claudius
"To lay our service freely at your feet"

TEXT ACT 2 scene 2

GERTRUDE
Thanks, Guildenstern, and gentle Rosencrantz.
And I beseech you instantly to visit
My too much chang'd son. Go, some of you,
And bring these gentlemen where Hamlet is.

GUILDENSTERN
Heavens make our presence and our practices
Pleasant and helpful to him!

GERTRUDE
Ay, amen!

*<Exeunt **ROSENCRANTZ** and **GUILDENSTERN**, escorted by attendants>*

*<Enter **POLONIUS**>*

POLONIUS
Th' ambassadors from Norway, my good lord,
Are joyfully returned.

CLAUDIUS
Thou still hast been the father of good news.

POLONIUS
Have I, my lord? I assure my good liege,
I hold my duty as I hold my soul,
Both to my God and to my gracious king.
And I do think—or else this brain of mine
Hunts not the trail of policy so sure
As it hath used to do—that I have found
The very cause of Hamlet's lunacy.

CLAUDIUS
Oh, speak of that. That do I long to hear.

POLONIUS
Give first admittance to th' ambassadors.
My news shall be the fruit to that great feast.

CLAUDIUS
Thyself do grace to them, and bring them in.

*<Exit **POLONIUS**>*

He tells me, my dear Gertrude, he hath found
The head and source of all your son's distemper.

GERTRUDE
I doubt it is no other but the main:
His father's death and our o'er-hasty marriage.

EXPLANATION

Both men very obligingly accede to the king's and queen's request to help them restore Hamlet to his former self. Gertrude was very grateful and urges the men to meet Hamlet.

"And I beseech you instantly visit
My too much chang'd son"

Polonius tells the king that the ambassadors from Norway, has returned.

Shakespeare presents Polonius as a very fickle character bordering on comic because he assumes an air of authority, yet all his actions are questionable and destructive, and he pays dearly for it later in the play.

He is quite content at being flattered by the king when the king says,

"Thou still has been the father of good news"

Once again, he conjures up false information about Hamlet to present to the king hence trying to gain the king's approval.

"that I have found
The very cause of Hamlet's lunacy"

The king is excited, and this news is,

"That do I long to hear"

Polonius boasts,

"My news shall be the fruit to that great feast"

Claudius tells Gertrude that Polonius,

"hath found
The head and source of your son's distemper"

Gertrude now admits that their,

"o'er hasty marriage"

is the cause of Hamlet's woes. We can detect a sense of regret in her tone.

CLAUDIUS
Well, we shall sift him.

*<Enter **POLONIUS** with ambassadors **VOLTEMAND** and **CORNELIUS**>*

—Welcome, my good friends!
Say, Voltemand, what from our brother Norway?

VOLTEMAND
Most fair return of greetings and desires.
Upon our first, he sent out to suppress
His nephew's levies, which to him appeared
To be a preparation 'gainst the Polack,
But, better looked into, he truly found
It was against your highness. Whereat grieved—
That so his sickness, age, and impotence
Was falsely borne in hand—sends out arrests
On Fortinbras, which he, in brief, obeys,
Receives rebuke from Norway, and in fine
Makes vow before his uncle never more
To give th' assay of arms against your majesty.
Whereon old Norway, overcome with joy,
Gives him three thousand crowns in annual fee
And his commission to employ those soldiers,
So levied as before, against the Polack,
With an entreaty, herein further shown,
That it might please you to give quiet pass
Through your dominions for this enterprise,
On such regards of safety and allowance
As therein are set down.

(*VOLTEMAND gives CLAUDIUS a document*)

CLAUDIUS
It likes us well,
And at our more considered time we'll read,
Answer, and think upon this business.
Meantime we thank you for your well-took labour.
Go to your rest. At night we'll feast together.
Most welcome home!

*<Exeunt **VOLTEMAND** and **CORNELIUS**>*

EXPLANATION

Claudius greets Voltemand and Cornelius with much zest and vigour. They tell him that the king of Norway is very annoyed about his nephew's preparation for war against Denmark. He is also disgruntled that Fortinbras took advantage of his,

"sickness, age, and impotence"

to wage war and he had ordered his arrest.

Fortinbras promised that he would not threaten Denmark again.

"Makes vows before his uncle never more
To give th' assay of arms against your majesty"

The king was so excited at this promise that he gave Fortinbras a huge annual fee.

Claudius is thrilled at this news,

"It likes us well"

and promised to read the document sent by the king.

"Meantime we thank you for your well-took labour"

Polonius is anxious to speak to the king and queen about his daughter's encounter with Hamlet.

POLONIUS speaks with CLAUDIUS and GERTRUDE about Hamlet's insane behaviour towards his daughter Ophelia

POLONIUS
This business is well ended.
My liege and madam, to expostulate
What majesty should be, what duty is,
Why day is day, night night, and time is time,
Were nothing but to waste night, day, and time.
Therefore, since brevity is the soul of wit
And tediousness the limbs and outward flourishes,
I will be brief: your noble son is mad.
Mad call I it, for, to define true madness,
What is 't but to be nothing else but mad?
But let that go.
GERTRUDE
More matter, with less art.
POLONIUS
Madam, I swear I use no art at all.
That he is mad, 'tis true. Tis true, 'tis pity,
And pity 'tis 'tis true—a foolish figure,
But farewell it, for I will use no art.
Mad let us grant him then. And now remains
That we find out the cause of this effect,
Or rather say, the cause of this defect,
For this effect defective comes by cause.
Thus it remains, and the remainder thus.
Perpend.
(*He produces a letter*)
I have a daughter—have while she is mine—
Who in her duty and obedience, mark,
Hath given me this. Now gather and surmise

(*He reads a letter*)

"To the celestial and my soul's idol, the most
beautified Ophelia"—
That's an ill phrase, a vile phrase.
"Beautified" is a vile phrase.
But you shall hear.

(*He continues to read the letter*)

"In her excellent white bosom, these," etc.—
GERTRUDE
Came this from Hamlet to her?

Once again, we see Polonius making himself look and sound comical. Gertrude is anxious for the news about her son's deranged behaviour, yet Polonius presents her with a long-drawn boring speech before he comes to the point.

She becomes rather irate at his silly antics to curry favour that she retorts,

"More matter, with less art"

She is very clearly accusing him of play-acting which he vehemently denies.

"Madam, I swear I use no art at all"

He tells them that Hamlet is mad because his daughter rejected his love. He also says that a solution needs to be sourced to end his madness.

He then produces a love letter written by Hamlet to Ophelia. He is very proud about how obedient and submissive his daughter is to his demands.

"Who in her duty and obedience, mark,
Hath given me this"

He is also dramatic when he reads the letter, and he scorns Hamlet for using the phrase

"beautified"

calling it,

"an ill phrase, a vile phrase"

CLAUDIUS listens as POLONIUS reads Hamlet's love letter to Ophelia

POLONIUS (*continues*)

Good madam, stay a while. I will be faithful.

(He *continues to read the letter*)

"Doubt thou the stars are fire,
Doubt that the sun doth move,
Doubt truth to be a liar,
But never doubt I love."
O dear Ophelia, I am ill at these numbers.
I have not art to reckon my groans,
but that I love thee best,
oh, most best, believe it. Adieu.

(*He continues to read the letter*)

Thine evermore, most dear lady,
whilst this machine is to him, Hamlet.

This in obedience hath my daughter shown me,
And more above, hath his solicitings,
As they fell out by time, by means, and place,
All given to mine ear.

CLAUDIUS

But how hath she received his love?

POLONIUS

What do you think of me?

CLAUDIUS

As of a man faithful and honorable.

Polonius has now taken centre stage and he wants to be reassured by the king and queen that they appreciate his loyalty.

"Good Madam, stay a while. I will be faithful"

We must note how Polonius is 'in his element.'

He is lapping up all the attention he is getting but he is doing it on his daughter's strength – the letter. He seems to have the king and queen at his 'mercy' because they are desperate for news and Polonius got the 'answer.'

Polonius continues to read Hamlet's very emotional letter. Even in his love life we see a very confused, isolated character because he says that he cannot express his love adequately to Ophelia. We tend to pity Hamlet here because he is 'swimming in an ocean full of sharks. He is about to be betrayed by everyone close to him. Even in life in general, he cannot express his pain and sadness to anyone. He must fight his battles alone. Everyone seems to be capitalising on his grief and his weakness as Polonius is shamefully doing here.

'I have no art to reckon my groans'

This letter peaked Claudius' interest and he asks,

"But how Hath she received his love?"

GERTRUDE, CLAUDIUS, POLONIUS discussing the intent expressed in the letter, "But how Hath she received his love?"

TEXT ACT 2 scene 2

POLONIUS
I would fain prove so. But what might you think,
When I had seen this hot love on the wing—
As I perceived it, I must tell you that,
Before my daughter told me—what might you,
Or my dear majesty your queen here, think,
If I had played the desk or table-book,
Or given my heart a winking, mute and dumb,Or
looked upon this love with idle sight?
What might you think? No, I went round to work,
And my young mistress thus I did bespeak:
"Lord Hamlet is a prince out of thy star.
This must not be." And then I prescripts gave her,
That she should lock herself from his resort,
Admit no messengers, receive no tokens.
Which done, she took the fruits of my advice,
And he, repelled—a short tale to make—
Fell into a sadness, then into a fast,
Thence to a watch, thence into a weakness,
Thence to a lightness, and, by this declension,
Into the madness wherein now he raves
And all we mourn for.

CLAUDIUS
(*to Gertrude*) Do you think 'tis this?

GERTRUDE
It may be, very like.

POLONIUS
Hath there been such a time —
I would fain know that —
That I have positively said, " 'Tis so,"
When it proved otherwise?

CLAUDIUS
Not that I know.

POLONIUS
(*points to his head and shoulders*)
Take this from this if this be otherwise.
If circumstances lead me, I will find
Where truth is hid, though it were hid indeed
Within the center.

CLAUDIUS
How may we try it further?

POLONIUS
You know sometimes he walks four hours togetherHere in the lobby.

GERTRUDE
So he does indeed.

EXPLANATION

Polonius tells him that he bade his daughter not to see Hamlet or welcome any attention from Him.

This has caused Hamlet to sink into the 'depths of despair' and this is the reason for his crazy behaviour. Shakespeare gives us a peek into Polonius' distorted mind. Everything that he is saying is merely a figment of his imagination and an urgent need to feel important. He is unaware that Hamlet is merely acting crazy.

It can foreshadow Hamlet's confused state of mind. We are given an insight into the character's psychological dilemmas in this play. It seems to be an exploration of their minds rather than their characters.

Polonius goes on and on 'blowing his own trumpet' about his loyalty and his total control of his daughter and how she,

"took the fruits of his advice"

When he gave her instructions to totally reject Hamlet's attention and advances.

Polonius is still harping about what a loyal servant he is and emphatically states that he never lies, yet he just asked Renaldo to lie when he spies on his son in France.

"That I have positively said 'Tis so
When it proved otherwise?"

Polonius' colourful and verbose character helps to cut the tension in the play because his utterances have a comic flavour to them. Claudius and Polonius plan to spy on Hamlet.

TEXT ACT 2 scene 2

POLONIUS
At such a time I'll loose my daughter to him.
(*to Claudius*) Be you and I behind an arras then
Mark the encounter. If he love her not
And be not from his reason fall'n thereon,
Let me be no assistant for a state
But keep a farm and carters.
CLAUDIUS
We will try it.

< *Enter **HAMLET**, reading on a book*>

*Enter **HAMLET**, reading on a book*

GERTRUDE
But look where sadly the poor wretch comes reading
POLONIUS
Away, I do beseech you, both away.
I'll board him presently. O, give me leave.

< *Exeunt **CLAUDIUS** and **GERTRUDE**>*

How does my good Lord Hamlet?
HAMLET
Well, God-'a'-mercy.
POLONIUS
Do you know me, my lord?
HAMLET
Excellent well. You are a fishmonger.
POLONIUS
Not I, my lord.
HAMLET
Then I would you were so honest a man.
POLONIUS
Honest, my lord?

EXPLANATION

Polonius says that when Hamlet walks in the lobby he will,

"loose my daughter to him"

Polonius delights in using his daughter as a pawn as though she is a commodity to be toyed with. In act 1, he referred to her virginity as though it was merchandise to be traded for a high price.

Here he is talking about 'losing his daughter' to Hamlet as though she is on sale. The fact that Hamlet calls him a 'fishmonger' can also suggest this. It's obvious that Polonius is using her to further his ambition and gain favour with the king and queen.

It is also symbolic of how trapped Ophelia is - like a caged bird let loose to do a specific job. Polonius is so sure that Hamlet's love for Ophelia has caused his madness and if proved otherwise then he is prepared to lose his job,

"Let me be no assistant for a state
But keep a farm and carters"

Hamlet is feigning insanity and he uses this opportunity to speak his mind and let people know about how he feels about their hypocritical ways.

Shakespeare points out the hypocrisy in characters like Polonius because he 'runs with the hares and hunts with the hounds'. Just now he was berating Hamlet in front of his parents yet immediately he assumes a different character on meeting Hamlet.
He is acting all kind and friendly.

"How does my good Lord Hamlet?"

Shakespeare cuts the tension by adding some humour here when Hamlet accuses Polonius of being a fishmonger.

There are many things that are plaguing Hamlet's mind, like lies, deceit, and immorality. He attacks Polonius' lying nature when confronted with him.

TEXT	EXPLANATION
HAMLET Ay, sir. To be honest, as this world goes, Is to be one man picked out of ten thousand. **POLONIUS** That's very true, my lord. **HAMLET** For if the sun breed maggots in a dead dog, Being a good kissing carrion— Have you a daughter? **POLONIUS** I have, my lord. **HAMLET** Let her not walk i' th' sun. Conception is a blessing, but, as your daughter may conceive— Friend, look to 't. (*He reads again*) **POLONIUS** *(aside)* How say you by that? Still harping on my daughter. Yet he knew me not at first. He said I was a fishmonger. He is far gone, far gone. And truly in my youth I suffered much extremity for love, very near this. I'll speak to him again. — (*to Hamlet*) What do you read, my lord? **HAMLET** Words, words, words. **POLONIUS** What is the matter, my lord? **HAMLET** Between who? **POLONIUS** I mean, the matter that you read, my lord. **HAMLET** Slanders, sir. For the satirical rogue says here That old men have grey beards, That their faces are wrinkled, Their eyes purging thick amber and plum- tree gum, And that they have a plentiful lack of wit, Together with most weak hams—all which, sir, Though I most powerfully and potently believe, Yet I hold it not honesty to have it Thus set down; for yourself, sir, should be old as I am If like a crab youcould go backward. (*He reads again*)	Hamlet says that there are very few men who are honest in the world, "To be honest, as this world goes, Is to be one man picked out of ten thousand" Hamlet shows his disgust for man's scheming nature by using a graphic, vile imagery, "For if the sun breed maggots in a dead dog, Being a good kissing carrion" His reasoning for this imagery is that the sun is such a beautiful spectacle, yet it can produce something so horrible like maggots to feed on a carcass. In the same way people are born beautiful, 'conception is a blessing', but have the innate ability to lie and kill and feast on the death of their prey, just like how Claudius killed his brother and is feasting on his power and wealth. Of course, Polonius misunderstands Hamlet's reasoning and still insists that he is mad because of his daughter's rejection of him. Hamlet tells Polonius that he is reading lies from his book. He further verbally attacks Polonius by saying that old men have no wit or wisdom and that their faces are wrinkled and that they have weak legs. "That old men have grey beards, That their faces are wrinkled" He believes these facts to be true but since Polonius is an old man, he thinks it is rude to expose him to such slander. It's quite funny how cleverly Hamlet uses the play on words and alliterative devices to expose Polonius' fraudulent behaviour. He knows that he is working deviously for the king. "Though I most powerfully and potently believe, Yet hold it not honesty to have it Thus set down"

POLONIUS
(*aside*) Though this be madness,
Yet there is method in 't.—
(*to* HAMLET) Will you walk out of the air, my lord?
HAMLET
Into my grave.
POLONIUS
Indeed, that is out of the air. (*aside*)
How pregnant sometimes his replies are.
A happiness that often madness hits on,
Which reason and sanity could not so prosperously
Be delivered of. I will leave him
And suddenly contrive the means of meeting
Between him and my daughter. —
(*to* HAMLET) My honorable lord,
I will most humbly take my leave of you.
HAMLET
You cannot, sir, take from me any thing
That I will more willingly part withal—
Except my life, except mylife, except my life.
POLONIUS
Fare you well, my lord.
HAMLET
(*aside*) These tedious old fools!

< *Enter **ROSENCRANTZ** and **GUILDENSTERN*** >

POLONIUS
You go to seek the Lord Hamlet. There he is.
ROSENCRANTZ
God save you, sir!

< *Exit **POLONIUS*** >

GUILDENSTERN
My honored lord!
ROSENCRANTZ
My most dear lord!
HAMLET
My excellent good friends! How dost thou,
Guildenstern? Ah, Rosencrantz! Good lads, how
do you both?
ROSENCRANTZ
As the indifferent children of the earth.
GUILDENSTERN
Happy, in that we are not over-happy.
On Fortune's cap we are not the very button.
HAMLET
Nor the soles of her shoes?

POLONIUS tries to get HAMLET to reveal his true intent

The play is full of pretentious behaviour.

First we saw it in Claudius, then Polonius and now his friends - all directed towards Hamlet.

We pity Hamlet because his mission is to restore dignity, morality, and truth in a diseased Denmark, but he bears all the brunt of these atrocities, and the burden is too heavy to carry all alone.

He is bombarded with it from all sides creating a sense of revulsion and disgust in him.

Shakespeare presents us with all these false characters – even the queen was 'seeming' to be mourning her husband's death.

These vile and pretentious characters are symbolic of the moral, social, and psychological degradation of Denmark.

ROSENCRANTZ, GUILDENSTERN, POLONIUS attempting to discover HAMLET's madness

TEXT ACT 2 scene 2

ROSENCRANTZ
Neither, my lord.
HAMLET
Then you live about her waist,
Or in the middle of her favours?
GUILDENSTERN
Faith, her privates we.
HAMLET
In the secret parts of Fortune? Oh, most true.
She is a strumpet. What news?
ROSENCRANTZ
None, my lord, but that the world's grown honest.
HAMLET
Then is doomsday near.
But your news is not true.
Let me question more in particular.
What have you, my good friends,
Deserved at the hands of fortune that she sends
You to prison hither?
GUILDENSTERN
Prison, my lord?
HAMLET
Denmark's a prison.
ROSENCRANTZ
Then is the world one.
HAMLET
A goodly one, in which there are many confines,
wards, and dungeons,
Denmark being one o' th'worst.
ROSENCRANTZ
We think not so, my lord.
HAMLET
Why, then, 'tis none to you,
for there is nothing either good or bad,
but thinking makes it so.
To me it is a prison.
ROSENCRANTZ
Why then, your ambition makes it one.
'Tis too narrow for your mind.
HAMLET
O God, I could be bounded in a nutshell
And count myself a king of infinite space,
Were it not that I have bad dreams?
GUILDENSTERN
Which dreams indeed are ambition,
for the very substance of the ambitious
is merely the shadow of a dream.

EXPLANATION

One may ask the question, if all the important figures in Hamlet's life is so morally corrupt, how can Hamlet cope in his mammoth task to restore Denmark to a normal state?

As we know that he is a man who reflects on these atrocities, and he is not a man of action. He is a man with a conscience.

Will he become a victim of his innocence and his quest for truth and morality?

Rosencrantz and Guildenstern meet Hamlet and they greet him very cordially.

There's some light banter about them being,

"In the secret parts of Fortune?"

Hamlet goes on to say that Lady Luck is a strumpet. Hamlet's reference to Lady Luck being a loose woman can be attributed to his anger towards his mother. He is furious with her indiscretions with his uncle,

"She is a strumpet"

When Rosencrantz said that,

"the world's grown honest"

Hamlet was very sceptical and asks,

"Then is doomsday near"

He refused to believe that there is any honesty in the world. And he also said that,

"Denmark's a prison"

He uses this imagery to describe the decay and decadent state that Denmark is imprisoned by, which is fuelled by the head – the king.

HAMLET
A dream itself is but a shadow.
ROSENCRANTZ
Truly, and I hold ambition of so airy and light a quality that it is but a shadow's shadow.
HAMLET
Then are our beggars' bodies, and our monarchs
And outstretched heroes the beggars' shadows.
Shall we to th' court? For by my fay, I cannot reason.
ROSENCRANTZ, GUILDENSTERN
We'll wait upon you.
HAMLET
No such matter. I will not sort you with the rest of my servants, for, to speak to you like an honest man,
I am most dreadfully attended.
But in the beaten way of friendship,
What make you at Elsinore?
ROSENCRANTZ
To visit you, my lord, no other occasion.
HAMLET
Beggar that I am, I am even poor in thanks,
But I thank you, and sure, dear friends,
My thanks are too dear a halfpenny.
Were you not sent for? Is it your own inclining?
Is it a free visitation?
Come, come, deal justly with me.
Come, come. Nay, speak.
GUILDENSTERN
What should we say, my lord?
HAMLET
Why, anything, but to th' purpose. You were sent for
and there is a kind of confession in your looks
your modesties have not craft enough to colour.
I know the good king and queen have sent for you.
ROSENCRANTZ
To what end, my lord?
HAMLET
That you must teach me.
But let me conjure you,
by the rights of our fellowship,
By the consonancy of our youth,
By the obligation of our ever-preserved love, and
By what more dear a better proposer
Could charge you withal: be even and direct with me
whether you were sent for or no.
ROSENCRANTZ
(to Guildenstern) What say you?

Rosencrantz and Guildenstern probe Hamlet's intent by engaging him in an abstract conversation on dreams. But Hamlet knowing their intent bamboozle them, so they cannot detect if he is suffering from true madness or not, as suspected by Claudius.

HAMLET debates with ROSENCRANTZ and GUILDENSTERN about the meaning of dreams

Hamlet is very perceptive and suspicious about his friends' motives and their sudden appearance.

He questioned them about the purpose of their visit and who had requested their visit.

He noticed their guilty looks and urged them to tell the truth since they were dear friends since their youth.

"Come, come, deal justly with me"

Hamlet was forthright and told them very candidly that the king and queen had sent for them. He remarked that their looks and pale faces made him believe that.

"I know the good king and queen have sent for you"

He urged them to be honest and direct with him, 'whether you were sent for or no.'

TEXT ACT 2 scene 2

HAMLET
(*aside*) Nay, then, I have an eye of you—
If you love me,hold not off.
GUILDENSTERN
My lord, we were sent for.
HAMLET
I will tell you why.
So shall my anticipation prevent you're discovery,
And your secrecy to the king
And queen moult no feather. I have of late—
But wherefore I know not—lost all my mirth,
Forgone all custom of exercises,
And indeed it goes so heavily with my disposition
That this goodly frame, the earth,
Seems to me a sterile promontory.
This most excellent canopy, the air—
Look you, this brave o'er-hanging firmament,
This majestical roof fretted with golden fire—
Why, it appears no other thing to me than a foul
And pestilent congregation of vapours.
What a piece of work is a man!
How noble in reason
How infinite in faculty! In form and moving
How express and admirable! In action
How like an angel, in apprehension
How like a god! The beauty of the world.
The paragon of animals. And yet, to me,
What is this quintessence of dust?
Man delights not me. No, nor woman neither,
though by your smiling you seem to say so.
ROSENCRANTZ
My lord, there was no such stuff in my thoughts.
HAMLET
Why did you laugh then,
When I said, "man delights not me"?
ROSENCRANTZ
To think, my lord, if you delight not in man,
What Lenten entertainment
The players shall receive from you
We coted them on the way,
And hither are they coming to offer you service?
HAMLET
He that plays the king shall be welcome.
His majesty shall have tribute of me.
The adventurous knight shall use his foil and target,
The lover shall not sigh gratis,

EXPLANATION

Hamlet prevents their discomfort by telling them that he knows the reason for their visit and hints that they are in liaison and have secrets with the king and queen.

"And your secrecy to the king
And queen moult no feather."

Hamlet has lost the will to live, lost his laughter, stopped exercising and the world has no meaning to him anymore.

"lost all my mirth,
Forgone all custom of exercises"

Even the sky with its beautiful golden sun has lost its beauty. To me it's nothing but a dirty and filthy, diseased filled air.

"This majestical roof fretted with golden fire"

He talks of man being perfect. He has reasoning power, dexterous in shape and movements 'like an angel' and he is superior to animals, 'The paragon of animals'.

"What a piece of work is man!
How noble in reason,
How infinite in faculty!"

Hamlet continues by saying no man or woman interests him anymore. We are just dust?

"What is this quintessence of dust?"

He uses a biblical imagery, when God created man, He used dust to do so. We are created with dust and when we die, we return to dust – the earth –
'Ashes to ashes, dust to dust'.

Rosencrantz tells him that they have met a group of actors who are on their way to entertain him.

Hamlet is keen to welcome the one who plays the king, and he intends to treat him like a real king. This foreshadows Hamlet's action towards the king later in the play.

HAMLET (*continues*)
The humorous man shall end his part in peace,
The clown shall make those laugh
Whose lungs are tickle o' th' sear,
And the lady shall say hermind freely,
Or the blank verse shall halt for 't.
What players are they?
ROSENCRANTZ
Even those you were wont to take delight in,
The Tragedians of the city.
HAMLET
How chances it they travel? Their residence,
Both in reputation and profit, was better both ways
ROSENCRANTZ
I think their inhibition comes
By the means of the late innovation.
HAMLET
Do they hold the same estimation they did When I was in the city? Are they so followed?
ROSENCRANTZ
No, indeed are they not.
HAMLET
How comes it? Do they grow rusty?
ROSENCRANTZ
Nay, their endeavor keeps in the wonted pace.
But there is, sir, an eyrie of children, little eyases,
That cry out on the top of question
And are most tyrannically clapped for 't.
These are now the fashion,
And so berattle the common stages—
So they call them—
That many wearing rapiers
Are afraid of goose quills
And dare scarce come thither.
HAMLET
What, are they children?
Who maintains 'em? How are they escoted?
Will they pursue the quality no longer
Than they can sing?
Will they not say afterwards?
If they should grow themselves to common players As it is most like if their means areno better,
Their writers do them wrong to make them
Exclaim against their own succession?
ROSENCRANTZ
Faith, there has been much to do on both sides,
And the nation holds it no sin
To tar them to controversy.

Hamlet makes known to Rosencrantz that the only pastime he is interested in is the theatre.

HAMLET and ROSENCRANTZ spot the Players arriving

THE PLAYERS recognise Hamlet

Hamlet remarks about the children,

"What, are they children?"

THE PLAYERS arrive at Elsinore Castle

TEXT ACT 2 scene 2

ROSENCRANTZ (*continues*)
There was, for a while, no money bid for argument
Unless the poet and the player went to cuffs
In the question.

HAMLET
Is 't possible?

GUILDENSTERN
O,there has been much throwing about of brains

HAMLET
Do the boys carry it away?

ROSENCRANTZ
Ay, that they do, my lord.
Hercules and his load too.

HAMLET
It is not very strange.
For my uncle is King of Denmark,
And those that would make mouths at him
While my father lived give twenty, forty, fifty,
A hundred ducats apiece for his picture in little.
'Sblood, there is something in this more than natural
If philosophy could find it out.

<*Flourish for the* ***PLAYERS*** *within*>

GUILDENSTERN
There are the players.

HAMLET
Gentlemen, you are welcome to Elsinore.
Your hands, come then.
Th' appurtenance of welcome is fashion
And ceremony.
Let me comply with you in this garb—
Lest my extent to the players, which,
I tell you, must show fairly outwards,
Should more appear like entertainment than yours.
You are welcome.
But my uncle-father and aunt-mother are deceived.

GUILDENSTERN
In what, my dear lord?

HAMLET
I am but mad north-north-west.
When the wind is southerly,
I know a hawk from a handsaw.

EXPLANATION

Hamlet asks many questions about the children's acting abilities because adults generally played these roles. Rosencrantz says that without the money earnt by using child actors there would have been a big fight between the poets (playwrights) and the adult players,

"There was, for a while, no money bid for argument
Unless the poet and the player went to cuffs"

Guildenstern concurs,

"O, there has been much throwing about of brains"

Rosencrantz tells Hamlet that the child actors (boys) have saved the poets from bankruptcy and are earning the money to keep the players afloat although it means extra hard work by them, as performed by Hercules in Greek myth.

"Ay, that they do, my lord.
Hercules and his load too"

Hamlet welcomes the players, but there is a tone of sarcasm in Hamlet's voice.

HAMLET welcomes THE PLAYERS to Elsinore "Gentlemen, you are welcome to Elsinore"

He scorns the superficial, polite customs,

"Th' appurtenance of welcome is fashion
And ceremony"

He says,
"You are welcome.
But my uncle-father and aunt-mother are deceived"

hinting at Claudius and Gertrude's unnatural union.

TEXT ACT 2 scene 2

POLONIUS
Well be with you, gentlemen
HAMLET
Hark you, Guildenstern, and you too—
at each ear a hearer. (*indicates Polonius*)
That great baby you see there
Is not yet out of his swaddling – clouts
ROSENCRANTZ
Happily he's the second time come to them,
for theysay an old man is twice a child.
HAMLET
(*Aside to Rosencrantz and Guildenstern*)
I will prophesy he comes to tell me of the players.
Mark it.
(*to Polonius*)— You say right, sir.
O' Monday morning, 'twas so indeed.
POLONIUS
My lord, I have news to tell you.
HAMLET
My lord, I have news to tell you.
When Roscius was an actor in Rome—
POLONIUS
The actors are com hither, my lord.
HAMLET
Buzz, buzz.
POLONIUS
Upon my honor—
HAMLET
Then came each actor on his ass—
POLONIUS
The best actors in the world,
either for tragedy, comedy,
history, pastoral, pastoral-comical,
historical-pastoral, tragical-historical,
tragical-comical-historical-pastoral,
scene individable, or poem unlimited.
Seneca cannot be too heavy, nor Plautus too light.
For the law of writ and the liberty,
These are the only men.
HAMLET
O Jephthah, judge of Israel,
What a treasure hadst thou!
POLONIUS
What a treasure had he, my lord?
HAMLET
Why,
One fair daughter and no more,
The which he loved passing well.

EXPLANATION

Hamlet constantly belittles Polonius. It's obvious that he is not in favour of his scheming, devious ways. He accuses him of being a baby who is still wearing his diapers.

"Is not yet out of his swaddling – clouts"

He makes fun of him, 'buzz, buzz,' when he tells him about the arrival of the actors which he already knew about.

"I will prophesy he comes to tell me of the players.
Mark it"

Hamlet sarcastically repeats Polonius' statement,

"My lord, I have news to tell you"

As if Hamlet's news is more important than Polonius' news.

Polonius draws Hamlet's attention to the arrival of the actors who he considers are 'the best in the world', not matter what the type of play.

Hamlet compares Polonius to the biblical character Jephthah who was a judge and warrior. He promised God that if he wins, he will sacrifice whoever meets him first. He ended up sacrificing his only daughter.

Similarly, Polonius unwittingly used his daughter as a pawn which led to her death.

"O Jephthah, judge of Israel,
What a treasure hadst thou!"

Hamlet's taunts are foreboding because Ophelia's life has a dramatic ending as Hamlet foresees because of Polonius' interference.

POLONIUS
(*aside*) Still on my daughter.
HAMLET
Am I not i' th' right, old Jephthah?
POLONIUS
If you call me Jephthah, my lord,
I have a daughter that I love passing well.
HAMLET
Nay, that follows not.
POLONIUS
What follows, then, my lord?
HAMLET
Why,
As by lot, God wot,
and then, you know,
It came to pass, as most like it was—
The first row of the pious chanson
Will show you more for look
Where my abridgement comes.

<*Enter the* ***PLAYERS***>

You are welcome, masters, welcome, all! —
I am glad to see thee well. —
Welcome, good friends. —O old friend?
Why, thy face is valenced since I saw thee last. Comest thou to beard me in Denmark? —
What, my young lady and mistress!
By 'r Lady, your ladyshipis nearer to heaven than When I saw you last, by the altitude of a chopine.
Pray God, your voice,
Like a piece of uncurrent gold,
Be not cracked within the ring. —
Masters, you are all welcome.
We'll e'en to 't like French falconers,
fly at anything we see.
We'll have a speech straight.
Come, give us a taste of your quality.
Come, a passionate speech.
FIRST PLAYER
What speech, my good lord?
HAMLET
I heard thee speak me a speech once,
But it was never acted.
Or, if it was, not above once, for the play,
I remember, pleased not the million,
'Twas caviary to the general.

POLONIUS tries to get HAMLET to admit he loves Ophelia

Hamlet welcomes and compliments the players dress, beards, and their appearance.

In the Elizabethan era women had no status and they were not allowed to participate in plays. Hence men played all the women's roles dressed up as women.

Hamlet requests a passionate speech from them. He remembers it very well, but it has never been enacted so he wants it enacted.

"masters, welcome, all! —
I am glad to see thee well. —"

Hamlet compares their voice to gold,

"your voice,
Like a piece of uncurrent gold"

Hamlet asks the First Player if he recalls a speech made by the player which was not acted, but received with much acclaim

"I heard thee speak me a speech once,
But it was never acted"

TEXT ACT 2 scene 2

HAMLET (*continues*)
But it was—as I received it, and others,
Whose judgments in such matters
Cried in the top of mine—an excellent play,
Well digested in the scenes,
Set down with as much modesty as cunning.
I remember, one said
There were no sallets in the lines
To make the matter savory,
Nor no matter in the phrase
That might indict the author of affectation,
But called it an honest method,
As wholesome as sweet,
And by very much more handsome than fine.
One speech in it I chiefly loved.
'Twas Aeneas' tale to Dido and thereabout of it,
Especially where he speaks of Priam's slaughter
If it live inyour memory, begin at this line—
Let me see, let me see —
The rugged Pyrrhus, like th' Hyrcanian beast—
It is not so. It begins with Pyrrhus—
The rugged Pyrrhus, he whose sable arms,
Black as his purpose, did the night resemble
When he lay couched in the ominous horse,
Hath now this dread and black complexion smeared
With heraldry more dismal. Head to foot
Now is he total gules, horridly tricked
With blood of fathers, mothers, daughters, sons,
Baked and impasted with the parching streets,
That lend a tyrannous and damn'd light
To their lord's murder. Roasted in wrath and fire,
And thus o'er-sized with coagulate gore,
With eyes like carbuncles, the hellish Pyrrhus
Old grandsire Priam seeks.
So, proceed you.

POLONIUS
'Fore God, my lord, well spoken,
With good accent and good discretion.

FIRST PLAYER
Anon he finds him
Striking too short at Greeks. His antique sword,
Rebellious to his arm, lies where it falls,
Repugnant to command. Unequal matched,

EXPLANATION

The critics called it,

"an excellent play,
Well-digested in the scenes"

The poem is modest as well as cunning because it tells a story, and it can tug at people's conscience.

"Set down with as much modesty as cunning"

It's "As wholesome as sweet"

and Hamlet seems to develop more confidence in his speech since the acting group arrived. There's a certain rhythm in his tone and he seems to be relishing the fact that he is now in control and can have a voice and express his opinion and give vent to his frustration whereas in Act 1 scene 2 line 159, in his soliloquy he says,

"But break, my heart, for I must hold my tongue."

His speech is very melodramatic, and he speaks in blank verse because he wants his message to 'go home'.

He very aptly chose the story of the Trojan horse where Pyrrhus, Archilles' son went to Troy to avenge his father's death by hiding in a Trojan horse. This can very well reflect Hamlet's life of betrayal and murder.

He was furious and strong,

"The rugged Pyrrhus, he whose sable arms,
Black as his purpose, did the night resemble"

Determined to avenge his father's death, he went in search of Priam,

"That lend a tyrannous and damn'd light
To their lord's murder"

Polonius was startled at this rendition but gives a compliment to Hamlet,

"Fore God, my lord, well spoken,
With good accent and good discretion."

TEXT ACT 2 scene 2

FIRST PLAYER
Pyrrhus at Priam drives, in rage strikes wide,
But with the whiff and wind of his fell sword
The unnerved father falls. Then senseless Ilium,
Seeming to feel this blow, with flaming top
Stoops to his base, and with a hideous crash
Takes prisoner Pyrrhus' ear. For, lo, his sword,
Which was declining on the milky head
Of reverend Priam, seemed i' th' air to stick.
So as a painted tyrant Pyrrhus stood,
And, like a neutral to his will and matter,
Did nothing.
But as we often see against some storm
A silence in the heavens, the rack stand still,
The bold winds speechless, and the orb below
As hush as death, anon the dreadful thunder
Doth rend the region. So, after Pyrrhus' pause,
Aroused vengeance sets him new a-work.
And never did the Cyclops' hammers fallOn
Mars's armour forged for proof eterne
With less remorse than Pyrrhus' bleeding sword
Now falls on Priam.
Out, out, thou strumpet Fortune!
All you godsIn general synod take away her power,
Break all the spokes and fellies from her wheel,
And bowl the round nave down the hill of heaven,
As low as to the fiends!

POLONIUS
This is too long.

HAMLET
It shall to the barber's, with your beard. —Prithee,say on.
He's for a jig or a tale of bawdry, or he sleeps.
Say on. Come to Hecuba.

FIRST PLAYER
But who, ah woe,
Who had seen the mobbled queen—

HAMLET
"The mobbled queen"?

POLONIUS
That's good. "mobbled queen" is good.

EXPLANATION

The play gives us a detailed visual picture of how Pyrrhus exacted revenge on the king who killed his father and how distraught the queen was.

This play can very well mirror Claudius' killing of the king and usurping the crown and Hamlet is bent on taking revenge for his father's death just like Pyrrhus.

"With less remorse than Pyrrhus' bleeding sword Now falls on Priam"

Once again, we see 'Lady Luck' called a 'strumpet', a whore,

"Out, out, thou strumpet Fortune!"

The Gods mudt punish her for her devious acts and take away all her fortune and power,

"take away her power,
Break all the spokes and fellies from her wheel"

The First Player mentioned the 'mobbled queen'
And the mention of the queen had Hamlet question, "The mobbled queen?"

This piqued his interest and he thought about how his mother 'mourned' was when her husband died.

She didn't even wear her black mourning clothes like Hamlet did.

TEXT ACT 2 scene 2

FIRST PLAYER

Run barefoot up and down, threatening the flames
With bisson rheum, a clout upon that head
Where late the diadem stood, and for a robe,
About her lank and all o'erteemed loins,
A blanket, in the alarm of fear caught up—
Who this had seen, with tongue in venom steeped,
'Gainst fortune's state
Would treason have pronounc'd.
But if the gods themselves did see her then
When she saw Pyrrhus make malicious sport
In mincing with his sword her husband's limbs,
The instant burst of clamour that she made,
Unless things mortal move them not at all
Would have made milch the burning eyes of heaven,
And passion in the gods.

POLONIUS

Look whe'e he has not turned his colour
And has tears in 's eyes. —Prithee, no more.

HAMLET

(*to First Player*) 'Tis well.
I'll have thee speak outthe rest soon.
(*to Polonius*) Good my lord,
Will you see the players well bestowed?
Do you hear, let them be well used?
For they are the abstract
And brief chronicles of the time.
After your death you were better have a bad epitaph
Than their ill report while you live.

POLONIUS

My lord, I will use them according to their desert

HAMLET

God's bodykins, man, much better.
Use every man after his desert,
And who should 'scape whipping?
Use them after your own honour and dignity.
The less they deserve,
The more merit is in your bounty.
Take them in.

POLONIUS

Come, sirs.

HAMLET

Follow him, friends.
We'll hear a play tomorrow.
(*to First Player*)— Dost thou hear me,old friend?
Can you play *The Murder of Gonzago*?

EXPLANATION

The First Player continues the dramatic action within the speech.

"Run barefoot up and down, threatening the flames"

The play gives details of the queen in utter shock at seeing her husband die a horrible death. She was running around crying profusely. She gave such a terrible cry which,

Would have made milch the burning eyes of heaven

Polonius is very uncomfortable with the play because he knows that it is directed towards the present king and queen who he is very loyal to, and he makes many attempts to stop it.

"Look whe'e he has not turned his colour
And has tears in 's eyes"

Hamlet urges Polonius to treat the players well and pay them more than what they deserve, as this will enhance his prestige,

"Use them after your own honour and dignity"

Before they leave Hamlet asks them to perform,

"Can you play *The Murder of Gonzago*?"

THE PLAYER KING inspects HAMLET's new version of *The Murder of Gonzago*

TEXT ACT 2 scene 2

FIRST PLAYER
Ay, my lord.
HAMLET
We'll ha 't tomorrow night.
You could, for a need, study a speech
Of some dozen or sixteen lines
Which I would set down and insert in 't,
Could you not?
FIRST PLAYER
Ay, my lord.
HAMLET
Very well.
Follow that lord,
and look you mock him not.

< *Exeunt* ***POLONIUS*** *and the* ***PLAYERS***>

(*to Rosencrantz and Guildenstern*)
My good friends, I'll leave you till night.
You are welcome to Elsinore.
ROSENCRANTZ
Good my lord.
HAMLET
Ay, so. Good-bye to you.

<*Exeunt* ***ROSENCRANTZ*** *and* ***GUILDENSTERN***>

Now I am alone.
Oh, what a rogue and peasant slave am I!
Is it not monstrous that this player here
But in a fiction, in a dream of passion,
Could force his soul so to his own conceit
That from her working all his visage wanned,
Tears in his eyes, distraction in his aspect,
A broken voice, and his whole function suiting
With forms to his conceit? And all for nothing—
For Hecuba!
What's Hecuba to him or he to Hecuba
That he should weep for her?
What would he do had he the motive
And the cue for passion that I have?
He would drown the stage with tears
And cleave the general ear with horrid speech,
Make mad the guilty and appall the free,
Confound the ignorant, and amaze indeed

EXPLANATION

We are delighted to see a very bold and energised Hamlet who is taking control.

He tells the players that he would like to write a speech and they must learn it by tomorrow.

He even has a sense of humour and even pokes fun at Polonius. He mockingly tells the men not to make fun of him,

"And look you mock him not"

In this soliloquy Hamlet speaks in blank verse. There is a certain rhythm in his speech. He reprimands himself for causing such grief to the player. He feels he made him cry and feel distraught for nothing.

"all for nothing –
For Hecuba!"

He is annoyed that the player cried for the queen Hecuba. Imagine if he felt the passion that I feel and endure the pain within me then he would,

"drown the stage with tears"

And he will shock the audience with his woeful tales of deceit and murder that really happened. He would surely amaze everyone.

He will seriously distract the audience with his 'broken voice' but this will be in vain

Hamlet compares Hecuba's terrible actions to that of his mother's. Both had affairs which resulted in the death of their husbands.

TEXT ACT 2 scene 2

HAMLET (*continues*)
The very faculties of eyes and ears. Yet I,
A dull and muddy-mettled rascal, peak
Like John-a-dreams, unpregnant of my cause,
And can say nothing—no, not for a king,
Upon whose property and most dear life
A damn'd defeat was made.
Am I a coward? Who calls me "villain"?
Breaks my pate across? Plucks off my beard
And blows it in my face?
Tweaks me by the nose?
Gives me the lie i' th' throat
As deep as to the lungs? Who does me this?
Ha!
'Swounds, I should take it, for it cannot be
But I am pigeon-livered and lack gall
To make oppression bitter, or ere this
I should have fatted all the region kites
With this slave's offal. Bloody, bawdy villain!
Remorseless, treacherous, lecherous,
Kindless villain! O vengeance!
Why, what an ass am I! This is most brave,
That I, the son of a dear father murdered,
Prompted to my revenge by heaven and hell,
Must, like a whore, unpack my heart with words
And fall a-cursing like a very drab,
A scullion! Fie upon 't, foh!
About, my brain.—Hum,
I have heard that guilty creatures sitting at a play
Have, by the very cunning of the scene,
Been struck so to the soul that presently They
have proclaimed their malefactions.
For murder, though it have no tongue, will speak
With most miraculous organ. I'll have these players
Play something like the murder of my father
Before mine uncle. I'll observe his looks.
I'll tent him to the quick. If he do blench,
I know my course. The spirit that I have seen
May be the devil, and the devil hath power
T' assume a pleasing shape. Yea, and perhaps
Out of my weakness and my melancholy,
As he is very potent with such spirits,
Abuses me to damn me. I'll have grounds
More relative than this. The play's the thing
Wherein I'll catch the conscience of the king.

< Exit >

EXPLANATION

He is berating himself for not acting for his father's murder. He just moans about this injustice and does nothing about it. He has no plans in place to exact revenge, as his father expects of him.

He accuses himself of being,

"Am I a coward? Who calls me "Villain "?

He is so angry with his weakness to act that he calls himself,

"pigeon-liveried and lack gall
To make oppression bitter"

He doesn't have the guts to take revenge otherwise he would have fattened the vultures with the intestines of that slave. He is furious with his uncle and levels obscenities at him"

"Bloody, bawdy villain!
Remorseless, treacherous, lecherous,
Kindless villain! O vengeance!

Hamlet uses repeated exclamation marks in his rant, and we can denote that he is giving vent to his frustration and fury against his uncle.

He is confident now and says that,

"I know my course"

Now he doubts the ghost and thinks it's the devil who came in a disguise to 'damn-me' but he is assured that he got better ammunition and that is the play.

"I'll have grounds
More relative than this"

If he stages the play then his uncle will acknowledge his guilt and confess to his devious actions against his brother,

"The play's the thing
Wherein I'll catch the conscience of the king"

In Act 3 scene 1, the setting is a chamber inside the castle, the next day.

Enter the King, the Queen, Polonius, his daughter Ophelia, Rosencrantz and Guildenstern.

Claudius enquires if Rosencrantz and Guildenstern have discovered the reason for Hamlet's confused state of mind, but they could only detect a crafty madness.

Claudius asks them to press the matter, which they agree to. Exit Rosencrantz and Guildenstern.

Hamlet is sent for, and Claudius asks Gertrude to leave, while he and Polonius remain hidden to establish Hamlet's love for Ophelia.

Exit Gertrude.

Enter hamlet, philosophising, saying:

> *To be, or not to be: that is the question:*
> *Whether 'tis nobler in the mind to suffer*
> *The slings and arrows of outrageous fortune,*
> *Or to take arms against a sea of troubles,*
> ....

A soliloquy on living and dying.

Enter Ophelia, waiting for Hamlet to encounter her, as suggested she should do by her father Polonius with the approval of Claudius.

The exchange between the two, leaves Ophelia baffled and rejected as Hamlet at first denies the letter he gave her, and finally orders her to get to a nunnery.

Hamlet states before he exits that he will no more on it, as it hath made him mad.

Ophelia in a soliloquy expresses her dismay at being rejected by a noble mind.

Enter the King and Polonius to discuss what they have seen and heard between the two.

Claudius is sure Hamlet's malady is not love, but something else, and consequently he decides to remove any mad actions by sending Hamlet to England to collect neglected tribute, with the view that a change will expel his madness.

Polonius concurs, but thinks Hamlet's madness sprung from neglected love, and not Claudius.

To prove this, Polonius advises Claudius to wait until the play is ended, then let Hamlet's mother Queen Gertrude determine his grief while he, Polonius, listens hidden. And, if the madness is not love, then Hamlet should be sent to England.

Claudius remarks –

Madness in great ones must not unwatch'd go

TEXT ACT 3 scene 1

*< Enter **CLAUDIUS, GERTRUDE, POLONIUS, OPHELIA, ROSENCRANTZ,** and **GUILDENSTERN** >*

CLAUDIUS
And can you by no drift of conference
Get from him why he puts on this confusion,
Grating so harshly all his days of quiet
With turbulent and dangerous lunacy?
ROSENCRANTZ
He does confess he feels himself distracted.
But from what cause he will by no means speak.
GUILDENSTERN
Nor do we find him forward to be sounded.
But with a crafty madness keeps aloof
When we would bring him on to some confession
Of his true state.
GERTRUDE
Did he receive you well?
ROSENCRANTZ
Most like a gentleman.
GUILDENSTERN
But with much forcing of his disposition.
ROSENCRANTZ
Niggard of question, but of our demands
Most free in his reply.
GERTRUDE
Did you assay him?
To any pastime?
ROSENCRANTZ
Madam, it so fell out, that certain players
We o'er-raught on the way. Of these we told him,
And there did seem in him a kind of joy
To hear of it. They are about the court,
And, as I think, they have already order
This night to play before him.
POLONIUS
'Tis most true,
And he beseeched me to entreat your Majesties
To hear and see the matter.
CLAUDIUS
With all my heart, and it doth much content me
To hear him so inclin'd.
Good gentlemen, give him a further edge,
And drive his purpose on to these delights.
ROSENCRANTZ
We shall, my lord.

*< Exeunt **ROSENCRANTZ** and **GUILDENSTERN** >*

EXPLANATION

Claudius seems unnerved at Hamlet's crazy, and confused behaviour which is ruining his peace of mind.

"With turbulent and dangerous lunacy?"

Rosencrantz and Guildenstern are also at their wits end trying to find the root cause of Hamlet's irrational behaviour. They complain that he evades their questions and

"with a crafty madness keeps aloof"

when they ask him about his feelings?

Gertrude seems to be very concerned about her son's madness and she asks if they organised some entertainment for him.

"Did you assay him?
To any pastime?"

Claudius' glaring hypocrisy is evident here. He is feigning concern for Hamlet's welfare yet in fact he is concocting devious plans to harm him.

"With all my heart, and it doth much content me
To hear him so inclin'd"

Rosencrantz could only inform the king and queen that Hamlet's only joy was the players ordering of a play tonight.

GERTRUDE is pleased when ROSENCRANTZ tells her that Hamlet's joy is plays, "And there did seem in him a kind of joy"

TEXT ACT 3 scene 1

CLAUDIUS
Sweet Gertrude, leave us too,
For we have closely sent for Hamlet hither,
That he, as 'twere by accident, may here
Affront Ophelia.
Her father and myself, lawful espials
Will so bestow ourselves that, seeing unseen,
We may of their encounter frankly judge,
And gather by him, as he is behav'd,
If 't be the affliction of his love or no
That thus he suffers for.

GERTRUDE
I shall obey you.
And for your part, Ophelia, I do wish
That your good beauties be
The happy cause of Hamlet's wildness.
So shall I hope your virtues
Will bring him to his wonted way again,
To both your honours.

OPHELIA
Madam, I wish it may.

< *Exit* ***GERTRUDE***>

POLONIUS
Ophelia, walk you here.
(*to Claudius*) Gracious, so please you,
We will bestow ourselves.
(*to Ophelia*) Read on this book,
That show of such an exercise
May colour your loneliness. —
We are oft to blame in this,
'Tis too much prov'd, that with devotion's visage
And pious action we do sugar o'er the devil himself.

CLAUDIUS
(aside) Oh, 'tis too true!
How smart a lash
That speech doth give my conscience.
The harlot's cheek, beautied with plast'ring art,
Is not more ugly to the thing that helps it
Than is my deed to my most painted word.
O heavy burden!

POLONIUS
I hear him coming. Let's withdraw, my lord.

<***CLAUDIUS*** *and* ***POLONIUS*** *withdraw*>

EXPLANATION

Claudius asks Gertrude to leave because he has arranged for Hamlet to accidentally meet Ophelia. Polonius and him secretly plan to spy on Hamlet to ascertain whether it's love that is causing this madness. Gertrude obliges and say to Ophelia that she hopes that her beauty is the very reason for Hamlet's insanity.

"That your good beauties be
The happy cause of Hamlet's wildness"

She also hopes that Ophelia's virtues will restore him to normality again.

"So shall I hope your virtues
Will bring him to his wonted way again"

Ophelia is also pretending to be sincere when she says,

"Madam, I wish it may"

The theme of appearance versus reality is seen once again this time by Ophelia.

We see a flurry of activity in Polonius and his role in taking command. We are dismayed to see how Ophelia is groomed to carry out his vile actions to spy on Hamlet. Polonius gives her the bible to read which will suggest her loneliness,

"May colour your loneliness"

It's ironical when Polonius says that we pretend to be good and turn to God to hide our evil deeds.

"with devotion's visage
And pious action we do sugar o'er the devil himself"

Claudius' outburst is shocking, because he admits that Polonius' words tug at his conscience. And makes him feel guilty.

"How smart a lash
That speech doth give my conscience"

He compares the imagery of a harlot's painted face trying to hide its blemishes to his guilt that he is hiding.

TEXT ACT 3 scene 1

*<Enter **HAMLET**>*

HAMLET

To be, or not to be? That is the question—
Whether 'tis nobler in the mind to suffer
The slings and arrows of outrageous fortune,
Or to take arms against a sea of troubles,
And, by opposing, end them? To die, to sleep—
No more—and by a sleep to say we end
The heartache and the thousand natural shocks
That flesh is heir to—'tis a consummation
Devoutly to be wished! To die, to sleep.
To sleep, perchance to dream—ay, there's the rub,For in
that sleep of death what dreams may come
When we have shuffled off this mortal coil,
Must give us pause. There's the respect
That makes calamity of so long life.
For who would bear the whips and scorns of time,
Th' oppressor's wrong, the proud man's contumely,
Th' pangs of despised love, the law's delay,
The insolence of office, and the spurns
That patient merit of th' unworthy takes,
When he himself might his quietus make
With a bare bodkin? Who would fardels bear,
To grunt and sweat under a weary life,
But that the dread of something after death,
The undiscovered country from whose bourn
No traveler returns, puzzles the will
And makes us rather bear those ills we have
Than fly to others that we know not of?
Thus, conscience does make cowards of us all,
And thus, the native hue of resolution
Is sicklied o'er with the pale cast of thought,
And enterprises of great pith and moment
With this regard their currents turn awry,
And lose the name of action. —Soft you now,
The fair Ophelia! —Nymph, in thy orisons
Be all my sins remember'd.

EXPLANATION

In his famous soliloquy Hamlet's character – his confused psychological and mental state is exposed. His pace and tone vary here to that of his other soliloquies. His pace is even, and his tone is reflective, and the tempo is not hurried. He seems to be in serious and deep thoughts thinking philosophically about whether life is worth living. He contemplates the meaning of life and death. He is pondering his situation,

"To be, or not to be? That is the question—"

He is questioning a state of being versus a state of not being. He uses a vivid imagery to establish whether it's better to alienate himself from a sea of pain and trouble or oppose it and end his troubles.

"The slings and arrows of outrageous fortune,
Or to take arms against a sea of troubles."

In this metaphor he challenges whether it's nobler to endure the pain and suffering of life comparing it to 'a sea of troubles' or just end your life and so put an end to all the pain and misery. Death is empowering and by sleeping we end the heartaches. Living is a passive state whilst dying can be seen as an active state. It's difficult to put up with the calamities of life – the abuse, insults, unrequited love, and corruption of leadership,

"For who would bear the whips and scorns of time, Th' oppressor's wrong, the proud man's contumely, Th' pangs of despised love, the laws delay"

He makes a profound judgment,

"Thus, conscience does make cowards of us all."

TEXT ACT 3 scene 1

OPHELIA
Good my lord,
How does your honour for this many a day?
HAMLET
I humbly thank you. Well, well, well.
OPHELIA
My lord, I have remembrances of yoursThat I
have long'd long to redeliver.
I pray you now receive them.
HAMLET
No, not I.
I never gave you aught.
OPHELIA
My honour'd lord, you know right well you did,
And with them, words of so sweet breath compos'd
As made the things more rich. Their perfume lost,
Take these again, for to the noble mind
Rich gifts wax poor when givers prove unkind.
There, my lord.
HAMLET
Ha, ha, are you honest?
OPHELIA
My lord?
HAMLET
Are you fair?
OPHELIA
What means your lordship?
HAMLET
That if you be honest and fair,
Your honesty should admit
No discourse to your beauty.
OPHELIA
Could beauty, my lord,
Have better commerce than with honesty?
HAMLET
Ay, truly, for the power of beauty
Will sooner transform honesty
From what it is to a bawd
Than the force of honesty
Can translate beauty into his likeness.
This was sometime a paradox,
But now the time gives it proof.
I did love you once.

EXPLANATION

He fails to take actions because he makes excuses for not avenging his father's death, perhaps looking at the moral aspect of it. He also looks at the religious aspect of whether taking one's life is a sin. Ophelia gives Hamlet his gifts back to him. We see Ophelia is on a mission of deceit and pretence.

OPHELIA returns HAMLET's remembrances, "My lord, I have remembrances of yours"

Ophelia is making excuses to leave him, to carry out Claudius' and Polonius's plot. She says that the perfume is lost in his presents and one can infer that she means it's Hamlet's love that is lost and she wants to end the relationship.
She also accuses him of being unkind,

"for to the noble mind
Rich gifts wax poor when givers prove unkind"

Hamlet is aghast at Ophelia's sudden change in behaviour. He senses that she is being dishonest.
"That if you be honest and fair,
Your honesty should admit
No discourse to your beauty"

HAMLET denies he gave them to OPHELIA but admits, "I did love you once"

TEXT ACT 3 scene 1

OPHELIA
Indeed, my lord, you made me believe so.
HAMLET
You should not have believed me,
For virtue cannot so inoculate our old stock
But we shall relish of it. I loved you not.
OPHELIA
I was the more deceived.
HAMLET
Get thee to a nunnery.
Why wouldst thou be a breeder of sinners?
I am myself indifferent honest,
But yet I could accuse me of such things
that it were better my mother had not borne me.
I am very proud, revengeful, ambitious,
With more offences at my beck
Than I have thoughts to put them in,
Imagination to give them shape,
Or time to act them in.
What should such fellows
As I do crawling between earth and heaven?
We are arrant knaves all.
Believe none of us
Go thy ways to a nunnery
Where's your father?
OPHELIA
At home, my lord.
HAMLET
Let the doors be shut upon him,
That he may play the fool no where
But in 's own house.
Farewell.
OPHELIA
O, help him, you sweet heavens!
HAMLET
If thou dost marry,
I'll give thee this plague for thy dowry.
Be thou as chaste as ice, as pure as snow,
Thou shalt not escape calumny.
Get thee to a nunnery, go.
Farewell.
Or, if thou wilt needs marry, marry a fool,
For wise men know well enough
What monsters you make of them.
To a nunnery, go, and quickly too.
Farewell.

EXPLANATION

He is furious at her deceit and declares,

"I loved you not"

He tells her to go to a nunnery perhaps to cleanse herself of her lying nature and get closer to God.
She should not also have children because they will sin like her,

"Why wouldst thou be a breeder of sinners?"

Hamlet's need for purity and morality is evident in this speech.
He regrets his mother giving birth to him and he acknowledges his faults saying that he is proud, revengeful, and ambitious.

"I am very proud, Revengeful, ambitious,
With more offences at my beck."

He repeats his pleas for Ophelia to,

"Go thy ways to a nunnery."

This repetition suggests an urgency to cleanse Ophelia of her sins and the nunnery suggest purity and holiness. It's as though he is very disappointed that everyone closes to him betrayed him and now Ophelia is adding to his confusion and woes.

Hamlet is disillusioned and he vents his frustration towards Polonius when he asks that,

"Let doors be shut upon him,
That he may play the fool no where
But in his own house"

He is very wise and perceptive, and he is aware that Polonius is behind Ophelia's strange behaviour.

In his fury he again urges Ophelia to go to a convent at once to purge herself of this sin. If she gets married, she needs to marry a fool because,

"wise men know well enough
What monsters you make of them."

OPHELIA
Heavenly powers, restore him!
HAMLET
I have heard of your paintings too, well enough.
God has given you one face
And you make yourselves another.
You jig and amble, and you lisp,
You nickname God's creatures
And make your wantonness your ignorance.
Go to, I'll no more on't.
It hath made me mad.
I say, we will have no more marriages
Those that are married already,
all but one, shall live.
The rest shall keep as they are.
To a nunnery, go.
OPHELIA
Oh, what a noble mind is here o'erthrown!
The courtier's, soldier's, scholar's, eye, tongue, sword
Th' expectancy and rose of the fair state,
The glass of fashion and the mould of form,
Th' observed of all observers, quite, quite down!
And I, of ladies most deject and wretched,That
suck'd the honey of his music vows,
Now see that noble and most sovereign reason
Like sweet bells jangled, out of tune and harsh,
That unmatch'd form and feature of blown youth
Blasted with ecstasy. Oh, woe is me,
T' have seen what I have seen, see what I see!

< ***CLAUDIUS*** *and* ***POLONIUS*** *come forward* >

POLONIUS and CLAUDIUS listen in from above to the encounter between Ophelia and Hamlet

Once again, the theme of appearance versus reality surfaces because Hamlet accuses her of a disguise,

"God hath given you one face
And you make yourselves another"

He is referring to her lies and deception and her pretentious behaviour. He is furious and tells her that there will be no more marriages.

This constant repetition of urging Ophelia to go to a nunnery is suggesting that his anger and his concern for her soul is mounting. His concerns for morality and religion are paramount.

OPHELIA listens in torment as HAMLET tells her, "To a nunnery, go.

Ophelia is mourning Hamlet's change of disposition and character. He used to have a noble mind, bravery, brilliance, and a soldier's strength but now he is down.

"Oh, what a noble mind is here o'erthrown!"

She feels miserable at seeing him like this and recalls how melodiously he used to sing. Now his music is out of tune just like his mind.

"Like sweet bells jangled, out of tune and harsh"

TEXT ACT 3 scene 1

CLAUDIUS
Love? His affections do not that way tend.
Nor what he spake, though it lacked form a little,
Was not like madness.
There's something in his soul
O'er which his melancholy sits on brood,
And I do doubt the hatch and the disclose Will be
some danger—which for to prevent,
I have in quick determination
Thus, set it down: he shall with speed to England
For the demand of our neglected tribute.
Haply the seas and countries different,
With variable objects shall expel
This something-settled matter in his heart,
Whereon his brains still beating puts him thus
From fashion of himself.
What think you on 't?
POLONIUS
It shall do well. But yet do I believe
The origin and commencement of his grief
Sprung from neglected love. —
How now, Ophelia?
You need not tell us what Lord Hamlet said.
We heard it all. —
My lord, do as you please.
But, if you hold it fit, after the play
Let his queen mother
All alone entreat him to show his grief.
Let her be round with him,
And I'll be placed, so please you, in the ear
Of all their conference.
If she find him not,
To England send him or confine him
Where your wisdom best shall think.
CLAUDIUS
It shall be so.
Madness in great ones
Must not unwatched go.

< *Exeunt* >

EXPLANATION

Claudius is getting ever more edgy, and he has now gaged that Hamlet's show of madness is merely an act.

"Was not like madness.
There's something in his soul"

Claudius is nervous and he uses the imagery of an egg about to hatch and whatever will be hatched will be dangerous, so he made an instant decision to send Hamlet away to England.

"O'er which his melancholy sits on brood,
And I do doubt the hatch and the disclose
Will be some danger"

Claudius hopes that the change of scenery will 'expel' this matter that is closest to his heart.

Polonius is adamant that Hamlet's grief is

"Sprung from neglected love"

Polonius suggests that the queen should intercede and find out why he is grieving. She should,

"All alone entreat him to show his grief"

He will spy on the conversation and if she is unsuccessful, then the king should send him to England.

"To England send him or confine him
Where your wisdom best shall think"

Claudius is determined to find the cause of Hamlet's strange behaviour and says that,

"Madness in great ones
Must not unwatched go"

In Act 3 scene 2, the setting is on a stage inside the castle, the next day.

Enter Hamlet and three of the Players. Hamlet instructs the Players to not over play their parts, but let their own discretion be their tutor. Exit Players.

Enter Polonius with Rosencrantz and Guildenstern, to inform Hamlet to make haste as both the King and the Queen will attend the play later tonight. Exit Polonius and company.

Enter Horatio. Hamlet admonishes Horatio for his fatuous salutations, and then instructs him to watch the king's face for signs of guilt when in one scene the circumstance similar to King Hamlet's death, is enacted.

Enter trumpets, kettle drums and sound flourish.

Enter King, Queen, Polonius, Ophelia, Rosencrantz and Guildenstern, and other Lords, attendants with the King's Guard carrying torches.

Polonius brags he played Julius Caesar killed by Brutus, and the Queen invites Hamlet to sit by her, but instead lies down at Ophelia's feet harping on usurped love.

The trumpets sound. A dumb show (a mimed version of the main play) follows.

Enter the Player Queen and Player King. She kneels and makes a show of protestation. He takes her up and declines his head upon her neck. Later, as he sleeps upon a bank of flowers, a man takes off the King's crown, kisses it, pours poison in the King's ear. The Poisoner woos the widow Queen who eventually accepts his love. Exit the Players.

Ophelia asks Hamlet what means this. His replies Marry means mischief.

Enter the Player King and Queen to start the play which mirrors the dumb show. In the intermission, Hamlet asks Gertrude what she thinks about the Player Queen's declaration that she would not remarry should the Player King die. Gertrude replies:

> *The lady doth protest too much, methinks.*

Claudius asks Hamlet to name the play which he does as *The Mousetrap* based on the image of a murder done in Vienna. In a lewd exchange with Ophelia, Hamlet ends by saying women mistake their husbands, then deceive them.

As the play proceeds, Lucianus, the Player King's nephew, pours the poison in the sleeper's ears. At this, Hamlet remarks, his name is Gonzago, and the murderer gets the love of Gonzago's wife.

Claudius rises, causing concern among the audience, and departs.

Exit all but Hamlet and Horatio.

Hamlet exclaims to Horatio that he'll take the ghost's word for a thousand pounds.

Enter Rosencrantz and Guildenstern to tell Hamlet that the King is in distemper and the Queen desires to speak to him in her closet to which promises to do. Rosencrantz asks Hamlet the cause of his distemper, to which Hamlet remarks he lack advancement. Rosencrantz is baffled as Hamlet is next in line to the throne.

Enter The Players with recorders.

Hamlet seizes upon this interruption to berate Guildenstern, comparing his inability to play the recorder to the action of treating him like a musical instrument he cannot play.

Enter Polonius with a message that the Queen would speak with Hamlet now, but Hamlet toys with him, by saying that when the cloud yonder forms a particular shape he will come.

Exit all but Hamlet who starts a soliloquy where he will speak daggers to the Queen, but use none, and she be shent (reproached). Exit Hamlet.

TEXT ACT 3 scene 2

< *Enter **HAMLET** and **PLAYERS*** >

HAMLET (*To the **First Player***)
Speak the speech, I pray you,
As I pronounced it to you, trippingly on the tongue.
But if you mouth it, as many of your players do,
I had as lief the town crier spoke my lines.
Nor do not saw the air too much with your hand thus
But use all gently,
For in the very torrent, tempest,
And as I may say whirlwind of passion,
You must acquire and beget a temperance
That may give it smoothness.
Oh, it offends me to the soul to hear a robustious
Periwig-pated fellow tear a passion to tatters,
To very rags, to split the ears of the groundlings,
Who for the most part are capable of nothing,
But inexplicable dumb-shows and noise.
I would have such a fellow whipped
For o'er-doing Termagant.
It out-Herods Herod. Pray you, avoid it.
FIRST PLAYER
I warrant your honour.
HAMLET
Be not too tame neither,
But let your own discretion beyour tutor.
Suit the action to the word,
The word to the action,
With this special observance
That you o'er-step not the modesty of nature.
For anything so overdone is
From the purpose of playing,
Whose end, both at the first and now, was
And is to hold, as 'twere the mirror up to nature,
To show virtue her own feature,
Scorn her own image, and the very age and body
Of the time his form and pressure.
Now this overdone or come tardy off,
Though it makes the unskillful laugh,
Cannot but make the judicious grieve,
The censure of the which one must in your
Allowance o'er-weigh a whole theatre of others.
Oh, there be players that I have seen play
And heard others praise
And that highly – not to speak it profanely,

EXPLANATION

Hamlet speaks in blank verse. He is directing and preparing for the 'play-within-the-play'. Hamlet is so admirably assertive when directing the play.
He places emphasis on stage presence, passion, and emotions. He says that,

"It offends me to the soul"

To hear a robust actor in a wig,

"tear a passion to tatters,
To very rags, to split the ears of the groundlings"

He would whip an actor if he overacted the role of tyranny,

"I would have such a fellow whipped
For o'er-doing Termagant."

He does not want them to act like the old plays where king Herod ranted.

They must act accordingly, holding up a mirror to virtue and scorning vice. He personifies 'virtue' and 'vice'

"To show virtue her own feature,
Scorn her own image"

The PLAYERS instructed by Hamlet, "To show virtue her own feature,"

HAMLET (*continues*)
That, neither having th' accent of Christians
Nor the gait of Christian, pagan, nor man,
Have so strutted and bellowed
That I have thought some of nature's journeymen
Had made men and not made them well,
They imitated humanity so abominably.

FIRST PLAYER
I hope we have reformed
That indifferently with us, sir.

HAMLET
O, reform it altogether!
And let those that play your clowns
Speak no more than is set down for them,
For there be of them that will themselves laugh
To set on some quantity of barren spectators
To laugh too,
Though in the meantime some necessary
Question of the play be then to be considered.
That's villainous, and shows a most pitiful ambition
in the fool that uses it. Go, make you ready.

< *Exeunt* ***PLAYERS*** >
< *Enter* ***POLONIUS, ROSENCRANTZ*** and ***GUILDENSTERN*** >

How now, my lord!
Will the king hear this piece of work?

POLONIUS
And the queen too, and that presently.

HAMLET
Bid the players make haste.
< *Exit* ***POLONIUS*** >
Will you two help to hasten them?

ROSENCRANTZ
Ay, my lord.

< ***Exeunt ROSENCRANTZ and GUILDENSTERN*** >

HAMLET
What ho, Horatio!
< *Enter* ***HORATIO*** >

HORATIO
Here, sweet lord, at your service.

HAMLET
Horatio, thou art e'en as just a man
As e'er my conversation cop'd withal.

HORATIO
O my dear lord—

Hamlet continues the theme of righteousness in his instructions to the Players, to which the First Player responds,

"I hope we have reformed
That indifferently with us, sir"

Hamlet instructs all the Players to work together to promote reform.

"O, reform it altogether!"

But they must keep to the script set down by him,

"And let those that play your clowns
Speak no more than is set down for them"

Hamlet knows within the script the key lines will reveal Claudius' guilt. The irony is that the Players do not know, except for Hamlet's cryptic clue when he tells them

"That's villainous, and shows a most pitiful ambition
in the fool that uses it"

Hamlet is delighted to learn from Polonius that the king and queen are attending the performance. The trap is set to reveal Claudius' guilt!

Polonius greets Hamlet and introduces the Players to the audience.

POLONIUS introduces the PLAYERS

Hamlet is thrilled to see Horatio and he tells him that he is the most loyal friend that he had ever known,

"Horatio, thou art e'en as just a man
As ever my conversation cop'd withal"

TEXT ACT 3 scene 2

HAMLET

Nay do not think I flatter.
For what advancement may I hope from thee
That no revenue hast but thy good spirits,
To feed and clothe thee?
Why should the poor be flatter'd?
No, let the candied tongue lick absurd pomp,
And crook the pregnant hinges of the knee
Where thrift may follow fawning.
Dost, thou hear?
Since my dear soul was mistress of her choice
And could of men distinguish, her election
Hath sealed thee for herself, for thou hast been—
As one in suffering all that suffers nothing—
A man that Fortune's buffets and rewards
Hast ta'en with equal thanks. And blessed are those
Whose blood and judgment are so well commingled,
That they are not a pipe for Fortune's finger
To sound what stop she please.
Give me that man
That is not passion's slave, and I will wear him
In my heart's core, ay, in my heart of heart,
As I do thee. —Something too much of this. —
There is a play tonight before the king.
One scene of it comes near the circumstance
Which I have told thee of my father's death.
I prithee, when thou seest that act afoot,
Even with the very comment of thy soul
Observe mine uncle. If his occulted guilt
Do not itself unkennel in one speech,
It is a damn'd ghost that we have seen,
And my imaginations are as foul
As Vulcan's stithy. Give him heedful note
For I mine eyes will rivet to his face,
And after we will both our judgments join
In censure of his seeming.

HORATIO

Well, my lord.
If he steals aught the whilst this play is playing,
And 'scape detecting, I will pay the theft.

EXPLANATION

He tells Horatio that he is not flattering him and although he is poor, his good qualities are enough for him to survive,

"That no revenue hast but thy good spirits,
To feed and clothe thee"

Since he had the privilege of choosing his friends, he was glad to choose a friend like Horatio. He is the master of his emotions and not, 'passion's slave'

Hamlet enlists Horatio's help for the play.

HAMLET enlists HORATIO's help as a witness

One of the scenes is very closely related to his father's betrayal and death.

"One scene of it comes near the circumstance Which I have told thee of my father's death"

When he sees that scene, he must observe his uncle and his reaction. Hamlet is trying to establish his uncle's guilt for his father's murder,

"Even with the very comment of thy soul
Observe mine uncle"

If my uncle doesn't express his guilt, then the ghost is the devil and has misled me. And my imagination is foul and all wrong,

"It is a damn'd ghost that we have seen,
and my imaginations are as foul
As Vulcan's stithy"

He urges Horatio to, 'Give him needful note'. And he will observe his face for any guilt then they will compare their findings to establish his uncles' guilt,
"And after we will both our judgements join
In censure of his seeming"

TEXT ACT 3 scene 2

Danish march. Sound a flourish.

< Enter King ***CLAUDIUS,*** *Queen* ***GERTRUDE, POLONIUS, OPHELIA, ROSENCRANTZ, GUILDENSTERN*** *and other lords, attendant, guard carrying torches >*

HAMLET
They are coming to the play.
I must be idle.
Get you a place.
CLAUDIUS
How fares our cousin Hamlet?
HAMLET
Excellent, i' faith, of the chameleon's dish.
I eat the air, promise crammed.
You cannot feed capons so.
CLAUDIUS
I have nothing with this answer, Hamlet.
These words are not mine.
HAMLET
No, nor mine now.
(*to Polonius*) My lord,
You played once i' th' university, you say?
POLONIUS
That did I, my lord,
And was accounted a good actor.
HAMLET
What did you enact?
POLONIUS
I did enact Julius Caesar.
I was killed i' th' Capitol.
Brutus killed me.
HAMLET
It was a brute part of him to kill
So capital a calf there.
Be the players ready?
ROSENCRANTZ
Ay, my lord.
They stay upon your patience.

EXPLANATION

POLONIUS, CLAUDIUD, ROSENCRANTZ, GERTRUDE

This seems to be a pivotal point of the play laced with much tension and suspense. Hamlet gets ready to meet them.

Claudius once again pretends to be loyal and concerned. He greets Hamlet very 'cordially'

"How fares our cousin Hamlet?"

Hamlet aptly refers to a 'chameleon' which is known to change colour. This can be attributed to Claudius' two-faced, pretentious behaviour towards Hamlet.

"Excellent, i' faith, of the chameleon's dish"

Claudius is confused at Hamlet's response, but Hamlet quickly turns his attention to Polonius and asks,

"You played once in the university; you say?

Polonius brags about how good he was at playing Caesar and how Brutus killed him,

"I was killed I' th' Capitol.
Brutus killed me"

Ironically, we see betrayal and murder here which is reminiscent of what Hamlet's play is all about. Hamlet uses a pun on the word, 'brute' suggesting Brutus was a brute to kill a statesman. This can be directly linked to Claudius' brutish behaviour to kill the king. Hamlet uses a bitter tone and much sarcasm in this utterance.

GERTRUDE
Come hither, my dear Hamlet, sit by me.
HAMLET
No, good mother.
Here's metal more attractive.
(*He sits next to Ophelia*)
POLONIUS
(*Aside to Claudius*) Oh, ho, do you mark that?
HAMLET
(*Lying down at Ophelia's feet*)
Lady, shall I lie in your lap?
OPHELIA
No, my lord.
HAMLET
I mean, my head upon your lap?
OPHELIA
Ay, my lord.
HAMLET
Do you think I meant country matters?
OPHELIA
I think nothing, my lord.
HAMLET
That's a fair thought to lie between maids' legs.
OPHELIA
What is, my lord?
HAMLET
Nothing.
OPHELIA
You are merry, my lord.
HAMLET
Who, I?
OPHELIA
Ay, my lord.
HAMLET
O God, your only jig-maker.
What should a man dobut be merry?
For, look you, how cheerfully my mother looks,
And my father died within these two hours.

Gertrude invites Hamlet to sit next to her, but he declines, and he sits next to Ophelia.

"No, good mother.
Here's metal more attractive"

He refers to Ophelia being 'metal' suggesting her cold, steely feelings like metal.

HAMLET asks OPHELIA, "Lady, shall I lie in your lap?"

Polonius draws Claudius' attention to Hamlet's refusal to sit next to his mother. It's obvious that Polonius is 'stirring the pot of troubles.'

"Oh, ho, do you mark that?"

Hamlet very strangely approaches Ophelia with a rather bawdy proposition to lay his head upon her lap. He also makes sexual nuances about lying between maids' legs.

Ophelia is rather perplexed at his uncanny behaviour and asks if he is cheerful.

"You are merry, my Lord"

Hamlet then goes on to attack his mother's cheerful looks, hence hinting at her Hypocrisy,

"For, look you, how cheerfully my mother looks."

He makes a ridiculous statement that his father has died only two hours ago, and his mother is cheerful.

OPHELIA
Nay, 'tis twice two months, my lord.
HAMLET
So long?
Nay then, let the devil wear black,
For I'll have a suit of sables. O heavens!
Die two months ago and not forgotten yet?
Then there's hope a greatman's memory
May outlive his life half a year.
But, by 'r Lady, he must build churches then,
Or else shall he suffer not thinking on,
with the hobbyhorse, whose epitaph is
"For, oh, for, oh, the hobby-horse is forgot"

Trumpets sound.
The dumb show begins

Enter a King and a Queen very lovingly, the Queen embracing him and he her. She kneels and makes show of protestation unto him He takes her up and declines his head upon her neck, lays him down upon a bank of flowers.

She, seeing him asleep, leaves him. Anon comes in a fellow, takes off his crown, kisses it, pours poison in the King's ear and exits

The Queen returns, finds the King dead, and makes passionate action.

The Poisoner, with some two or three Mutes, comes in again, seeming to lament with her.

The dead body is carried away.

The Poisoner woos the Queen with gifts.

She seems loath and unwilling awhile, but in the end accepts his love

< *Exeunt* ***PLAYERS*** >

He is corrected by Ophelia that it's two months since his father's death,

"Nay, tis twice two months, my Lord"

Hamlet is pretending not to know the date of his father's death. He says he wants to cast off his mourning clothes because, he sarcastically says that his father should be forgotten by now. Once again hinting at his mother's haste in forgetting him and marrying so quickly,

"Nay then, let the devil wear black,
For I'll have a suit of sables. O heavens!
Die two months ago and not forgotten yet?"

Hamlet refers to dark imagery, 'black' and the 'devil' this can well be associated to his dark frame of mind and all the darkness surrounding him.
He goes on to juxtapose 'Heaven' and 'hell' and once again Shakespeare highlights Hamlet's desire for beliefs in morality and religion.

ENTER A KING AND A QUEEN

They lovingly embrace each other. He lay down on a bank of flowers and falls asleep. She leaves him. Another fellow comes in, takes the king's crown, kisses it, and pours poison in the King's ears, and exits.

The Queen returns and on seeing her husband dead, she becomes very distraught.

The poisoner comes in again and laments with her. He then woos the queen with gifts. At first, she refuses but is soon captivated and accepts his love.

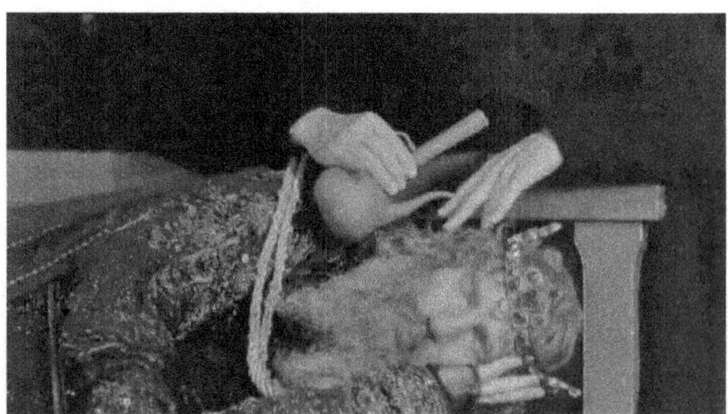

The Anon pours poison in the King's ear

OPHELIA
What means this, my lord?
HAMLET
Marry, this is *miching malhecho*.
It means mischief.
OPHELIA
Belike this show imports the argument of the play.

< *Enter **PROLOGUE*** >

HAMLET
We shall know by this fellow.
The players cannot keep counsel.
They'll tell all.
OPHELIA
Will he tell us what this show meant?
HAMLET
Ay, or any show that you will show him.
Be not you ashamed to show,
He'll not shame to tell you what it means.
OPHELIA
You are naught, you are naught.
I'll mark the play.
PROLOGUE
For us and for our tragedy,
Here stooping to your clemency,
We beg your hearing patiently.

< *Exit **PROLOGUE*** >

HAMLET
Is this a prologue or the posy of a ring?
OPHELIA
'Tis brief, my lord.
HAMLET
As woman's love.

Hamlet very beautifully and meticulously portrays the story of his father's betrayal and death by his mother and uncle in this most alluring play.

Shakespeare creates much tension and suspense here because we are curious to see the king and queen's reaction.

Ophelia is rather puzzled at this display, and she questions the legitimacy of it.

"What means this, my Lord?"

Hamlet cheekily says that it 'means mischief'.

He tells Ophelia that these actors cannot keep secrets. Everything will be exposed hinting at his uncle's murder of his dear father.

"The players cannot keep counsel.
They'll tell all"

Hamlet uses a lot of play on words and sexual innuendos. He tells her that the actors will not be ashamed to tell her what the play is about if she's not ashamed to show them anything. He seems to be demeaning her because of her sneaky behaviour towards him.

The prologue gives us a 'teeny weeny' bit of introduction before it exits. Hamlet uses its briefness to poke fun very sarcastically at his mother's promiscuity. He says,

"Is that a prologue or the posy of a ring?"

He attributes this very short introduction to a 'posy' which is a very very short verse inscribed inside a ring.

This is a direct and bitter outburst of his mother's short wedding to his uncle. He also describes the briefness of the prologue to his mother's superficial and brief love for his father she forgot him so quickly after he died and married his uncle.

TEXT ACT 3 scene 2

<*Enter* ***PLAYER KING*** *and* ***PLAYER QUEEN***>

PLAYER KING

Full thirty times hath Phoebus' cart gone round
Neptune's salt wash and Tellus' orbed ground,
And thirty dozen moons with borrowed sheen
About the world have times twelve thirties been,
Since love our hearts and Hymen did our hands
Unite commutual in most sacred bands.

PLAYER QUEEN

So many journeys may the sun and moon
Make us again count o'er ere love be done.
But woe is me! You are so sick of late,
So far from cheer and from your former state,
That I distrust you. Yet though I distrust,
Discomfort you, my lord, it nothing must.
For women fear too much, even as they love,
And women's fear and love hold quantity,
In neither aught, or in extremity.
Now what my love is, proof hath made you know,
And as my love is sized, my fear is so:
Where love is great, the littlest doubts are fear.
Where little fears grow great, great love grows there.

PLAYER KING

Faith, I must leave thee, love, and shortly too.
My operant powers their functions leave to do.
And thou shalt live in this fair world behind,
Honoured, beloved, and haply one as kind
For husband shalt thou—

PLAYER QUEEN

Oh, confound the rest!
Such love must needs be treason in my breast.
In second husband let me be accursed!
None wed the second but who killed the first.

HAMLET

(*aside*) That's wormwood.

PLAYER QUEEN

The instances that second marriage move
Are base respects of thrift, but none of love.
A second time I kill my husband dead
When second husband kisses me in bed.

EXPLANATION

This play is very carefully crafted by Hamlet to illicit a guilty response from the king to acknowledge his murder of his father. Both Hamlet and Claudius are playing a game of 'Cat and mouse.' Hamlet is trying to set a trap for Claudius and Claudius is trying to set a trap to detect Hamlet's insanity. Hamlet is thirty years old according to the gravedigger because he was born on the day-old Hamlet defeated old Fortinbras. (Act 5 scene 1 line 148)

"I have been sexton here, man and boy, thirty years"

The player king declares his undying love for the player queen for the past thirty years (the same number of years Hamlet's mother and father were married.) Note how the play is carefully devised to target the conscience of the king and the queen. Hamlet did not leave out any minor details to ensure this. The player queen also declares her undying love for the player king.

"So many journeys may the sun and moon
Make us again count o'er ere love be done"

He sadly tells her that he must leave her because he is sick and that she will find another husband.
Note the abrupt end to his incomplete sentence marked by a hyphen implying that he is too pained to imagine his queen with another man hence leaving his sentence in mid air. This is how Hamlet's father would have felt if he knew about the queen's disgusting affair with his own brother.

"For husband shalt thou —"
The player queen's retort about devotional love and loyalty seems to be very real. We see her heartfelt response to the true meaning of love yet, later she proves to be pretentious just like Gertrude when she betrays her husband's unconditional love.

"Oh, confound the rest!
Such love must be treason in my breast"

Hamlet is sceptical and he utters, "That's wormwood." Hamlet is referring to the biblical symbolism of 'wormwood' which represents the bitterness that will fill the earth during troubled times. Like the bitterness that he is experiencing from the display of the immorality and betrayal in the world around him.

TEXT ACT 3 scene 2

PLAYER KING

I do believe you think what now you speak,
But what we do determine oft we break.
Purpose is but the slave to memory,
Of violent birth, but poor validity,
Which now, like fruit unripe, sticks on the tree,
But fall, unshaken, when they mellow be.
Most necessary 'tis that we forget
To pay ourselves what to ourselves is debt.
What to ourselves in passion we propose,
The passion ending, doth the purpose lose.
The violence of either grief or joy
Their own enactures with themselves destroy.
Where joy most revels, grief doth most lament.
Grief joys, joy grieves on slender accident.
This world is not for aye, nor 'tis not strange
That even our loves should with our fortunes change.
For 'tis a question left us yet to prove,
Whether love lead fortune, or else fortune love.
The great man down, you mark his favourite flies.
The poor advanced makes friends of enemies.
And hitherto doth love on fortune tend,
For, who not needs shall never lack a friend,
And who in want a hollow friend doth try,
Directly seasons him his enemy.
But, orderly to end where I begun,
Our wills and fates do so contrary run
That our devices still are overthrown.
Our thoughts are ours,
their ends none of our own.
So think thou wilt no second husband wed,
But die thy thoughts when thy first lord is dead.

PLAYER QUEEN

Nor earth to me give food, nor heaven light.
Sport and repose lock from me day and night.
To desperation turn my trust and hope.
An anchor's cheer in prison be my scope.
Each opposite that blanks the face of joy
Meet what I would have well, and it destroy.
Both here and hence pursue me lasting strife
If, once a widow, ever I be wife!

HAMLET

If she should break it now!

EXPLANATION

The PLAYER KING and PLAYER QUEEN acting out the script rewritten by Hamlet to reveal to all how his uncle Claudius murdered King Hamlet by poison poured into the sleeping king's ear, to gain the throne and the queen, just as in the play.

The player King says that fate decides our futures and although you think that you won't marry now but when the first husband is dead you will change your thoughts and think otherwise.

"So think thou wilt no second husband wed,
But die thy thoughts when thy first lord is dead."

Hamlet has concocted this play with the intention of tugging at the king and queen's guilty conscience because he was convinced that (Act 2 Sc2 Li591)

"The play's the thing
Wherein I'll catch the conscience of the king."

The player queen is putting on such a dramatic performance of expressing her 'unwavering' love for her husband and making false vows.

"Both here and hence pursue me lasting strife
If, once a widow, ever I be wife!"

Hamlet is relishing this false exhibition of honesty by the player queen, exaggerating her uncompromising marital fidelity. He then makes a snide remark about her not keeping her promises and be damned. The player queen's performance is making his mother nervous,
"If she should break it now."

Hamlet taunts his mother because he can sense her unease at the play's uncanny resemblance of her.

TEXT ACT 3 scene 2

PLAYER KING
'Tis deeply sworn. Sweet, leave me here awhile.
My spirits grow dull, and fain I would beguile
The tedious day with sleep.

< *The* ***PLAYER KING*** *sleeps* >

PLAYER QUEEN
Sleep rock thy brain,
And never come mischance between us twain.

< *Exit* ***PLAYER QUEEN*** >

HAMLET
Madam, how like you this play?
GERTRUDE
The lady protests too much, methinks.
HAMLET
Oh, but she'll keep her word.
CLAUDIUS
Have you heard the argument?
Is there no offense in't?
HAMLET
No, no, they do but jest. Poison in jest.
No offense i'th' world.
CLAUDIUS
What do you call the play?
HAMLET
The Mousetrap. Marry, how? Tropically!
This play is the image of a murder done in Vienna.
HAMLET (*continues*)
Gonzago is the duke's name, his wife *Baptista*.
You shall see anon.
'Tis a knavish piece of work, but what o' that?
Your majesty and we that have free souls,
It touches us not.
Let the galled jade wince,
our withers are unwrung.

EXPLANATION

CLAUDIUS listens as HAMLET provokes GERTRUDE into understanding the play. "Madam, how like you this play?"

His mother expresses her dissatisfaction by saying that the lady is overplaying her role and remarks,

"The lady protests too much, methinks."

Hamlet taunts her further and he implies that unlike his mother, 'she'll keep her word.'
Claudius is also getting nervous, and he enquires of Hamlet if he knows the plot of the play and if it is offensive. He says it's just, 'poison in a jest'. All a joke but the poison he is referring to is his revenge.
Claudius asks what the name of the play is, and Hamlet ironically says, '*The mousetrap*'.

He sees his mother as a mouse trapped in Claudius' snare and Claudius trapped in his own guilt. He also calls Polonius 'a rat' when he kills him.
The imagery of the 'mouse' here suggests their vile, rattish deeds have caught up with them and they are all trapped in a net like a mouse.

Hamlet tells Claudius that the play is based on a murder in Vienna. *Gonzago* is the duke's name and his wife *Baptista*. It's a piece of nonsense, but who cares? You and I are honest people, so this silly play won't affect us,

"Your majesty and we that have free souls,
It touches us not"

Hamlet deliberately speaks to Claudius in riddles and jest to confuse and mislead him, whilst trying to get a guilty reaction from him.

*< Enter **LUCIANUS** >*

This is one Lucianus, nephew to the king.

OPHELIA

You are as good as a chorus, my lord.

HAMLET

I could interpret between you and your love,
If I couldsee the puppets dallying.

OPHELIA

You are keen, my lord, you are keen.

HAMLET

It would cost you a groaning to take off mine edge.

OPHELIA

Still better and worse.

HAMLET

So you must take your husbands. —
Begin, murderer.Pox,
leave thy damnable faces and begin. Come,
"The croaking raven doth bellow for revenge—"

LUCIANUS

Thoughts black, hands apt, drugs fit,
And time agreeing,
Confederate season, else no creature seeing,
Thou mixture rank, of midnight weeds collected,
With Hecate's ban thrice blasted, thrice infected,
Thy natural magic and dire property
On wholesome life usurp immediately.

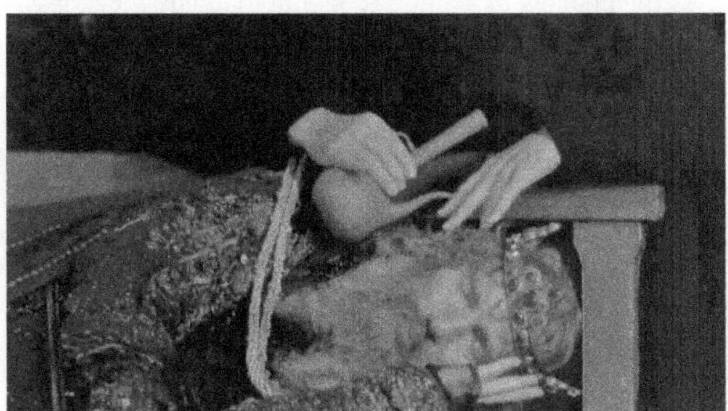

(*Pours poison into Player King's ears*)

HAMLET

He poisons him i' th' garden for 's estate.
His name'sGonzago.
The story is extant, and writ in choice Italian.
You shall see anon
How the murderer gets the love of Gonzago's wife.

OPHELIA

The king rises.

Hamlet's sharp, biting, retorts to Ophelia is shocking. He has come to realise that she too is a tool of betrayal, and he is bent on giving her a piece of his wrath. He makes fun of her flitting love for him, and he accuses her of 'dangling him like a puppet on a string',

"I could interpret between you and your love, if I could see the puppets dallying."

He uses the imagery of a 'raven' because in the Elizabethan era, they are believed to be a symbol of a bad omen heralding death. This could be a foreshadowing of Claudius' death later in the play.

Hamlet uses the metaphor of a raven to represent himself and his dire urge for revenge.

"The croaking raven doth bellow for revenge."

LUCIANUS SPEAKS

Ironically, Lucianus starts of his act with dark imagery. He introduces the supernatural and talks of his dark intentions to kill the king, willing hands, apt poison, and dark night so no one can see and the perfect poison which Hercate, goddess of witchcraft had concocted to pluck the life off a strong man.

"Thoughts black, hands apt, drugs fit,
And time agreeing"

Hamlet says that he poisons him in his own garden to usurp his estate which is exactly what Claudius did to his father in his own garden.

"He poisons him i'th' garden for' s estate."

The king rises, surely his action is seen as a sign of guilt. Hamlet says that he is frightened of a false alarm, 'false fire' and Gertrude is very concerned, and Polonius quickly stops the play.

HAMLET
What, frighted with false fire?
GERTRUDE
How fares my lord?
POLONIUS
Give o'er the play.
CLAUDIUS
Give me some light. Away!
POLONIUS
Lights, lights, lights!
Commotion
< *Exeunt all but **HAMLET** and **HORATIO*** >
HAMLET
Why, let the stricken deer go weep,
The hart ungall'd play.
For some must watch while some must sleep.
So runs the world away.
Would not this, sir, and a forest of feathers—
If the rest of my fortunes turn Turk with me—
With two Provincial roses on my razed shoes,
Get me a fellowship in a cry of players?
HORATIO
Half a share.
HAMLET
A whole one, I.
For thou dost know, O Damon dear,
This realm dismantled was
Of Jove himself.
And now reigns here
A very, very—pajock.
HORATIO
You might have rhymed.
HAMLET
O good Horatio,
I'll take the ghost's word for a thousand pound.
Didst perceive?
HORATIO
Very well, my lord.
HAMLET
Upon the talk of the poisoning?
HORATIO
I did very well note him.
HAMLET
Ah ha! Come, some music!
Come, the recorders!
For if the king like not the comedy,
Why then, belike, he likes it not, perdy.
Come, some music!

CLAUDIUS raises and staggers away from the play

Shakespeare uses light imagery when Claudius and Polonius ask for lights. They are desperate for lights and yell out,
"Give me some light, away!"

One can connote that they want to see the light and be cleansed of their sins. Both use exclamations suggesting their desperation.
Hamlet sings a little rhythmic, rhyming, jubilant song to express his excitement on his mission accomplished in getting a guilty response from Claudius. His anxiety and sudden abrupt departure from the play suggests this. He uses the imagery of a 'deer' to jeer at Claudius' weakness.
"Why, let the stricken deer go weep"

The imagery of the deer is symbolic because it is a hunted animal in the same way Claudius was hunted and his guilt revealed. Hamlet is now convinced that the ghost was right.
"O good Horatio,
I'll take the ghost's word for a thousand pound. Didst perceive"

Horatio also confirmed that when they were talking about poison, he noted Claudius' guilty response.
"I did very well note him"

Hamlet is elated at his success. He calls for music. Note his over-exuberant attitude in this utterance, 'Ah ha! – he is clearly rejoicing at his success.
"Ah ha! Come some music!"
"Come, the recorders!"
The repeated exclamation can suggest his overwhelming joy.

TEXT ACT 3 scene 2

< Enter ROSENCRANTZ and GUILDENSTERN >

GUILDENSTERN
Good my lord, vouchsafe me a word with you.
HAMLET
Sir, a whole history.
GUILDENSTERN
The king, sir—
HAMLET
Ay, sir, what of him?
GUILDENSTERN
Is in his retirement marvellous distemper'd.
HAMLET
With drink, sir?
GUILDENSTERN
No, my lord, with choler.
HAMLET
Your wisdom should show itself
More richer to signify this to the doctor.
For, for me to put him to his purgation
Would perhaps plunge him into far more choler.
GUILDENSTERN
Good my lord,
Put your discourse into some frame
And start not so wildly from my affair.
HAMLET
I am tame, sir. Pronounce.
GUILDENSTERN
The queen your mother,
In most great affliction of spirit,
Hath sent me to you.
HAMLET
You are welcome.
GUILDENSTERN
Nay, good my lord,
This courtesy is not of the right breed.
If it shall please you
To make me a wholesome answer
I will do your mother's commandment.
If not,your pardon and my return
Shall be the end of my business.
HAMLET
Sir, I cannot.
GUILDENSTERN
What, my lord?
HAMLET
Make you a wholesome answer.
My wits diseased.
But,sir, such answer as I can make,

EXPLANATION

We see Hamlet's excitement peak even further when Guildenstern asks for a word, and he offers to give him,

"Sir, a whole history"

Guildenstern informs Hamlet that the king has retired to his chambers, and he is extremely annoyed.

"Is in his retirement marvellous distemper'd"

Shakespeare cuts the tension in the more serious scenes to come by presenting Hamlet as a humorous and light hearted character.

Hamlet asks Guildenstern to tell a doctor about Claudius' ailment since he would only intensify his anger. Guildenstern is losing his patience with Hamlet's behaviour and urges him to think and respond properly.

"Put your discourse into some frame
And start not so wildly from my affair"

Guildenstern tells Hamlet that the queen is very annoyed and has sent him to see Hamlet.

"The queen your mother,
In most great affliction of spirit,
Hath sent me to you."

Guildenstern is fast becoming irate at Hamlet's irrational behaviour, and he reprimands him and tells him that his attitude is wrong.

If he will care to answer him with more politeness, then he will relay his mother's wish to him. If not, Guildenstern will not bother him and that will be the end of his business with Hamlet.

"Nay, good my Lord,
This courtesy is not of the right breed"

Hamlet tells him that he cannot make him a 'wholesome' answer because his 'wits' are diseased.

TEXT ACT 3 scene 2

HAMLET (*continues*)
You shall command –
Or, rather, as you say, my mother.
Therefore, no more, but to the matter.
My mother, you say—

ROSENCRANTZ
Then thus she says: your behaviour hath struck her
Into amazement and admiration.

HAMLET
O wonderful son that can so 'stonish a mother!
But is there no sequel
At the heels of this mother's admiration?
Impart.

ROSENCRANTZ
She desires to speak with you
In her closet ere you go to bed.

HAMLET
We shall obey, were she ten times our mother.
Have you any further trade with us?

ROSENCRANTZ
My lord, you once did love me.

HAMLET
And do still, by these pickers and stealers.

ROSENCRANTZ
Good my lord, what is your cause of distemper?
You do surely bar the door upon your own liberty
If you deny your griefs to your friend.

HAMLET
Sir, I lack advancement.

ROSENCRANTZ
How can that be,
when you have the voice of the king himself
for your succession in Denmark?

*< Re-enter the **PLAYERS** with recorders >*

HAMLET
Ay, sir, but "While the grass grows—"
The proverb is something musty—
Oh, the recorders! Let me see one.
(*He takes a recorder*)
(*Aside to Rosencrantz and Guildenstern*)
To withdraw with you,
Why do you go about to recover the wind of me
As if you would drive me into a toil?

EXPLANATION

ROSENCRANTZ and GUILDENSTERN tell Hamlet that his mother says his "behaviour hath struck her Into amazement and admiration"

Rosencrantz tells Hamlet that his mother thinks that his behaviour is astonishing and rather amazing,

"your behaviour Hath struck her
Into amazement and admiration."

She requests his presence in her bedroom.
Hamlet uses a rather sarcastic tone when he hears that his mother admired him, and he wants to know the reason for her admiration.

"O wonderful son that can so 'stonish a mother!"

Rosencrantz tries to find out what is troubling Hamlet,

"You do surely bar the door upon your own liberty If you deny your griefs to your friends"

Hamlet is troubled that he 'lacks advancement' but Rosencrantz says that the king had promised him succession to the throne in Denmark.

Hamlet is angry with Guildenstern because he is spying for the king. He very rudely asks him why he is hovering so close to him.

"Why do you go about to recover the wind of me
As if you would drive me into a toil?"

GUILDENSTERN
O my lord, if my duty be too bold,
My love is too unmannerly
HAMLET
I do not well understand that.
Will you play upon this pipe?
GUILDENSTERN
My lord, I cannot.
HAMLET
I pray you.
GUILDENSTERN
Believe me, I cannot.
HAMLET
I do beseech you.
GUILDENSTERN
I know no touch of it, my lord.
HAMLET
It is as easy as lying.
Govern these ventages with your fingers and thumb,
Give it breath with your mouth,
And it will discourse most eloquent music.
Look you, these are the stops.
GUILDENSTERN
But these cannot I command
To any utterance of harmony.
I have not the skill.
HAMLET
Why, look you now,
How unworthy a thing you makeof me!
You would play upon me.
You would seem toknow my stops.
You would pluck out the heart of my mystery.
You would sound me
From my lowest note to the top of my compass.
And there is much music,
Excellent voice, in this little organ,
Yet cannot you make it speak?
'Sblood, do you think
I am easier to be played on than a pipe.
Call me what instrument you will,
Though you can fret me,
Yet you cannot play upon me.

< Enter ***POLONIUS*** *>*

God bless you, sir.
POLONIUS
My lord,
The queen would speak with you, and presently.

HAMLET tells Guildenstern that playing the pipe is "as easy as lying"

Hamlet forces Guildenstern to play the recorder but he is adamant that he can't play. Hamlet attacks his character by insinuating that he is a liar,

"It's as easy as lying"

Hamlet very bitterly compares Guildenstern's treatment of him to a recorder. He speaks in blank verse and puns to verbally attack him.

"Why look you now,
How unworthy a thing you make of me!"

He accuses Guildenstern of playing him, knowing his movements, and manipulating him yet he is incapable of making music from a small instrument. You can take me for a fool, says Hamlet, but you cannot play upon me,

"Call me what instrument you will,
Though you can't fret me,
Yet you cannot play upon me."

Polonius enters and tells Hamlet, as did Rosencrantz and Guildenstern, that,

"The queen would speak with you, and presently"

TEXT ACT 3 scene 2

HAMLET
Do you see yonder cloud
that's almost in shape of a camel?

POLONIUS
By th' mass, and 'tis like a camel indeed.

HAMLET
Methinks it is like a weasel.

POLONIUS
It is backed like a weasel.

HAMLET
Or like a whale.

POLONIUS
Very like a whale.

HAMLET
Then I will come to my mother by and by.
(*aside*) They fool me to the top of my bent. —
I will come by and by.

POLONIUS
I will say so.

< *Exit* ***POLONIUS*** >

HAMLET
"By and by" is easily said.
Leave me, friends.

< *Exeunt all but* ***HAMLET*** >

'Tis now the very witching time of night,
When churchyards yawn
And hell, itself breathes out Contagion to this world.
Now could I drink hot blood
And do such bitter business as the bitter day
Would quake to look on.
Soft, now to my mother. —
O heart, lose not thy nature. Let not ever
The soul of Nero enters this firm bosom.
Let me be cruel, not unnatural.
I will speak daggers to her but use none.
My tongue and soul in this be hypocrites.
How in my words somever she be shent,
To give them seals never, my soul, consent.

< *Exit* >

EXPLANATION

When Polonius enters, Hamlet immediately seizes the opportunity to belittle him. He asks him if he can see a cloud which looks like a camel and Polonius says that he can,

"By th' mass, and 'tis like a camel indeed"

But Hamlet counteracts it by saying that,

"Methinks it is like a weasel"

and it has a back like a whale. He once again uses puns and metaphors to attack Polonius' character and his looks. The term 'weasel' is generally associated with a dishonest person like Polonius and reference to a 'whales back' can mean someone with a huge bottom like Polonius' which Hamlet makes fun of.

Hamlet agrees to see his mother. He said that they test his patience to the hilt.

"Then I will come to my mother by and by.
They fool me to the top of my bent"

In this very telling soliloquy, Hamlet seems to be plunged into a supernatural world. His bizarre thoughts are geared towards witches, graveyards, and hell.

We look at Hamlet's curious philosophical mind – yearning also to understand the metaphysical world where ghosts, witches and the devil lurk. He has brought Claudius to his 'very knees' and almost made him confess. Shakespeare used a lot of suspense and tension here as the play reached its climax.

Hamlet certainly does not have the gall to commit murder and says that he will speak in a harsh way to his mother, but he will not use the dagger on her,

"I will speak daggers to her but use none"

We are now curious to see what Hamlet's next steps are.

In Act 3 scene 3, the setting is a chamber inside the castle, later in the day.

Enter Claudius, Rosencrantz and Guildenstern.

The King instructs Rosencrantz and Guildenstern to take Hamlet to England forthwith as he is a threat to his life and the throne, and they concur.

Exit Rosencrantz and Guildenstern.

Enter Polonius who informs the King that Hamlet will soon visit his mother, the Queen, and that he will hide behind the Arras to gain further information as to Hamlet's intent.

Exit Polonius.

Claudius in a soliloquy where he admits his guilt to the murder of his brother and asks what form of payer can forgive this foul murder. He kneels in prayer.

Enter Hamlet who see the King in prayer, draws his sword, but in a soliloquy, reasons that by killing Claudius in prayer would be an act against heaven. Instead, much better to take revenge when the King is drunk or in the incestuous pleasure of the bed.

< Enter ***CLAUDIUS, ROSENCRANTZ***
and ***GUILDENSTERN*** *>*

CLAUDIUS
I like him not, nor stands it safe with us
To let his madness range.
Therefore prepare you.
I your commission will forthwith dispatch,
And he to England shall along with you.
The terms of our estate may not endure
Hazard so dangerous as doth hourly grow
Out of his lunacies.

GUILDENSTERN
We will ourselves provide.
Most holy and religious fear it is
To keep those many, many bodies safe
That live and feed upon your majesty.

ROSENCRANTZ
The single and peculiar life is bound
With all the strength and armour of the mind
To keep itself from noyance, but much more
That spirit upon whose weal depends and rest
The lives of many. The cease of majesty
Dies not alone, but, like a gulf, doth draw
What's near it with it. Or it is a massy wheel
Fix'd on the summit of the highest mount,
To whose huge spokes ten thousand lesser things
Are mortised and adjoined, which, when it falls,
Each small annexment, petty consequence,
Attends the boist'rous ruin. Never alone
Did the king sigh, but with a general groan?

CLAUDIUS
Arm you, I pray you, to this speedy voyage.
For we will fetters put upon this fear,
Which now goes too free-footed.

ROSENCRANTZ, GUILDENSTERN
We will haste us.

<Exeunt ***ROSENCRANTZ, GUILDENSTERN>***

From a powerful and strong man Claudius now appears like a dejected, defeated man.

We can juxtapose his earlier reactions to situations in Act 1. He was level-headed and in full control of his responsibilities.

Even his calm, calculated and persuasive speech was admirable, speaking very cordially to Hamlet although he bore a grudge against him.

But now he appears vulnerable and nervous, and he is desperate to put an end to Hamlet's 'lunacy' which is dangerous for him and to secure his status as king again.

He decides to send Hamlet away to England on a diplomatic mission.

"I your commission will forthwith dispatch,
And he to England shall along with you"

Explaining the danger and why he must send Hamlet away.

"The terms of our estate may not endure
Hazard so dangerous as doth hourly grow
Out of his lunacie"

Guildenstern promises the king that he and Rosencrantz will do their duty and fulfil the king's request.

"We will ourselves provide"

Claudius asks Rosencrantz and Guildenstern to arm themselves, but he is creating the opportunity for them to get rid of Hamlet by themselves if they desire.

"Arm you, I pray you, to this speedy voyage"

Both are not aware that the diplomatic letters that they carry to the King of England order the immediate execution of Hamlet, so if their desire fails, Claudius knows that Hamlet's demise is guaranteed.

< *Enter* ***POLONIUS*** >

POLONIUS

My lord, he's going to his mother's closet.
Behind the arras I'll convey myself
To hear the process.
I'll warrant she'll tax him home.
And, as you said – and wisely was it said –
'Tis meet that some more audience than a mother—
Since nature makes them partial—should o'erhear
The speech, of vantage.
Fare you well, my liege.
I'll call upon you ere you go to bed
And tell you what I know.

CLAUDIUS

Thanks, dear my lord.

< *Exit* ***POLONIUS*** >

Oh, my offence is rank. It smells to heaven.
It hath the primal eldest curse upon 't,
A brother's murder.
Pray can I not.
Though inclination be as sharp as will,
My stronger guilt defeats my strong intent,
And, like a man to double business bound,
I stand in pause where I shall first begin,
And both neglect. What if this cursed hand
Were thicker than itself with brother's blood?
Is there not rain enough in the sweet heavens
To wash it white as snow?
Where to serves mercy
But to confront the visage of offence?
And what's in prayer but this twofold force,
To be fore-stalled ere we come to fall
Or pardoned being down?
Then I'll look up. My fault is past.
But oh, what form of prayer
Can serve my turn, "Forgive me my foul murder"?
That cannot be, since I am still possess'd
Of those effects for which I did the murder:
My crown, mine own ambition, and my queen.

Polonius enters and tells Claudius that Hamlet is going to see his mother and he will hide behind the curtains and eavesdrop on their conversation.
Ironically, he promises to report to Claudius about the proceedings of their conversation.

"I'll call upon you ere you go to bed
And tell you what I know"

Claudius' soliloquy is perhaps the most poignant and riveting in the play. His use of spell-binding imagery and epic language as he exposes his guilty conscience, gives us a sense of satisfaction that justice will soon be done, as this Machiavellian character slowly reveals his true nature.

His anguish is clearly visible as he grapples with his guilty conscience and his fear of divine judgment. He starts his soliloquy off with a very emotive and dramatic biblical imagery. The murder of Cain killing his brother Abel. He says that his sins stink and heaven certainly frown upon it.

"Oh, my offence is rank. It smells to heaven.
It hath the primal eldest curse upon 't,
A brother's murder."

If we look closely, we will notice that despite his dejected state, Claudius seem to possess a sense of arrogance. His Machiavellian pragmatism is clearly visible because he appears to be challenging God, which can be denoted by the many questions he asks,

"What if this cursed hand
Were thicker than itself with brother's blood?"
"Is there not rain enough in the sweet heavens
To wash it white as snow?"

He intends to ask for forgiveness and keep the fruits of his vile deed,

"Forgive me my foul murder" And keep,

"My crown, mine own ambition, and my queen"

CLAUDIUS (*continues*)
May one be pardoned and retain th' offense?
In the corrupted currents of this world
Offense's gilded hand may shove by justice,
And oft 'tis seen the wicked prize itself
Buys out the law. But 'tis not so above.
There is no shuffling. There the action lies
In his true nature, and we ourselves compell'd,
Even to the teeth and forehead of our faults,
To give in evidence. What then? What rests?
Try what repentance can. What can it not?
Yet what can it when one cannot repent?
O wretched state! O bosom black as death!
O limed soul that, struggling to be free,
Art more engaged!
Help, angels. Make assay.
Bow, stubborn knees,
And heart with strings of steel,
Be soft as sinews of the newborn babe.
All may be well.
(kneels)

< *Enter* ***HAMLET*** >

HAMLET
Now might I do it pat.
(*Hamlet draws his sword*)

His many uses of all the anguished punctuation and dark imagery reveals a very tortured soul,

"What then? What rests?"

"O wretched state! O bosom black as death!"

Claudius' heartfelt plea to the angels is almost comical. He urges the angels to relent and throw away their stubbornness in forgiving him and soften their heart of steel like that of a newborn baby.
"Help, angels. Make assay.
Bow, stubborn knees,
And heart with strings of steel,
Be soft as sinews of the newborn babe."
Claudius seek redemption, so he prays.

CLAUDIUS seeks forgiveness for killing his brother

Hamlet draws his sword ready to take revenge, but stays his hand, as it might make Claudius a martyr murdered on hallowed ground.

HAMLET thinks twice, and decides it may make Claudius a martyr

Now he is a-praying. And now I'll do 't.
And so he goes to heaven.
And so am I reveng'd.—
That would be scann'd.
A villain kills my father, and, for that,
I, his sole son, do this same villain send to heaven.
Oh, this is hire and salary, not revenge.
He took my father grossly, full of bread,
With all his crimes broad blown, as flush as May.
And how his audit stands who knows save heaven?
But in our circumstance and course of thought
'Tis heavy with him. And am I then reveng'd
To take him in the purging of his soul
When is he fit and seasoned for his passage? No
Up, sword, and know thou a more horrid hent.
When he is drunk asleep, or in his rage,
Or in th' incestuous pleasure of his bed,
At game a-swearing, or about some act
That has no relish of salvation in 't—
Then trip him, that his heels may kick at heaven,
And that his soul may be as damn'd and black
As hell, whereto it goes. My mother stays
This physic but prolongs thy sickly days.

< *Exit* ***HAMLET*** >

CLAUDIUS
(rises) My words fly up, my thoughts remain below.
Words without thoughts never to heaven go.

< *Exit* >

Hamlet's reaction here is debatable. He refuses to kill Claudius at his most vulnerable moment whilst he is praying. One may argue if he is really taking the prospect of Divine judgment into consideration,

"To take him in the purging of his soul."

or is he considering the moral aspect which he holds very dear to his heart - not to kill, which is also one of God's commandments: "Thou shalt not kill."

He is afraid that if he kills Claudius while he is praying then his soul will be purged, and he will go to heaven.

"A villain kills my father, and, for that,
I, his sole son, do this same villain send to heaven"

He shelves his idea of killing Claudius now and puts his sword away. He plans to kill him if he is in the midst of some unwholesome behaviour that's not pleasing in the sight of God. He intends to kill him,

in th' incestuous pleasure of his bed,
At game a-swearing

And make sure that,

"his heels may kick at heaven,
And that his soul may be as damn'd and black
As hell"

CLAUDIUS admitting his guilt to heaven

Claudius gives up his failed attempt to be redeemed of his sins. Words without any meaning can never go to heaven,

"Words without thoughts never to heaven go"

In Act 3 scene 4, the setting is the Queen's chamber inside the castle, later in the day.

Enter Gertrude and Polonius who then hides behind the Arras.

Enter Hamlet who demands to know what's the matter. His mother tells him that the King his uncle is much offended but Hamlet retorts that she has offended her deceased husband by this marriage to the King.

Hamlet tells the Queen to sit, and not budge until she sees the inmost part of herself. The Queen asks what Hamlet will do and if he wilts murder her. She yells Help. Polonius yells Help, and Hamlet draws his sword and stabs Polonius through the Arras thinking it is Claudius behind it.

Hamlet lifts up the Arras and finds Polonius, dead.

The Queen is shocked and asks, 'What a rash and bloody deed is this!'

Hamlet retorts, 'A bloody deed. Almost as bad, good mother, As kill a king and marry with his brother'.

Hamlet tells Gertrude to look upon the picture of King hamlet in splendour and then his brother who he likened to the mildew infecting her deceased husband ear. He accuses Gertrude of incest. The Queen response by asking Hamlet to speak no more, as his words are like daggers entering in her ears.

Enter the Ghost who instructs Hamlet to sharpen his purpose by not berating his mother. Gertrude asks Hamlet to whom does he speak. Hamlet can see the ghost, but Gertrude cannot. Exit the Ghost.

Hamlet rejects his mother inference of madness, asking her to repent the past, and discover the truth for herself. She asks what she should do. Hamlet tells her not to go to the King's bed but assume a virtue.

Gertrude confirms she knows Hamlet is to be sent to England with his friends Rosencrantz and Guildenstern. Hamlet does not trust either friend, convinced that they are marshalling him into Knavery (a trap), but will hoist them with their petard.

Exit Hamlet lugging the body of Polonius.

TEXT ACT 3 scene 4

The Queen's closet hung with an arras

*< Enter **GERTRUDE** and **POLONIUS** >*

POLONIUS
He will come straight. Look you lay home to him.
Tell him his pranks have been too broad to bear with,
And that your grace hath screen'd
And stood between much heat and him.
I'll silence me even here.
Pray you, be round with him.

HAMLET
(within) Mother, mother, mother!

GERTRUDE
I'll warrant you. Fear me not.
Withdraw, I hear him coming.

*< **POLONIUS** hides behind the arras >*

*< Enter **HAMLET** >*

HAMLET
Now mother, what's the matter?

GERTRUDE
Hamlet, thou hast thy father much offended.

HAMLET
Mother, you have my father much offended.

GERTRUDE
Come, come, you answer with an idle tongue.

HAMLET
Go, go, you question with a wicked tongue.

GERTRUDE
Why, how now, Hamlet?

HAMLET
What's the matter now?

GERTRUDE
Have you forgot me?

HAMLET
No, by the rood, not so.
You are the queen, your husband's brother's wife,
And—would it were not so, you are my mother.

EXPLANATION

POLONIUS discussing with GERTRUDE what to tell Hamlet when he arrives, "Tell him his pranks have been too broad to bear with"

If we assess Gertrude's behaviour, then we will understand and empathise with Hamlet's sense of loneliness and apprehension about his mother's loyalty. She seems to be collaborating with Polonius against her son and later we see that she betrayed Hamlet's trust as well.

"I'll warrant you. Fear me not.
Withdraw, I hear him coming."

Hamlet's bold and brazen verbal attack on his mother is shocking. His caustic biting wit, candid questioning and his sharp tit for tat answers seems to have got Hamlet the craving for revenge on his mother, for betraying his father.

His mother tells him that he has offended the king and he points out that she had wronged his father.

"Mother, you have my father much offended."

He also accuses her of having a wicked tongue. He is very sarcastic and bitter when he says that she is

"the queen, your husband's brother's wife"

He makes her feel guilty by pointing out the incestuous relationship ties between him and his mother.

GERTRUDE
Nay, then I'll set those to you that can speak.
HAMLET
Come, come, and sit you down.
You shall not budge.
You go not till I set you up a glass
Where you may see the inmost part of you.
GERTRUDE
What wilt thou do?
Thou wilt not murder me?
Help, help, ho!
POLONIUS
(from behind the arras) What, ho? Help, help, help!
HAMLET
How now, a rat?
Dead for a ducat, dead!
(stabs his sword through the arras
And kills ***POLONIUS****)*
POLONIUS
(from behind the arras) Oh, I am slain.
GERTRUDE
O me, what hast thou done?
HAMLET
Nay, I know not. Is it the king?
GERTRUDE
Oh, what a rash and bloody deed is this!
HAMLET
A bloody deed?
Almost as bad, good mother,
As kill a king and marry with his brother.
GERTRUDE
As kill a king?
HAMLET
Ay, lady, 'twas my word.

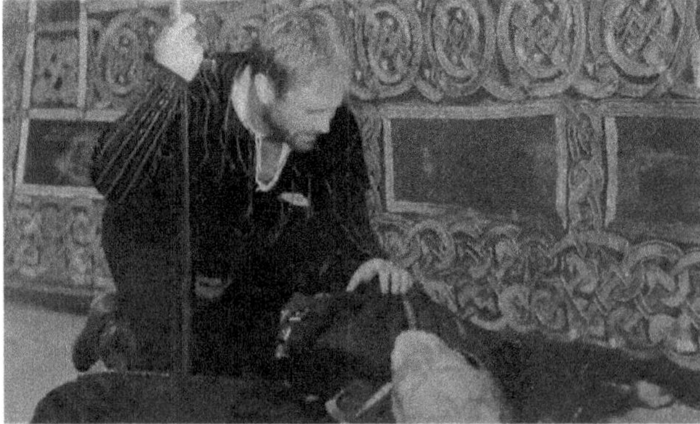

< ***HAMLET*** *draws back the arras and discovers* ***POLONIUS****, dead >*

Gertrude is alarmed at Hamlet's strange behaviour, and she insists on having someone who can speak to him, but he orders her to,

"not budge,
You go not till I set you up a glass,
Where you may see the inmost part of you."

He wants her to look into her soul and acknowledge her sins. Maybe in some way he wants her to redeem herself of her guilt.

HAMLET threatens his mother GERTRUDE

Gertrude is afraid and she yells for help.

Polonius then shouts for help from behind the curtain. Hamlet stabs his sword through the curtain and kills Polonius calling him a 'rat'.

Hamlet mistakes Polonius for Claudius when he struck.

Gertrude is horrified and cries out,
"Oh, what a rash and bloody deed is this?"

Hamlet retorts very briskly,
"A bloody deed?
Almost as bad, good mother
As kill a king and marry with his brother."

Gertrude's response is shocking,
"As kill a king?"

This response gives us reason to believe that she had no knowledge of Claudius' devious actions to kill her husband and she shared no part in it."

Thou wretched, rash, intruding fool, farewell.
I took thee for thy better. Take thy fortune.
Thou find'st to be too busy is some danger.
(*to Gertrude*) Leave wringing of your hands.
Peace. Sit you down
And let me wring your heart.
For so I shall, if it be made of penetrable stuff,
If damn'd custom have not braz'd it so
That it is proof and bulwark against sense.

GERTRUDE
What have I done, that thou dar'st wag thy tongue
In noise so rude against me?

HAMLET
Such an act
That blurs the grace and blush of modesty,
Calls virtue hypocrite, takes off the rose
From the fair forehead of an innocent love
And sets a blister there, makes marriage vows
As false as dicers' oaths—oh, such a deed
As from the body of contraction plucks
The very soul, and sweet religion makes
A rhapsody of words. Heaven's face doth glow
O'er this solidity and compound mass
With tristful visage, as against the doom,
Is thought-sick at the act.

GERTRUDE
Ay me, what act
That roars so loud and thunders in the index?

Drawing back the arras, Hamlet discovers it is Polonius' he has killed instead of Claudius, and he hurls a tirade of abuse at the body.

"Thou wretched, rash, intruding fool, farewell"

He then quickly focuses his attention back to his mother and commands her to,

"Leave wringing of your hands.
Peace. Sit you down
And let me wring your heart."

Note Hamlet's pun on the verb, 'wring'.
Gertrude is wringing her hands out of nervousness, but Hamlet is intending to 'wring her heart', make her feel guilty for her actions.

Gertrude enquires why he is so hostile towards her, and Hamlet tells her that her actions was beyond modesty, lacked virtue, destroyed and tainted true love and made a mockery of her marriage vows.

"Such an act
That blurs the grace and blush of modesty,
Calls virtue hypocrite"

Slowly the saga of this family's upheaval unfolds, and the plot thickens as it plods towards its fatal denouement. The death of Polonius is a twist in the plot. What Next?

Hamlet's religious conscience surfaces once again when he uses biblical reference to expose his mother's guilt. Heaven scorns her behaviour, and he personifies heaven's face saying,

"Heaven's face doth glow
O'er this solidity and compound mass
With tristful visage, as against the doom,
Is thought sick of the act."

TEXT ACT 3 scene 4 **EXPLANATION**

HAMLET

Look here upon this picture and on this,
The counterfeit presentment of two brothers.
See, what a grace was seated on this brow?
Hyperion's curls, the front of Jove himself,
An eye like Mars to threaten and command,
A station like the herald Mercury
New-lighted on a heaven-kissing hill—
A combination and a form indeed
Where every god did seem to set his seal
To give the world assurance of a man.
This was your husband. Look you now, what follows.
Here is your husband, like a mildewed ear
Blasting his wholesome brother.
Have you eyes?
Could you on this fair mountain leave to feed
And batten on this moor? Ha, have you eyes?
You cannot call it love, for at your age
The heyday in the blood is tame, it's humble,
And waits upon the judgment.
And what judgment would step from this to this?
Sense sure you have,
Else could you not have motion.
But sure that sense is apoplex'd,
For madness would not err,
Nor sense to ecstasy was ne'er so thrall'd,
But it reserved some quantity of choice
To serve in such a difference. What devil was 't
That thus hath cozen'd you at hoodman-blind?
Eyes without feeling, feeling without sight,
Ears without hands or eyes, smelling sans all, Or
but a sickly part of one true sense
Could not so mope. O shame, where is thy blush?
Rebellious hell,
If thou canst mutine in a matron's bones,
To flaming youth let virtue be as wax
And melt in her own fire. Proclaim no shame
When the compulsive ardour gives the charge,
Since frost itself as actively doth burn,
And reason panders will.

GERTRUDE

O Hamlet, speak no more!
Thou turn'st mine eyes into my very soul,
And there I see such black and grained spots
As will not leave their tinct.

He targets his mother's conscience by showing her pictures of both his father and his uncle. He comments positively on his father's physical attributes and negatively on his uncle's. He also draws a juxtaposition on the two men's differing character traits.

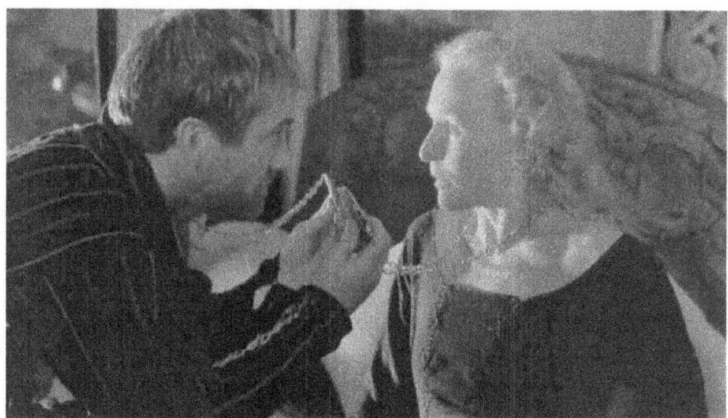

"Look here upon this picture and on this,
The counterfeit presentment of two brothers"

Hamlet acclaims his mother's first husband, his father, as a Greek god with all the endowments,

"See, what a grace was seated on this brow?Hyperion's curls, the front of Jove himself,
An eye like Mars to threaten and command,
A station like the herald Mercury
New-lighted on a heaven-kissing hill"

He disclaims her second husband as like a mildewed ear.

"Look you now, what follows.
Here is your husband, like a mildewed ear"

Hamlet's taunting of his mother with the two pictures of the brothers seems to have worked. Gertrude is acknowledging her guilt. She uses rather graphic imagery to express her shame. She looks into her soul and sees black marks and spots resembling her sins and they can never be erased.

"Thou turn'st mine eyes into my very soul,
And there I see such black and grained spots"

TEXT ACT 3 scene 4

HAMLET
Nay, but to live
In the rank sweat of an enseam'd bed,
Stewed in corruption, honeying and making love
Over the nasty sty—

GERTRUDE
O, speak to me no more!
These words like daggers enter in my ears.
No more, sweet Hamlet.

HAMLET
A murderer and a villain,
A slave that is not twentieth part the tithe
Of your precedent lord, a vice of kings,
A cutpurse of the empire and the rule,
That from a shelf the precious diadem stole,
And put it in his pocket—

GERTRUDE
No more!

HAMLET
A king of shreds and patches—

*< Enter **GHOST** >*

Save me and hover o'er me with your wings,
You heavenly guards! —
What would your gracious figure?

GERTRUDE
Alas, he's mad!

HAMLET
Do you not come your tardy son to chide,
That, laps'd in time and passion, lets go by
The important acting of your dread command?
O, say!

GHOST
Do not forget. This visitation
Is but to whet thy almost blunted purpose.
But look, amazement on thy mother sits.
O, step between her and her fighting soul.
Conceit in weakest bodies strongest works.
Speak to her, Hamlet.

EXPLANATION

Hamlet's speech to his mother is very lurid and explicit. He accuses her of making love in dirty sheets and sweat. The 'dirty sheets' is associated to a 'sty' which is full of Claudius' corruption.

"In the rank sweat of an endeared bed,
Stewed in corruption, honeying and making love
Over the nasty sty – "

Gertrude is aghast and urges him not to taunt her any further because his words are pricking her ears and her conscience.

"O, speak to me no more!
These words like daggers enter in my ears"

The GHOST only Hamlet can see and talk to but not Gertrude

The ghosts' demands are questionable because he is egging Hamlet on to murder. He is pushing him to flout God's law of, "Thou shalt not kill."

Hamlet asks the ghost if he came to reprimand him for dragging his feet and not carrying out his command to kill Claudius.

"Do you not come your tardy son to chide,
That lapsed in time and passion."

The ghost tells him that this visit is just a reminder.

"Is but to whet thy almost blunted purpose"

"Speak to her, Hamlet"

HAMLET
How is it with you, lady?
GERTRUDE
Alas, how is 't with you,
That you do bend your eye on vacancy
And with th' incorporal air do hold discourse?
Forth at your eyes your spirits wildly peep,
And, as the sleeping soldiers in th' alarm,
Your bedded hair, like life in excrements,
Starts up and stands on end. O gentle son,
Upon the heat and flame of thy distemper
Sprinkle cool patience. Whereon do you look?
HAMLET
On him, on him!
Look you, how pale he glares!
His form and cause conjoin'd, preaching to stones,
Would make them capable.
(*to Ghost*) Do not look upon me,
Lest with this piteous action you convert
My stern effects. Then what I have to do
Will want true color—tears perchance for blood.
GERTRUDE
To whom do you speak this?
HAMLET
Do you see nothing there?
GERTRUDE
Nothing at all, yet all that is I see.
HAMLET
Nor did you nothing hear?
GERTRUDE
No, nothing but ourselves.
HAMLET
Why, look you there! Look how it steals away—
My father, in his habit as he liv'd—
Look where he goes, even now, out at the portal!

< *Exit **GHOST*** >

GERTRUDE
This the very coinage of your brain.
This bodiless creation ecstasy
Is very cunning in.
HAMLET
Ecstasy?
My pulse as yours doth temperately keep time
And makes as healthful music. It is not madness
That I have utter'd. Bring me to the test,
And I the matter will re-word, which madness

Hamlet is not sure if Gertrude is frightened by the Ghost,

"How is it with you, lady?"

But she replies,

"O gentle son,
Upon the heat and flame of thy distemper
Sprinkle cool patience. Whereon do you look?"

She asks,

"To whom do you speak this?"

She confirms she see and hears nothing except Hamlet talking to empty space,

"No, nothing but ourselves"

HAMLET see and hears the Ghost but Gertrude does not

Hamlet is communicating with the ghost and Gertrude is now convinced that Hamlet is definitely gone crazy. She accuses him of imagining things.

"This is the very coinage of thy brain."

HAMLET (*continues*)
Would gambol from. Mother, for love of grace,
Lay not that flattering unction to your soul.
That not your trespass but my madness speaks.
It will but skin and film the ulcerous place
Whilst rank corruption, mining all within,
Infects unseen. Confess yourself to heaven.
Repent what's past. Avoid what is to come.
And do not spread the compost on the weeds
To make them ranker. Forgive me this my virtue,
For in the fatness of these pursy times
Virtue itself of vice must pardon beg,
Yea, curb and woo for leave to do him good.
GERTRUDE
O Hamlet, thou hast cleft my heart in twain.
HAMLET
Oh, throw away the worser part of it,
And live the purer with the other half.
Good night—but go not to mine uncle's bed.
Assume a virtue if you have it not.
That monster, custom, who all sense doth eat,
Of habits devil, is angel yet in this:
That to the use of actions fair and good
He likewise gives a frock or livery
That aptly is put on. Refrain tonight,
And that shall lend a kind of easiness
To the next abstinence, the next more easy.
For use almost can change the stamp of nature,
And either rein the devil or throw him out
With wondrous potency.
Once more, good night,
And when you are desirous to be blessed,
I'll blessing beg of you.
(*points to Polonius*) For this same lord,
I do repent.
But heaven hath pleas'd it so,
To punish me with this and this with me,
That I must be their scourge and minister.
I will bestow him and will answer well
The death I gave him.
So, again, good night.
I must be cruel only to be kind.
Thus bad begins and worse remains behind.
One word more, good lady—
GERTRUDE
What shall I do?

We look at Hamlet's lengthy blank- versed speeches to his mother. One can infer that it is a desperate attempt to make her see the light and redeem herself. The ghost as well made it clear that it is worried about her soul. He says, (Act 3 scene 4 line 115), 'speak to her Hamlet'.

"Confess yourself to heaven.
Repent what's past. Avoid what is to come"

He asks her not to,

"spread the compost on the weeds
To make them ranker"

The imagery of the compost and the weeds can be associated to Claudius. He is the weed which causes destruction and Hamlet warns that if she waters the weeds (ignore his uncle's crime) then Claudius' deeds will become even more dirtier.

He urges his mother to throw away the past and advance towards purity and seek purging for her iniquities,

"Oh, throw away the worser part of it,
And live the purer with the other half."

HAMLET listens as GERTRUDE asks, "What shall I do?"

Gertrude is desperate to right the wrong done to her son Hamlet caused by power and lust. She asks Hamlet for guidance,

"What shall I do?"

TEXT ACT 3 scene 4

HAMLET
Not this, by no means, that I bid you do—
Let the bloat king tempt you again to bed,
Pinch wanton on your cheek, call you his mouse,
And let him, for a pair of reechy kisses
Or paddling in your neck with his damn'd fingers,
Make you to ravel all this matter out:
That I essentially am not in madness
But mad in craft.
'Twere good you let him know,
For who that's but a queen, fair, sober, wise,
Would from a paddock, from a bat, a gib,
Such dear concernings hide? Who would do so?
No, in despite of sense and secrecy,
Unpeg the basket on the house's top.
Let the birds fly, and like the famous ape,
To try conclusions, in the basket creep
And break your own neck down.

GERTRUDE
Be thou assur'd, if words be made of breath
And breath of life, I have no life to breathe
What thou hast said to me.

HAMLET
I must to England, you know that?

GERTRUDE
Alack,
I had forgot. 'Tis so concluded on.

HAMLET
There's letters sealed, and my two schoolfellows,
Whom I will trust as I will adder's fang'd,
They bear the mandate. They must sweep my way
And marshal me to knavery. Let it work,
For 'tis the sport to have the engineer
Hoist with his own petard. And 't shall go hard,
But I will delve one yard below their mines,
And blow them at the moon. Oh, 'tis most sweet
When in one line two crafts directly meet.
(indicates Polonius)
This man shall set me packing.
I'll lug the guts into the neighbour room.
Mother, good night. Indeed this counselor
Is now most still, most secret, and most grave
Who was in life a foolish prating knave. —
Come, sir, to draw toward an end with you.—
Good night, mother.

*< Exeunt, **HAMLET** lugging in **POLONIUS** >*

EXPLANATION

Hamlet instructs her not to do Claudius' bidding but reveals all about his madness as a ploy to seek revenge, thus winning Claudius' trust.

"Make you to ravel all this matter out:
That I essentially am not in madness
But mad in craft"

Gertrude refuses, saying if words are made of breath, her breath has no life. So, she will not reveal what Hamlet has told her.

"I have no life to breathe
What thou hast said to me"

In other words, she will be loyal to Hamlet not her husband Claudius.

Hamlet confirms to Gertrude that

"I must to England, you know that?"

Something she had forgot, in all the turmoil.

Hamlet prepares to leave for England. He uses the imagery of a snake to describe his friends – Rosencrantz and Guildenstern. He says that he doesn't trust them because they have forked tongues like a snake. Being friendly to him but collaborating with his uncle against him.

HAMLET drags away POLONIUS' lifeless body

Whom I will trust as I will adder's fang'd

He says that Polonius is quiet now, but he was,

"in life a foolish prating knave"

In Act 4 scene 1, the setting is the Queen's chamber inside the castle, a few hours later.

Enter Claudius with Rosencrantz and Guildenstern.

Claudius asks Gertrude where Hamlet is. In reply, Gertrude asks Rosencrantz and Guildenstern to leave so she can speak to the King in private.

Exit Rosencrantz and Guildenstern.

Gertrude tells Claudius that Hamlet in his lawless fit on hearing something stirring behind the Arras had drawn his rapier and inadvertently kill Polonius.

Claudius remarks that Hamlet's liberty is full of threats to all, and Gertrude tells Claudius that Hamlet had lugged away the body.

Enter Rosencrantz and Guildenstern by command of the King who tells them that Hamlet had slain Polonius and then instructs both to seek the body and bring it into the chapel.

Exit Rosencrantz and Guildenstern.

Claudius tells Gertrude that they will calls up wisest friends to determine what to do. He then instructs her to come away, and remarks his soul is full of discord and dismay.

Exit Claudius and Gertrude.

TEXT ACT 4 scene 1

*Enter King **CLAUDIUS** and Queen **GERTRUDE**,with **ROSENCRANTZ** and **GUILDENSTERN***

CLAUDIUS
(*to Gertrude*) There's matter in these sighs,
These profound heaves.
You must translate.
'Tis fit we understand them.
Where is your son?
GERTRUDE
(*to Rosencrantz and Guildenstern*)
Bestow this place on us a little while.

<*Exeunt **ROSENCRANTZ** and **GUILDENSTERN***>

Ah, my good lord, what have I seen tonight!
CLAUDIUS
What, Gertrude?
How does Hamlet?
GERTRUDE
Mad as the sea and wind when both contend
Which is the mightier. In his lawless fit,
Behind the arras hearing something stir,
Whips out his rapier, cries, "A rat, a rat!"
And in this brainish apprehension kills
The unseen good old man.
CLAUDIUS
O heavy deed!
It had been so with us, had we been there.
His liberty is full of threats to all—
To you yourself, to us, to everyone.
Alas, how shall this bloody deed be answer'd?
It will be laid to us, whose providence
Should have kept short, restrain'd and out of haunt,
This mad young man. But so much was our love,
We would not understand what was most fit,
But, like the owner of a foul disease,
To keep it from divulging, let it feed
Even on the pith of life. Where is he gone?
GERTRUDE
To draw apart the body he hath kill'd,
O'er whom his very madness, like some ore
Among a mineral of metals base,
Shows itself pure. He weeps for what is done.

EXPLANATION

Claudius tells Gertrude that her heaving sighs mean something, and he urges her to tell him what it is,

"There's matter in these sighs,
These profound heaves.
You must translate."

Gertrude relays to Claudius how Hamlet in his deranged state killed Polonius. She uses the imagery of the raging, tumultuous sea to describe Hamlet's craziness,

"Mad as the sea and wind when both contend
Which is the mightier."

Claudius seizes this opportunity to put his vile plan into action. He insists that Hamlet's insanity is a big threat to everyone.

"His liberty is full of threats to all"

He said that it was his duty to keep Hamlet's behaviour under control.

"It will be laid to us, whose providence
Should have kept short, restrained and out of haunt,
This mad young man."

Once again, we see the theme of appearance versus reality when Claudius pretends to 'love' Hamlet.

"But so much was our love"

He loved him so much that he didn't want his insanity to be divulged. He uses the imagery of a disease where the owner tries to keep it a secret.

"But like the owner of a foul disease,
To keep it from divulging"

He feels he is responsible to let it fester and reach dangerous heights which resulted in murder.

"Let it feed
Even on the pith of life"

TEXT ACT 4 scene 1

CLAUDIUS
O Gertrude, come away!
The sun no sooner shall the mountains touch
But we will ship him hence, and this vile deed
We must, with all our majesty and skill,
Both countenance and excuse. —
Ho, Guildenstern!

*<Enter **ROSENCRANTZ** and **GUILDENSTERN**>*

Friends both, go join you with some further aid.
Hamlet in madness hath Polonius slain,
And from his mother's closet hath he dragg'd him.
Go seek him out, speak fair, and bring the body
Into the chapel. I pray you, haste in this.

*<Exeunt **ROSENCRANTZ** and **GUILDENSTERN**>*

Come, Gertrude,
We'll call up our wisest friends,
And let them know both what we mean to do
And what's untimely done.
So dreaded slander—
Whose whisper o'er the world's diameter,
As level as the cannon to his blank,
Transports the poisoned sh't—
May miss our name
And hit the woundless air.
Oh, come away!
My soul is full of discord and dismay.

< Exeunt >

EXPLANATION

GERTRUDE and CLAUDIUS survey the blood

Claudius tells Gertrude that as soon as the sun set in the mountains, they will ship Hamlet off to England,
"The sun no sooner shall the mountains touch,
But we will ship him hence"

CLAUDIUS orders, "Go seek him out"

Claudius asks Rosencrantz and Guildenstern to remove Polonius' dead body from Gertrude's room. He tells them to speak politely to Hamlet,

"Go seek him out, speak fair and bring the body
Into the chapel"

Claudius is very conscious of own and Gertrude's status and appearance. He is worried that Hamlet's actions will taint their 'perfect' character, and about the gossip that will spread far and wide, blackening their names.

"So dreaded slander –
Whose whisper o'er the world's diameter"

Claudius is clearly unnerved here, and he is trying to make sense of these new turn of events. He feels very distraught and says,
"My soul is full of discourse and dismay"

In Act 4 scene 2, the setting is another chamber inside the castle, a few hours later.

Enter Hamlet. Voices outside calls Hamlet's name.

Enter Rosencrantz and Guildenstern and Others.

Rosencrantz is insistent that Hamlet must tell him where the body of Polonium is as it is the King's wish that it be laid in the chapel.

Hamlet tells Rosencrantz that he is no more than sponge which the King will rung dry.

Hamlet is cryptic in his replies by saying the body is with the king, but the king is not with the body. Hamlet tells Guildenstern to bring him to the king.

Exit all.

TEXT ACT 4 scene 2

Another room of the castle

*< Enter **HAMLET** >*

HAMLET
Safely stowed.
GENTLEMEN
(from within) Hamlet! Lord Hamlet!
HAMLET
But soft, what noise?
Who calls on Hamlet?
Oh, here they come.

*< Enter **ROSENCRANTZ**,*
***GUILDENSTERN**, and Others >*

ROSENCRANTZ
What have you done, my lord, with the dead body?
HAMLET
Compounded it with dust, where to 'tis kin.
ROSENCRANTZ
Tell us where 'tis, that we may take it thence
And bear it to the chapel.
HAMLET
Do not believe it.
ROSENCRANTZ
Believe what?
HAMLET
That I can keep your counsel and not mine own.
Besides, to be demanded of a sponge!
What replication should be made
by the son of a king?
ROSENCRANTZ
Take you me for a sponge, my lord?
HAMLET
Ay, sir, that soaks up the king's countenance,
His rewards, his authorities.
But such officers do the king best service in the end.
He keeps them, like an ape, in the corner of his jaw –
First mouthed, to be last swallowed.
When he needs what you have gleaned,
It is but squeezing you
And, sponge, you shall be dry again

EXPLANATION

Hamlet hides Polonius' body and when Rosencrantz asks him what he had done with the body, he uses a very poignant biblical imagery,

"Ashes to ashes, dust to dust."

When God created man, he took the dust from the earth, blew into it, and created Adam – the first man. He then said,

GUILDENSTERN and ROSENCRANTZ search for Hamlet and the body of Polonius

Man was made from dust and when he dies, he will return to the earth, as did his kin.

"Compounded it with dust, where to tis kin"

Hamlet speaks bitterly to Rosencrantz, accusing him of being a sponge. He soaks up the king's rewards and approval,

"Ay sir, that soaks up the king's countenance,
His rewards, his authorities"

Officers like that will give the best service and loyalty to the king to the very end.

"But such officers do the king best service in the end"

He compares Rosencrantz to an ape to be used by the king for his dirty jobs and being swallowed by the king. Then after he has used him, he will squeeze him like a sponge, and he will be dry again.

"He keeps them, like an ape in the corner of his jaw,
First mouthed to be the last swallowed"

TEXT ACT 4 scene 2

ROSENCRANTZ
I understand you not, my lord.
HAMLET
I am glad of it.
A knavish speech sleeps in a foolish ear.
ROSENCRANTZ
My lord, you must tell us where the body is
And go with us to the king.
HAMLET
The body is with the king,
But the king is not with the body.
The king is a thing—
GUILDENSTERN
A thing, my lord?
HAMLET
Of nothing. Bring me to him.
Hide, fox, and all after.

< Exeunt >

EXPLANATION

Rosencrantz is confused about Hamlet's reasoning of his character, but Hamlet tells him that he is too foolish to understand his reasoning,

"A knavish speech sleeps in a foolish ear"

Rosencrantz insists that Hamlet tells him where Polonius' body is and he must go with them to the king.

In reply, Hamlet speaks in riddles,

"The body is with the king,
But the king is not with the body"

Concluding,

"The king is a thing—"

Guildenstern echoes Hamlet's words in admonishment,

"A thing, my lord?"

Hamlet is dismissive, replying,

"Of nothing. Bring me to him"

In Act 4 scene 3, the setting is the hall of the castle, a few hours later.

Enter Claudius and three Lords.

Claudius informs all present that he has sent for Hamlet who due to his dangerous nature is to be sent away.

Enter Rosencrantz and Others.

Enter Hamlet with Guildenstern.

The Kings orders Hamlet to tell him where the body is, but Hamlet is evasive citing obscure places, even heaven, before revealing that it might be found as you go upstairs into the lobby.

Exit Attendants to recover the body.

The King tells Hamlet he is to be sent to England for his transgression. Hamlet bids farewell to his mother.

Exit Hamlet.

The King demand haste for Hamlet's departure.

Exit all but the King.

Claudius in a soliloquy, expects England to pay homage as a defeated nation, and effect Hamlet's death as authorise by letters congruing to that effect, and cure him of this hectic otherwise he joys would never begin.

TEXT ACT 4 scene 3

The Hall of the castle

< *Enter King **CLAUDIUS** and two or three **LORDS*** >

CLAUDIUS
I have sent to seek him and to find the body.
How dangerous is it that this man goes loose!
Yet must not we put the strong law on him.
He's loved of the distracted multitude,
Who like not in their judgment, but their eyes.
And where 'tis so, th' offender's scourge is weigh'd,
But never the offense.
To bear all smooth and even,
This sudden sending him away must seem
Deliberate pause. Diseases desperate grown
By desperate appliance are reliev'd,
Or not at all.

< *Enter **ROSENCRANTZ** and others* >

How now, what hath befall'n?
ROSENCRANTZ
Where the dead body is bestow'd, my lord,
We cannot get from him.
CLAUDIUS
But where is he?
ROSENCRANTZ
Without, my lord; guarded, to know your pleasure.
CLAUDIUS
Bring him before us.
ROSENCRANTZ
Ho, Guildenstern! Bring in my lord.

< *Enter **HAMLET** and **GUILDENSTERN*** >

CLAUDIUS
Now, Hamlet, where's Polonius?
HAMLET
At supper.
CLAUDIUS
At supper? Where?

EXPLANATION

After many a sluggish slow-paced scene, this scene takes on a different, sombre mood and a frenzied pace. It's as though the action must move quickly towards its dramatic climax.

Both Claudius and Hamlet are 'fanning the flames', acting 'with fiery quickness', to the play's final denouement with their volatile actions. Hamlet killed Polonius in a fit of passion and his nonchalant attitude towards his death is indicative of a man with an unrelenting desire for revenge and Claudius' confidence is now wavering.

He is no more the confident, strong leader who could manipulate any situation. He cannot punish Hamlet with the law but must carefully consider his move.

"This sudden sending him away must seem
Deliberate pause"

ROSENCRANTZ and GUILDENSTERN tell Claudius,
"Where the dead body is bestow'd, my lord,
We cannot get from him."

Claudius very impatiently enquires where Hamlet is, suggesting his nervousness and fear of what Hamlet is capable of doing next,

"But where is he?"

Claudius summons Hamlet to his presence.

Hamlet's response when Claudius asks for Polonius' body is filled with puns and double meaning, spoken deliberately to confuse Claudius.

TEXT ACT 4 scene 3

HAMLET
Not where he eats, but where he is eaten.
A certain convocation
Of politic worms are e'en at him.
Your worm is your only emperor for diet.
We fat all creatures else to fat us,
and we fat ourselves for maggots.
Your fat king and your lean beggar is
But variable service—
Two dishes, but to one table.
That's the end.

CLAUDIUS
Alas, alas!

HAMLET
A man may fish with the worm
That hath eat of a king, and eat of the fish
That hath fed of that worm.

CLAUDIUS
What dost you mean by this?

HAMLET
Nothing but to show you
How a king may go a progress
Through the guts of a beggar.

CLAUDIUS
Where is Polonius?

HAMLET
In heaven.
Send hither to see.
If your messenger find him not there,
Seek him i' th' other place yourself.
But if indeed you find him not within this month,
You shall nose him as you go
Up the stairs into the lobby.

CLAUDIUS
(*to attendants*) Go seek him there.

HAMLET
He will stay till ye come.

< *Exeunt some attendants* >

EXPLANATION

CLAUDIUS interrogating HAMLET on the where abouts of Polonius' body

Polonius is at supper being eaten by worms because when we die the worms devour us. One can connote that,

"A certain convocation
Of politic worms are e'en at him"

Is referring to Polonius who became a 'political' dinner for the worms because of his role in politics and Claudius can also be seen as the political worm who preyed on Polonius' loyalty to him.

"We fat all creatures else to fat us,
We fat ourselves for maggots"

We are faced with the two heroes of the play sizing up each other (it's like a game of chess waiting for moves). Claudius the 'Tragic Hero' and Hamlet the revenge hero. Shakespeare creates a dramatic tension here as these two square each other up.

Hamlet's repetition of the adjective 'fat' is significant here. In the Bible story of the 'Prodigal son' the father kills the 'fatted calf' when his long-lost son, returns to celebrate. Here Hamlet refers to Claudius as 'fat king' because he stole the crown and is fattening himself with the proceeds of his terrible crime, only to be food for the worms whom we fatten.

CLAUDIUS
Hamlet, this deed, for thine especial safety –
Which we do tender as we dearly grieve—
For that which thou hast done—
Must send thee hence
With fiery quickness.
Therefore, prepare thyself.
The bark is ready and the wind at help,
Th' associates tend, and everything is bent
For England.
HAMLET
For England?
CLAUDIUS
Ay, Hamlet.
HAMLET
Good.
CLAUDIUS
So is it, if thou knew'st our purposes
HAMLET
I see a cherub that sees them.
But come, for England.
Farewell, dear mother.
CLAUDIUS
Thy loving father, Hamlet.
HAMLET
My mother. Father and mother is man and wife,
Man and wife is one flesh, and so, my mother. —
Come, for England!

< *Exit **HAMLET*** >

CLAUDIUS
Follow him at foot.
Tempt him with speed aboard.
Delay it not –
I'll have him hence tonight.
Away! For everything is seal'd and done
That else leans on th' affair.
Pray you, make haste.

< *Exeunt all but **CLAUDIUS*** >

Claudius is nervous and afraid of Hamlet's response. He says that Polonius is in heaven and that he must send a messenger to find him there. Claudius tells Hamlet that he has to send him away to England for his own safety and he must prepare,

"Hamlet this deed, for thine especial safety –"

Hamlet bids farewell to his mother and prepares to leave for England. Claudius is feigning sincerity once more by declaring his love for Hamlet.

"Thy loving father, Hamlet"

Hamlet sarcastically uses biblical reference and tells Claudius that he is both his 'mother' and 'father' because when he married his mother, he became 'one flesh' with his mother, according to the biblical marriage vows.

"Father and mother is man and wife,
Man and wife is one flesh"

The pace here is racing just like Claudius' mind. He sets the events of Hamlet's departure in motion. The use of his short, snappy sentences increases the pace and the urgency of his situation,

"Follow him at foot.
Tempt him with speed aboard.
Delay it not –
I'll have him hence tonight."

HAMLET departing for England, accompanied by Rosencrantz and Guildenstern

CLAUDIUS (*continues*)

And, England, if my love thou hold'st at aught—
As my great power thereof may give thee sense,
Since yet thy cicatrice looks raw and red
After the Danish sword and thy free awe
Pays homage to us—thou mayst not coldly set
Our sovereign process, which imports at full,
By letters congruing to that effect,
The present death of Hamlet.
Do it, England,
For like the hectic in my blood he rages,
And thou must cure me.
Till I know 'tis done,
Howe'er my haps, my joys were ne'er begun.

< *Exit* >

Claudius stand dejected, scared, and nervous in this melodramatic soliloquy. The only way out of this precarious situation is to have Hamlet killed. Once again, we see Claudius' ruthlessness at play.

He wrote to the King of England to have Hamlet killed.

"By letters congruing to that effect,
The present death of Hamlet."

CLAUDIUS hands on the letters condemning Hamlet to death by the King of England

He is like a disease in his blood, and he can't cope with this illness. He urges England to cure him of Hamlet, who he refers to as a disease.

Note the 'disease' theme of Denmark 'being rotten' that is prevalent throughout the play. Claudius caused this 'disease' by killing the king and he is still creating 'disease' in Denmark by wanting Hamlet killed.

"For like the hectic in my blood he rages"

In Act 4 scene 4, the setting is open ground on the road to England, a few days later.

Enter Prince Fortinbras, his captain, and other soldiers of his Army.

Fortinbras instructs his captain to greet the Danish King and crave conveyance to march through Denmark.

Exit all but the captain.

Enter Hamlet, Rosencrantz, and Others.

The captain tells Hamlet the Army is commanded by the nephew to old Norway, Fortinbras, and they march to Poland to gain a little patch of ground worth five ducats, not worth farming.

Hamlet see no sense in this military action where two thousand souls and twenty thousand ducats will not resolute this trivial issue.

Exit the Captain.

Rosencrantz asks Hamlet to go.

Exit all but Hamlet, who in a soliloquy, questions his resolve to take revenge on his father's murderer but is inspired by Fortinbras's honour and duty, and so decides to do or die saying from this time forth my thoughts be bloody or be nothing worth.

Exit Hamlet.

TEXT ACT 4 scene 4

Open ground

*< Enter **FORTINBRAS**, his **CAPTAIN**,*
*and other **SOLDIERS** of his army >*

FORTINBRAS
Go, Captain, from me greet the Danish king
Tell him that, by his license, Fortinbras
Craves the conveyance of a promised march
Over his kingdom. You know the rendezvous.
If that his majesty would aught with us,
We shall express our duty in his eye,
And let him know so.
CAPTAIN
I will do 't, my lord.
FORTINBRAS
Go softly on.

*< Exeunt all except the **CAPTAIN** >*
*< Enter **HAMLET, ROSENCRANTZ, GUILDENSTERN**, and others >*

HAMLET
Good sir, whose powers are these?
CAPTAIN
They are of Norway, sir.
HAMLET
How purpos'd, sir, I pray you?
CAPTAIN
Against some part of Poland.
HAMLET
Who commands them, sir?
CAPTAIN
The nephew to old Norway, Fortinbras.
HAMLET
Goes it against the main of Poland, sir,
Or for some frontier?
CAPTAIN
Truly to speak, and with no addition,
We go to gain a little patch of ground
That hath in it no profit but the name.
To pay five ducats, five, I would not farm it.
Nor will it yield to Norway or the Pole
A ranker rate, should it be sold in fee.
HAMLET
Why, then the Polack never will defend it.
CAPTAIN
Yes, it is already garrison'd.

EXPLANATION

Fortinbras has arrived in Denmark and requests permission from the king to March over his kingdom. He promises to reward him if he is given permission by the king,

"If that his majesty would aught with us,
We shall express our duty in his eye"

Fortinbras is young, erratic, and impulsive, unlike his level-headed father. It will be interesting to draw a juxtaposition between the characters of Hamlet and Fortinbras. They both share a common purpose- to avenge the wrongs done to their father's.

The Captain greets Hamlet and his companions, explaining that Forbinbras' army goes to Poland

"to gain a little patch of ground"

worth only five ducats, saying

"I would not farm it"

Yet, the Polack will defend it, despite its worth.

"Yes, it is already garrison'd"

Fortinbras' army destined to Poland to "gain a little patch of ground" **not worth farming**

Hamlet is surprised that they are just fighting for a small piece of insignificant land that is worthless.

HAMLET
Two thousand souls and twenty thousand ducats
Will not debate the question of this straw.
This is th' impostume of much wealth and peace,
That inward breaks, and shows no cause without
Why the man dies. — I humbly thank you, sir.
CAPTAIN
God be wi' you, sir.

< Exit ***CAPTAIN*** *>*

ROSENCRANTZ
Will 't please you go, my lord?
HAMLET
I'll be with you straight. Go a little before.

< Exeunt all except ***HAMLET*** *>*

How all occasions do inform against me,
And spur my dull revenge!
What is a man
If his chief good and market of his time
Be but to sleep and feed?
A beast, no more.
Sure, he that made us with such large discourse,
Looking before and after, gave us not
That capability and godlike reason
To fust in us unus'd. Now, whether it be
Bestial oblivion, or some craven scruple
Of thinking too precisely on th' event—
A thought which, quarter'd,
Hath but one part wisdom
And ever three parts coward — I do not know
Why yet I live to say "This thing's to do,"
Sith I have cause and will
And strength and means to do 't.
Examples gross as earth exhort me.
Witness this army of such mass and charge,
Led by a delicate and tender prince,
Whose spirit with divine ambition puff'd
Makes mouths at the invisible event,
Exposing what is mortal and unsure
To all that fortune, death, and danger dare,
Even for an eggshell.
Rightly to be great
Is not to stir without great argument,

Hamlet remarks about how many lives and the enormous amount of money that will be lost for a fruitless venture. This is what happens when countries have,

"Much wealth and peace"

This soliloquy reflects Hamlet's thoughts and a mirror into his mind. He lays bare his innermost feelings about his mission for revenge. Everything he experiences and sees tells him that he is wrong. He has been delaying his revenge for too long.

"How all occasions do inform against me,
And spur my dull revenge!"

A man is not a man if he is not productive. If he only eats and sleeps then he is nothing but 'a beast' God gave us reasoning power and other capabilities to be used and enhance ourselves.

"gave us not
That capability and godlike reason
To fust in us unus'd."

He doesn't know why he is alive to say,

"This thing's to do"

Instead of having already done the deed.

He has the willpower, strength, and the means to do it, yet he is 'dragging his feet.'

"Sith I have cause and will
And strength and means to do 't"

He is fascinated by this army who is led by a 'delicate and tender' prince Fortinbras who is brave enough to put his young life at risk for something as insignificant, valueless and thin like an 'eggshell'.

"To all that fortune, death and danger dare,
Even for an eggshell.
Righty to be great."

TEXT ACT 4 scene 4

HAMLET (*continues*)

But greatly to find quarrel in a straw
When honour's at the stake.
How stand I then,
That have a father killed, a mother stain'd,
Excitements of my reason and my blood,
And let all sleep—
While, to my shame, I see
The imminent death of twenty thousand men,
That for a fantasy and trick of fame
Go to their graves like beds, fight for a plot
Whereon the numbers cannot try the cause,
Which is not tomb enough and continent
To hide the slain?
Oh, from this time forth,
My thoughts be bloody or be nothing worth!

< *Exit* >

EXPLANATION

Hamlet continues berating himself for his lack of action in seeking revenge. It's as though he is seeking our sympathy and approval. His father has been wronged, his mother defiled and yet he ignores this emotional and psychological trauma that he is experiencing.

"That have a father killed, a mother stain'd,
Excitements of my reason and my blood,
And let all sleep –"

Yet these soldiers of Fortinbras are prepared to die for a tiny, worthless plot of land which can't even bury them.

He vows that from now on if his thoughts are not about killing and bloody, then it's worthless.

"Oh from this time forth,
My thoughts be bloody or be nothing worth!"

In Act 4 scene 5, the setting is a room inside Elsinore castle, a few days later.

The Gentleman speaks of Ophelia's grief at the loss of her father Polonius; her mood will need to be pitied.

Claudius commands Horatio to follow and watch Ophelia as he much concerned by her grief. Exit Horatio.

Claudius then tells Gertrude that the poison for this deep grief springs first from Polonius death, next her son Hamlet exiled for the violent murder, then the people muddled with unwholesome thoughts and whispers for good Polonius' death.

Claudius tells Gertrude of Laertes secret return from France and fears pestilent speeches by him for his father's death.

A noise within the castle causes Claudius to call for his Swiss guards.

Enter a Messenger who tells Claudius to save himself as a riotous rabble demanding Laertes be made King, is about to break in.

Claudius tells Gertrude to let him rail, telling Laertes that he is guiltless of his father's death and feels pain at this loss.

Outside the room, Ophelia is heard singing.

Laertes is distraught at his sister's distress and madness, as she hands out flowers, muses about nature, and sings about death and its finality.

Claudius tells Laertes to go to his wisest friends and judge his guilt. If they find him implicated, he will forfeit his kingdom, otherwise be content and lend his patience so together they can avenge Polonius' death.

Laertes concurs, stating the means of death, obscure (secret) funeral, nor hatchment (coat of arms) over his bones, no noble rite, nor formal ostentation must not be called into questioned. The King agrees, and where it is, then the great axe will fall.

TEXT ACT 4 scene 5

A room in the castle of Elsinore
*< Enter **HORATIO, GERTRUDE,** and a **GENTLEMAN** >*

GERTRUDE
I will not speak with her.
GENTLEMAN
She is importunate,
Indeed distract. Her mood will needs be pitied.
GERTRUDE
What would she have?
GENTLEMAN
She speaks much of her father, says she hears
There's tricks i' th' world,
And hems, and beats her heart,
Spurns enviously at straws,
Speaks things in doubt
That carry but half sense.
Her speech is nothing,
Yet the unshaped use of it doth move
The hearers to collection.
They aim at it,
And botch the words up
Fit to their own thoughts,
Which, as her winks and nods
And gestures yield them,
Indeed, would make one think
There might be thought,
Though nothing sure,
Yet much unhappily.
HORATIO
'Twere good she were spoken with,
For she may strew
Dangerous conjectures in ill-breeding minds.
GERTRUDE
Let her come in.

*< Exit **GENTLEMAN** >*

(aside) To my sick soul, as sin's true nature is,
Each toy seems prologue to some great amiss.
So full of artless jealousy is guilt,
It spills itself in fearing to be spilt.

*< Enter **OPHELIA,** distracted >*

OPHELIA
Where is the beauteous majesty of Denmark?

EXPLANATION

A gentleman comes in and tell Gertrude that Ophelia is acting crazy and distracted and she needs to talk to her but Gertrude refuses,

"She is importunate,
Indeed distract. Her mood will needs be pitied"

She speaks of her father and beats her heart. She speaks things in doubt, and it is senseless babbling, yet her listeners take heed of what she is saying.

All her gestures, winks and nods suggest that she wants to convey a message and it is not pleasant.

"Which as her winks and nods
And gestures yield them"

Shakespeare gives Gertrude a very short soliloquy and this reflects for the first time her true inner feelings.

She bares all and says that her soul is sick. She predicts that there is some great calamity to follow.

"To my sick soul, as sin's true nature is,
Each toy seems prologue to some great amiss"

Guilt is a terrible thing because it makes you admit your guilt because you are always afraid of getting caught.

"So full of artless jealousy is guilt,
It spills itself in fearing to be spilt"

*Enter **OPHELIA,** distracted*

GERTRUDE
How now, Ophelia?
OPHELIA
(sings)
How should I your true love know
From another one?
By his cockle hat and staff,
And his sandal shoon.
GERTRUDE
Alas, sweet lady, what imports this song?
OPHELIA
Say you? Nay, pray you, mark.
(sings)
He is dead and gone, lady,
He is dead and gone,
At his head a grass-green turf,
At his heels a stone.
Oh, ho!
GERTRUDE
Nay, but Ophelia—
OPHELIA
Pray you, mark.
(sings)
White his shroud as the mountain snow—

< *Enter* ***CLAUDIUS*** >

GERTRUDE
Alas, look here, my lord.
OPHELIA
(sings)
Larded all with sweet flowers,
Which bewept to the ground did not go
With true-love showers.
CLAUDIUS
How do you, pretty lady?
OPHELIA
Well, God dild you!
They say the owl was a baker's daughter.
Lord, we know what we are,
But know not what we may be.
God be at your table.
CLAUDIUS
Conceit upon her father.
OPHELIA
Pray you,
Let's have no words of this,
But when theyask you what it means,

She is deluded and she acts strangely. She begins to sing a heartfelt song for her father's demise. She is distraught and she uses a simile to compare his shroud to snow.

"*White his shroud as the mountain snow—*"

Gertrude is quite alarmed at Ophelia's deranged state,

"Alas, look here my lord."

But Claudius is very cold and detached towards Ophelia. He tries to flatter Ophelia by calling her, 'pretty lady' but Ophelia's words unnerve him,

"Lord, we know what we are,
But know not what we may be"

It's like an ominous warning to Claudius of what's to come.

In her very sombre and emotional songs, Ophelia, babbles about loss of virginity and marriage. Her songs ring of sexual nuances and one can connote that it is a reference to her sexual relationship with Hamlet. (*see next page*)

"*Before you tumbled me,*
You promised me to wed"

Ophelia seems to also foreshadow her own death when she says (*see next page*)

"Indeed, without an oath I'll make an end on it"

GERTRUDE, CLAUDIUS, OPHELIA in a distressed State, and HORATIO looking on

OPHELIA (*continues*)
say you this:
(sings)
Tomorrow is Saint Valentine's Day,
All in the morning betime,
And I a maid at your window,
To be your Valentine.
Then up he rose, and donned his clothes,
And dupped the chamber door.
Let in the maid that out a maid
Never departed more.

CLAUDIUS
Pretty Ophelia—

OPHELIA
Indeed, without an oath I'll make an end on 't:
(sings)
By Gis and by Saint Charity,
Alack, and fie, for shame!
Young men will do 't, if they come to 't.
By Cock, they are to blame.
Quoth she, "Before you tumbled me,
You promised me to wed."
He answers,
"So would I ha' done, by yonder sun,
And thou hadst not come to my bed."

CLAUDIUS
How long hath she been thus?

OPHELIA
I hope all will be well.
We must be patient,
But I cannot choose but weep,
To think they should lay him i' th' cold ground.
My brother shall know of it,
And so I thank you for your good counsel.
Come, my coach! Good night, ladies.
Good night, sweet ladies.
Good night, good night.

< *Exit* ***OPHELIA*** >

CLAUDIUS
Follow her close.
Give her good watch,
I pray you.

In her very emotive song, she talks about betrayal and using beautiful natural imagery like flowers and the sun. Her utterances are candid and biting and she tells Claudius,

"I hope all will be well"

God will give you what you deserve.

Sadly, Ophelia became a victim of her father's indiscretion. We can even infer that she was so well groomed by her father to follow his instructions that now his demise is having a negative impact on her. She cannot make decisions on her own and fend for herself.

"I cannot choose but weep
To think they should lay him in th' cold ground"

She sends a subtle warning to Claudius that her brother will know about their father's death and take action.

Claudius is becoming nervous after witnessing Ophelia's strange and uncanny behaviour. It was the same kind of behaviour in Hamlet which posed a problem to him, and he had to eliminate it in a hurry.

Now Ophelia has become vocal in her madness, no more the docile girl taking instructions from him to destroy Hamlet. She has taken on a completely new persona.

Polonius tried to control the actions and minds of his children. We will look at the younger generation as revenge heroes and juxtapose their passionate reaction to that of the older generation.

Here Ophelia appears very calm and restrained and does not possess the driving, wild passion like her brother but ironically conveys a very deadly message to Claudius using song, hence creating pathos and an emotional response from the audience.

Claudius' nervousness is increasing, and he wants this threat closely monitored.

"Follow her close.
Give her good watch"

CLAUDIUS (*continues*)
Oh, this is the poison of deep grief.
It springs all from her father's death,
And now behold!
O Gertrude, Gertrude,
When sorrows come, they come not single spiesBut in
battalions.
First, her father slain.
Next, your son gone, and he most violent author
Of his own just remove, the people muddied,
Thick, and unwholesome
in their thoughts and whispers
For good Polonius' death,
And we have done but greenly
In hugger-mugger to inter him.
Poor Ophelia divided from herself
And her fair judgment,
Without the which we are pictures,
Or mere beasts.
Last—and as much containing as all these—
Her brother is in secret come from France,
Feeds on his wonder,
Keeps himself in clouds,
And wants not buzzers to infect his ear
With pestilent speeches of his father's death,
Wherein necessity, of matter beggar'd,
Will nothing stick our person to arraign
In ear and ear.
O my dear Gertrude, this,
Like to a murdering piece, in many places
Gives me superfluous death.

(A noise within)

GERTRUDE
Alack, what noise is this?
CLAUDIUS
Attend!
Where are my Switzers?
Let them guard the door.

< *Enter a* ***MESSENGER*** >

What is the matter?
MESSENGER
Save yourself, my lord.
The ocean, overpeering of his list,

In his grief we see Claudius turning to Gertrude for consolation. It's the first time we see a camaraderie between the two. He cries out to her in anguish, that it never rains but pours. Problems come in armies not in singles.

"When sorrows come, they come not single spies But in battalions"

He tells Gertrude that Ophelia had suffered many blows – first her father was killed, Hamlet gone and now she's insane - robbed of her faculties.

The pace is moving furiously, and the events are moving so quickly that Claudius' woes are becoming overwhelming. Earlier Hamlet told Rosencrantz and Guildenstern that they will be used by the king like sponges and drained dry and discarded. We see how Claudius so coldly and disrespectfully discarded Polonius' body and didn't even give him a decent burial despite him being so loyal to him.

"For good Polonius' death,
And we have done but greenly
In hugger-mugger to inter him."

All the young revenge heroes were auricularly infected about what they heard about their father's being deceived and killed. They feel bound to act in a feverishly impulsive, erratic, and passionate manner as we see Laertes doing here. He is bent on avenging his father's death.

"And wants not buzzers to infect his ear
With pestilent speeches of his father's death"

Claudius informs Gertrude of Laertes' secret return from France.

Now Claudius is trying to play the victim and he wants Gertrude's sympathy because he says that he will be blamed for Polonius' death, and he feels like he is being murdered.

"Like to a murdering piece, in many places
Gives me superfluous death."

A messenger brings news that boisterous Laertes has returned.

MESSENGER (*continues*)
Eats not the flats with more impetuous haste
Than young Laertes, in a riotous head,
O'erbears your officers.
The rabble call him "lord" –
And as the world were now but to begin,
Antiquity forgot, custom not known,
The ratifiers and props of every word—
They cry, "Choose we! Laertes shall be king!"
Caps, hands, and tongues applaud it to the clouds:
"Laertes shall be king, Laertes king!"

GERTRUDE
How cheerfully on the false trail they cry?
O, this is counter, you false Danish dogs!

(A noise within)

CLAUDIUS
The doors are broke.

< *Enter* ***LAERTES****, armed with several* ***DANES*** >

LAERTES
Where is this king? —
Sirs, stand you all without.

DANES
No, let's come in!

LAERTES
I pray you, give me leave.

DANES
We will, we will.

LAERTES
I thank you. Keep the door

< *Exeunt* ***DANES*** >

(*to Claudius*) O thou vile king,
Give me my father!

GERTRUDE
(*holding Laertes*) Calmly, good Laertes.

LAERTES
That drop of blood
That's calm proclaims me bast'rd,
Cries "Cuckold!" to my father, brands the "harlot"
Even here between the chaste unsmirch'd brow
Of my true mother.

He is furious and like a raging and over flooding ocean, he is leading a rebellion against Claudius,

"Than young Laertes, in a riotous head,
O'erbears your officers."

The people cheer him and shout,

"Laertes shall be king, Laertes king!"

Gertrude's response is puzzling because she vehemently defends Claudius, calling them 'dogs', yet she is fully aware that Claudius killed her husband. Her reaction here can condone Hamlet's animosity towards her. She is proving to be disloyal to both her son and her late husband. She was never so vocal before in defending them but is ever ready to defend Claudius.

"O, this is counter, you false Danish dogs!"

Enter ***LAERTES****, armed with several* ***DANES***

Laertes confronts Claudius in fury calling him,

"O thou vile king"

CLAUDIUS threatened by LAERTES' sword, saying "O thou vile king"

TEXT ACT 4 scene 5

CLAUDIUS
What is the cause, Laertes?
That thy rebellion looks so giant-like? —
Let him go, Gertrude.
Do not fear our person.
There's such divinity doth hedge a king
That treason can but peep to what it would,
Acts little of his will. —
Tell me, Laertes,
Why thou art thus incens'd. —
Let him go, Gertrude. —
Speak, man.
LAERTES
Where is my father?
CLAUDIUS
Dead!
GERTRUDE
But not by him.
CLAUDIUS
Let him demand his fill.
LAERTES
How came he dead?
I'll not be juggled with.
To hell, allegiance!
Vows, to the blackest devil!
Conscience and grace,
To the profoundest pit!
I dare damnation.
To this point I stand
That both the worlds I give to negligence.
Let come what comes,
Only I'll be reveng'd
Most thoroughly for my father.
CLAUDIUS
Who shall stay you?
LAERTES
My will, not all the world.
And for my means,
I'll husband them so well,
They shall go far with little.
CLAUDIUS
Good Laertes,
If you desire to know the certainty
Of your dear father's death,
is 't writ in your revenge,
That, swoopstake, you will draw both friend and foe,
Winner and loser?

EXPLANATION

Claudius has once again resumed his calm and collected composure. He is trying to calm the raging waters by being level-headed and cordial towards Laertes.

It is interesting to note the many hyphens that are used at the end of Claudius' sentences. One can connote that Claudius is trying to control his temper and is trying to take control and appear bold and brave in a very precarious situation – hence the pauses. He is on one of his pretences again – acting all caring and loving.

He asks Laertes about his anger,

"Why thou art thus incens'd –"

He calmly tells Gertrude to let Laertes have his say and get the answers he needs.

Laertes is livid and he unleashes a tirade of abuse at Claudius. He said that he doesn't care about allegiance to the king, conscience and the grave. He doesn't even care about damnation, but he wants revenge for his father's death.

"I'll not be juggled with.
To hell, allegiance!
Vows to the blackest devil!
Conscience and grace"

We should draw a juxtaposition between the actions and characters of the two revenge heroes in exacting revenge for their father's deaths.

Hamlet goes about it in a more calm and diplomatic manner by acting insane and using the play to determine Claudius' guilt whilst Laertes is passionate, mouthy, and aggressive in his quest for justice. He is firm and robust in his conversation with Claudius, and he wants immediate action to avenge his father's death.

"Let come what comes,
Only I'll be reveng'd."

Claudius asks Laertes if he is prepared to hurt his father's friends and foe alike.

"That, swoops take you will draw both friend & foe
Winner or loser?"

LAERTES
None but his enemies.
CLAUDIUS
Will you know them then?
LAERTES
To his good friends thus wide I'll ope my arms
And, like the kind life-rend'ring pelican,
Repast them with my blood.
CLAUDIUS
Why, now you speak
Like a good child and a true gentleman.
That I am guiltless of your father's death
And am most sensible in grief for it,
It shall as level to your judgment pierce
As day does to your eye.

< A noise within
***OPHELIA** is heard singing >*

Let her come in!
LAERTES
How now? What noise is that?

< *Enter **OPHELIA** holding flowers* >

O heat, dry up my brains! Tears seven times salt,
Burn out the sense and virtue of mine eye!
By heaven, thy madness shall be paid by weight,
Till our scale turn the beam.
O rose of May!
Dear maid, kind sister, sweet Ophelia!
O heavens, is 't possible a young maid's wits
Should be as mortal as an old man's life?
Nature is fine in love, and where 'tis fine,
It sends some precious instance of itself
After the thing it loves.
OPHELIA
(sings)
They bore him barefaced on the bier,
Hey, non nonny, nonny, hey, nonny,
And in his grave rained many a tear.
Fare you well, my dove.
LAERTES
Hadst thou thy wits,
And didst persuade revenge,
It could not move thus.

Laertes says that he will open his arms to his father's friends, and he uses the imagery of a mother pelican who gives her blood for her kids to feed on.

"To his good friends thus wide I'll ope my arms."

Claudius tells him that he speaks like a 'true gentleman'. He is guiltless of his father's death, and he suffers profuse grief over it.

"I am guiltless of your father's death,
And am most sensible in grief for it"

Symbolically Ophelia is holding flowers which can represent death or purity. Laertes speech to his sister is emotive and heart-rendering. All his bitter exclamations suggest this,

O heat, dry up my brains! Tears seven times salt,
Burn out the sense and virtue of mine eye!
By heaven, thy madness shall be paid by weight

His gut-wrenching pain is felt here, and he is determined to take revenge. He couldn't believe how a young mind can diminish so easily like an old man's life.

"O heavens is 't possible a young maid's wits
Should be as mortal as an old man's life"

He draws a comparison between a virgin who gives away a precious part of her to her beloved and Ophelia giving her sanity away to her dead father.

"It sends some precious instance of itself
After the thing it loves."

Ophelia sings a sad song to her father which saddens Laertes. She uses the imagery of a 'dove' suggesting that her father is free of Claudius' schemes and tricks which he was a slave to.

"Fare you well, my dove"

Laertes is shocked at how precise Ophelia's speech is and he says that if she was sane and asked him to take revenge, she couldn't be more persuasive than she is now in her mental state.

OPHELIA
You must sing *A-down a-down—*
And you, *Call him a- down-a—*
Oh, how the wheel becomes it!
It is the false steward
That stole his master's daughter.

LAERTES
This nothing's more than matter.

OPHELIA
There's rosemary, that's for remembrance –
Pray you, love, remember.
And there is pansies, that's for thoughts.

LAERTES
A document in madness.
Thoughts and remembrance fitted.

OPHELIA
There's fennel for you, and columbines. —
There's rue for you, and here's some for me.
We may call it "herb of grace" o' Sundays. —
Oh, you must wear your rue with a difference. —
There's a daisy. I would give you some violets,
But they withered all when my father died.
They say he made a good end
(sings)
For bonny sweet Robin is all my joy—

LAERTES
Thought and affliction, passion, hell itself,
She turns to favour and to prettiness.

OPHELIA
(sings)
And will he not come again?
And will he not come again?
No, no, he is dead,
Go to thy deathbed.
He never will come again.

His beard was as white as snow,
All flaxen was his poll.
He is gone, he is gone,
And we cast away moan,
God ha' mercy on his soul. —
And of all Christian souls, I pray God.
God be wi' ye.

< *Exit* ***OPHELIA*** >

GERTRUDE accepts flowers from OPHELIA

OPHELIA gives flowers to CLAUDIUS

LEARTES is shocked to see his sister OPHELIA in such a depressed state

Exit ***OPHELIA, singing as she leaves***

LAERTES
Do you see this, O God?
CLAUDIUS
Laertes, I must commune with your grief,
Or you deny me right.
Go but apart,
Make choice of whom
Your wisest friends you will.
And they shall hear and judge 'twixt you and me.
If by direct or by collateral hand
They find us touch'd,
We will our kingdom give,
Our crown, our life,
And all that we can ours,
To you in satisfaction.
But if not,
Be you content to lend your patience to us,
And we shall jointly labour with your soul
To give it due content.
LAERTES
Let this be so.
His means of death, his obscure funeral—
No trophy, sword, nor hatchment o'er his bones,
No noble rite nor formal ostentation—
Cry to be heard as 'twere from heaven to earth,
That I must call 't in question.
CLAUDIUS
So, you shall.
And where the offense is,
Let the great axe fall.
I pray you, go with me.

< Exeunt >

Claudius seizes this opportunity to use Laertes to get his revenge on Hamlet. In a conspiratorial tone he eggs Laertes on and asks him to get his wisest friends to make a judgment about who killed his father.

"And they shall hear and judge 'twixt you and me."

If they find me guilty then I will give up my kingdom, crown, and life to make restitution.

"They find us touch'd,
We will our kingdom give,
Our crown, our life."

But if not, he tells Laertes that they will work jointly to ensure that Polonius' killer is brought to justice.

"And we shall jointly labour with your soul
To give it due content"

Laertes is content with this proposal, and he expresses his sadness at how disrespectful Polonius was treated at death. The hyphens can suggest his grief and his pauses to visualise how sad and lonely his father's funeral was.

"His means of death, his obscure funeral —
No trophy, sword, nor hatchment o'er his bones,
No noble rite nor formal ostentation — "

Claudius agrees with Laertes and promises that the culprit who killed his father will be put to death.

"And where the offense is,
Let the great axe fall"

In Act 4 scene 6, the setting is the courtyard in Elsinore castle, a few days later.

Enter Horatio and a Servant.

The Servant tells Horatio, Seafaring men have letters to give to him.

Exit Servant.

Enter Sailors with a letter from the Ambassador bound for England.

Horatio reads the letter and discovers that Hamlet two days out to sea, his ship too slow of sail, fought a valiant action against pirates.

He boarded the pirate ship on the instant his ship got clear, so alone he became their prisoner. In exchange for his liberty, he is to repay the debt.

Horatio is to let the king have the other letters and make much speed to him as directed by these good fellows, as he has words to speak of import.

He concludes by writing Rosencrantz and Guildenstern hold their course for England, of them he has much to tell.

Horatio directs the Seafarers to the king, and then departs with them to rendezvous with Hamlet.

TEXT ACT 4 scene 6

< *Enter **HORATIO** and a **SERVANT*** >

HORATIO
What are they that would speak with me?
SERVANT
Seafaring men, sir.
They say they have letters for you.
HORATIO
Let them come in.

< *Exit **SERVANT*** >

I do not know from what part of the world
I should be greeted, if not from Lord Hamlet.

< *Enter **SAILORS*** >

SAILOR
God bless you, sir.
HORATIO
Let him bless thee too.
SAILOR
He shall, sir, an 't please him.
There's a letter for you, sir —
It comes from th' ambassador
That was bound for England—
If your name be Horatio,
As I am let to know it is.

(*gives Horatio a letter*)

HORATIO
(reads the letter)
"Horatio,
When thou shalt have overlooked this,
give these fellows some means to the king.
They have letters for him. Ere we were two
days old at sea, a pirate of very warlike
appointment gave us chase. Finding ourselves
too slow of sail, we put on a compelled valour,
and in the grapple I boarded them. On the
instant, they got clear of our ship, so I alone
became their prisoner. They have dealt with me
like thieves of mercy, but they knew what they
did; I am to do a good turn for them.

EXPLANATION

ENTER HORATIO AND A SERVANT

The sailors bring letters from Hamlet to Horatio. He tells him how they were confronted by a pirate ship, and he became their prisoner. He asks Horatio to give the sailors passage to the king to deliver his letters.

"I do not know from what part of the world
I should be greeted, if not from Lord Hamlet"

Ship taking Hamlet and his schoolfellows Rosencrantz and Guildenstern to England by order of Claudius

Horatio reads the letter and learns that Hamlet's ship was too slow to escape the pirate ship, so they were forced to fight.

'we put on a compelled valour,
and in the grapple I boarded them'

Hamlet's letter reveals that the pirates treated him fairly

'They have dealt with me
like thieves of mercy,

but expect him to do something for them in the future.

'but they knew what they did;
I am to do a good turn for them.'

TEXT ACT 4 scene 6

HORATIO *(continues)*

Let the king have the letters I have sent, and repair thou to me with as much speed as thou wouldst fly death. I have words to speak in thine ear will make thee dumb, yet are they much too light for the bore of the matter. These good fellows will bring thee where Iam. Rosencrantz and Guildenstern hold their course for England. Of them I have much to tell thee. Farewell.

He that thou knowest thine,
Hamlet."

Come, I will give you way for these your letters,
And do 't the speedier, that you may direct me
To him fromwhom you brought them.

< Exeunt >

EXPLANATION

Hamlet tells Horatio that he must hurry to him because he has things to tell him that will leave him speechless.

"repair thou to me with as much speed as thou wouldst fly death. I have words to speak in thine ear will make thee dumb"

He also has very much to say about Rosencrantz and Guildenstern who are 'loyal' citizens to England."

"Rosencrantz and Guildenstern hold their course for England. Of them I have much to tell thee"

Horatio asks the sailors to take him to Hamlet. Horatio proved to be the most loyal subject to Hamlet and he is the only one he can trust.

"He that thou knowest thine"

In Act 4 scene 7, the setting is the King's chamber in Elsinore castle, later in the day.

Enter Claudius and Laertes.

Claudius tells Laertes his conscience must now acquit him of his father's murder, having heard that Hamlet did the deed, and who now pursues the King's life.

Laertes asks why the King takes no action against these feats so crimeful and so capital in nature.

Claudius replies, for two special reasons: the queen his mother adores him and the public who convert his gyves (faults) to graces, so the arrows would revert to the bow not its intended target.

Claudius assures Laertes for a noble father lost and a sister driven to madness, his revenge will come, and he will hear more shortly (execution of Hamlet by the King of England, Act 4 scene 3).

Enter a Messenger with a letter for the king and another for the queen.

Claudius asks who brought them, the Messenger replies by Claudio who received them from Sailors. Claudius tells Laertes to stay and hear their contents.

Exit the Messenger.

Claudius reads the letter in which Hamlet declares he is back in Denmark, and begs leave to see the king tomorrow, when he will be asking the king's pardon, thereunto recount the occasion of his sudden and more strange return.

Claudius asks Laertes if he will be ruled by him. Laertes agrees.

Claudius recounts how two months since a Norman gentleman named Lamord had visited the castle and made confession of Laertes' masterly skills with a rapier which did cause Hamlet envy and desire to test his skills.

Claudius questions Laertes as to how far he would go to avenge his father's death.

Laertes replies he would cut murderer's throat in the church, but the King replies this is no place indeed to commit murder even though revenge should have no bounds.

Instead, Laertes should stay in his chamber until a friendly duel arranged which Hamlet, where the wager will be in your favour.

Hamlet will be remiss, most generous, and free from all contriving, thus will not inspect the foils, making it easier to pick the unbated (untipped) foil and in a pass of practice cause death.

Laertes replies he will do that, but to make certain, he will dip the foil in an unction (ointment) supplied by a mountebank (quack doctor) so if he is galled slightly, it may be death.

Claudius adds if this should fail, he will call for drink to quench Hamlet's thirst, and prepare him a chalice laced with poison for the nounce (time-out session).

Enter Gertrude the queen to inform Laertes that his sister had drowned while making flower garlands on the branch of a willow tree which broke causing her to fall into the weeping brook where her garments kept her afloat until heavy with water she sank to a muddy death.

Laertes is distraught, forbids himself to weep, but weeps, and bids Adieu.

Exit Laertes.

Exit Claudius and Gertrude to calm his rage.

TEXT ACT 4 scene 7

*< Enter **CLAUDIUS** and **LAERTES** >*

CLAUDIUS
Now must your conscience my acquaintance seal,
And you must put me in your heart for friend,
Sith you have heard, and with a knowing ear,
That he which hath your noble father slain
Pursu'd my life.

LAERTES
It well appears. But tell me
Why you proceeded not against these feats,
So criminal and so capital in nature,
As by your safety, wisdom, all things else,
You mainly were stirred up.

CLAUDIUS
Oh, for two special reasons,
Which may to you perhaps seem much unsinw'd,
But yet to me they are strong.
The queen his mother
Lives almost by his looks, and for myself—
My virtue or my plague, be it either which
She's so conjunctive to my life and soul,
That, as the star moves not but, in his sphere,
I could not but by her. The other motive
Why to a public count I might not go,
Is the great love the general gender bear him
Who, dipping all his faults in their affection,
Would, like the spring that turneth wood to stone
Convert his gyves to graces—so that my arrows,
Too slightly timbered for so loud a wind,
Would have reverted to my bow again,
And not where I had aimed them.

LAERTES
And so have I a noble father lost,
A sister driven into desp'rate terms,
Whose worth, if praises may go back again,
Stood challenger on mount of all the age
For her perfections. But my revenge will come.

CLAUDIUS
Break not your sleeps for that.
You must not think
That we are made of stuff so flat and dull
That we can let our beard be shook with danger
And think it pastime. You shortly shall hear more.
I loved your father, and we love ourself.
And that, I hope, will teach you to imagine—

EXPLANATION

Claudius is trying very hard to gain Laertes' confidence and friendship. He asks him to be his friend since he now knows that the person who killed his father was also pursuing his life.

"And you must put me in your heart for friend"

Laertes questions Claudius about his lack of action against the person who killed his father since his safety, wisdom, and everything else was at stake.

"As by your safety, wisdom, all things else,
You mainly were stirred up"

Claudius explains the reasons why he didn't act. Firstly, he takes his marriage vows very seriously, his mother dotes on Hamlet, 'lives almost by his looks', and Gertrude is dear to his heart and soul.

"She's so conjunctive to my life and soul"

The other motive was that the public loves him dearly,

"Is the great love the general gender bear him"

Claudius uses a simile to explain that the public loves Hamlet so much that they will turn all his faults into graces.

"Would like the spring that turneth wood to stone"

Claudius' words and actions against Hamlet will turn against him and hurt him instead of hurting Hamlet. Laertes is bent on seeking revenge because he lost a dear father and a sister who was perfect.

"Stood challenger on mount of all the age
For her perfections. But my revenge will come."

Claudius consoles him saying that he mustn't think that he is 'flat and dull' and that he can be easily threatened. He loved Polonius and himself and he will certainly take appropriate action.

"I loved your father, and we love ourself"

CLAUDIUS (*continues*)

< *Enter a* ***MESSENGER*** *with letters* >

How now, what news?
MESSENGER
Letters, my lord, from Hamlet.
This to your majesty, this to the queen.

*[*He gives Claudius Hamlet's letters*]*

CLAUDIUS
From Hamlet? Who brought them?
MESSENGER
Sailors, my lord, they say.
I saw them not.
They were given me by Claudio.
He received them of him that brought them.
CLAUDIUS
Laertes, you shall hear them. —Leave us.

< *Exit* ***MESSENGER*** >

[reads]
"High and mighty,
You shall know I am set naked on your kingdom.
Tomorrow shall I beg leave to see
your kingly eyes, when I shall, first asking
your pardon there unto, recount the
occasion of my sudden and more strange
return.
Hamlet."

What should this mean?
Are all the rest come back?
Or is it some abuse, and no such thing?
LAERTES
Know you the hand?
CLAUDIUS
'Tis Hamlet's character. *"naked"*?
And in a postscript here, he says *"alone"*
Can you advise me?
LAERTES
I'm lost in it, my lord.
But let him come.
It warms the very sickness in my heart
That I shall live and tell him to his teeth,
"Thus diest thou."

Claudius asks the messenger "what news?"

The messenger gives Hamlet's letters to Claudius, and he asks Laertes to hear the contents of it.
Claudius is perturbed to receive letters from Hamlet who he thought had been put to death as by his instructions to the King of England, his vassal
Claudius reads Hamlet's letters with foreboding.

CLAUDIUS reads Hamlet's letter

Hamlet's letters really puzzle Claudius and the use of all the questioning can suggest this,
"What should this mean?
Are all the rest come back?
Or is it some abuse, and no such thing."

He desperately asks Laertes for help in unravelling this puzzle, but he doesn't know. The words *'naked'* and *'alone'* poses a dilemma to Claudius. Laertes says that it warms his seething heart to know that he shall look him straight and ask,
"Thus diest thou"

CLAUDIUS
If it be so, Laertes—
As how should it be so?
How otherwise? —
Will you be ruled by me?
LAERTES
Ay, my lord—
So you will not o'er-rule me to a peace.
CLAUDIUS
To thine own peace. If he be now return'd,
As checking at his voyage, and that he means
No more to undertake it, I will work him
To an exploit, now ripe in my devise,
Under the which he shall not choose but fall.
And for his death no wind of blame shall breathe,
But even his mother shall uncharge the practice
And call it accident.
LAERTES
My lord, I will be ruled
The rather if you could devise it so
That I might be the organ.
CLAUDIUS
It falls right.
You have been talk'd of since your travel much—
And that in Hamlet's hearing—for a quality
Wherein, they say, you shine. Your sum of parts
Did not together pluck such envy from him
As did that one, and that, in my regard,
Of the unworthiest siege.
LAERTES
What part is that my lord?
CLAUDIUS
A very ribbon in the cap of youth,
Yet needful too, for youth no less becomes
The light and careless livery that it wears
Than settled age his sables and his weeds,
Importing health and graveness.
Two months since,
Here was a gentleman of Normandy.
I've seen myself, and served against, the French,And
they can well on horseback.
But this gallant had witchcraft in't.
He grew unto his seat,
And to such wondrous doing brought his horse
As he had been incorps'd and demi-natur'd
With the brave beast.

Claudius is becoming 'hot under the collar', and he is nervous once again. The pace is flying furiously because too many events have occurred within a short space of time and Claudius is 'out of breath.' He must act quickly to secure his crown, so he asks Laertes to join him to kill Hamlet.

"Will you be ruled by me?"

Laertes agrees but on one condition, Claudius does not steer him towards peace with Hamlet.

"Ay, my lord—
So you will not o'er-rule me to a peace"

He promises to drive him towards his own peace of mind. Claudius says that he has devised a cunning and devious plan, one which is guaranteed to kill Hamlet. Claudius is using Laertes' passionate and naïve disposition to secure his 'nest egg' – his crown. He says that the plan is so watertight that nobody will be blamed, even his own mother will think that it was a mere accident.

"And for his death no wind of blame shall breathe,
But even his mother shall uncharge the practice
And call it accident."

Laertes is just like his father, and he is prepared to be used by Claudius to carry out his dirty deeds. Claudius flatters Laertes about his expert fencing skills. He says that when Hamlet heard this he was really envious – 'Pluck such envy from him'.
"for a quality
Wherein, they say, you shine"

He is slyly engineering a deadly plot with Laertes. He said that he met a gentleman from Normandy, and he was a very skilled rider.

"But this gallant had witchcraft in it"

Claudius is very crafty and he 'beats about the bush' by talking about the rider's skills and he doesn't come to the point. He is trying to 'whet his appetite' for action and to prove his skills as a fencer, by challenging Hamlet and killing him.

CLAUDIUS (*continues*)
So far, he topp'd my thought,
That I, in forgery of shapes and tricks,
Come short of what he did.
LAERTES
A Norman was 't?
CLAUDIUS
A Norman.
LAERTES
Upon my life, Lamond!
CLAUDIUS
The very same.
LAERTES
I know him well.
He is the brooch indeed
And gem of all the nation.
CLAUDIUS
He made confession of you,
And gave you such a masterly report
For art and exercise in your defense,
And for your rapier most especially,
That he cried out 'twould be a sight indeed
If one could match you.
The 'scrimers of their nation,
He swore, had had neither motion, guard, nor eye,
If you oppos'd them.
Sir, this report of his
Did Hamlet so envenom with his envy
That he could nothing do but wish and beg
Your sudden coming o'er, to play with him.
Now, out of this—
LAERTES
What out of this, my lord?
CLAUDIUS
Laertes, was your father dear to you?
Or are you like, the painting of a sorrow,
A face without a heart?
LAERTES
Why ask you this?
CLAUDIUS
Not that I think you did not love your father
But that I know love is begun by time,
And that I see, in passages of proof,
Time qualifies the spark and fire of it.
There lives within the very flame of love
A kind of wick or snuff that will abate it.
And nothing is at a like goodness still.

LAERTES listens to Claudius scheme to take revenge on Hamlet

CLAUDIUS explains his scheme for Laertes to take revenge on Hamlet

Claudius says that the rider held him in high esteem and praised his fencing skills to the hilt. Hamlet was so envious when he heard this that he wanted to challenge him,
"This report of his
Did Hamlet so envenom with his envy"

Claudius' devious and manipulative skills shocks the audience. He is so craftily and deviously leading Laertes astray to commit murder. He uses a very sincere and cajoling tone to persuade Laertes.
He suddenly changes the subject to Laertes' love for his father. He targets his vulnerability, and he questions Laertes if his love for his father is genuine or just 'the painting of sorrow'. Once again, he is targeting Laertes emotions and his weakness.
"Laertes, was your father dear to you?
Or are you like, the painting of a sorrow,
A face without a heart."

Claudius is trying to solidify his devious plan by testing Laertes' determination and strength.

TEXT ACT 4 scene 7

CLAUDIUS (*continues*)
For goodness, growing to a pleurisy,
Dies in his own too-much.
That we would do,
We should do when we would,
For this "would"changes
And hath abatements and delays as many
As there are tongues, are hands, are accidents.
And then this "should" is like a spendthrift sigh
That hurts by easing. —
But to the quick of th' ulcer:
Hamlet comes back.
What would you undertake
To show yourself in deed your father's son
More than in words?
LAERTES
To cut his throat i' th' church.
CLAUDIUS
No place indeed should murder sanctuarize.
Revenge should have no bounds.
But, good Laertes,
Will you do this, keep close within your chamber.
Hamlet return'd shall know you are come home.
We'll put on those shall praise your excellence
And set a double varnish on the fame
The Frenchman gave you, bring you in fine together
And wager on your heads. He, being remiss,
Most generous and free from all contriving,
Will not peruse the foils; so that, with ease,
Or with a little shuffling, you may choose
A sword unbated, and in a pass of practice
Requite him for your father.
LAERTES
I will do't.
And for that purpose I'll anoint my sword.
I bought an unction of a mountebank,
So mortal that, but dip a knife in it,
Where it draws blood no cataplasm so rare,
Collected from all simples that have virtue
Under the moon, can save the thing from death
That is but scratched withal.
I'll touch my point
With this contagion,
That if I gall him slightly,
It may be death.

EXPLANATION

He tells Laertes that they should not regret their actions but act fast and do it right.
"We should do when we would,
For this 'would' changes
And hath abatements and delays"

Claudius tells Laertes that Hamlet is coming back, and Claudius targets his weak spot – his love for his father to try to coax him to kill Hamlet.

"To show yourself in deed your father's son"

He demands to know what physical action Laertes will take and not just words to eliminate Hamlet.

"More than in words"

Claudius is content that Laertes is determined so he starts to put his vile plan into action. Revenge shall be boundless. Claudius says that even the church should scorn Hamlet and not offer him refuge.

"No place indeed should murder sanctuarize"

Claudius coaxes Laertes by flattering him. Everyone will praise him and even place bets on him. Hamlet won't suspect anything so Laertes can choose a sharpened tip sword and take his revenge.

LAERTES holding "an unction of a mountebank"

Eagerly Laertes agrees immediately, and he spices it up by adding that he will dab it with a deadly poison that even a small scratch will prove fatal.
"That if I gall him slightly,
It may be death"

TEXT ACT 4 scene 7

CLAUDIUS
Let's further think of this,
Weigh what convenience both of time and means
May fit us to our shape.
If this should fail,
And that our drift look through our bad performance
'Twere better not essay'd.
Therefore this project
Should have a back or second that might hold
If this should blast in proof. —
Soft, let me see. —
We'll make a solemn wager on your cunnings.-
I ha 't!
When in your motion you are hot and dry –
As make your bouts more violent to that end –
And that he calls for drink,
I'll have prepared him
A chalice for the nonce, whereon but sipping,
If he by chance escape your venom'd stuck,
Our purpose may hold there. —
But stay, what noise?

< *Enter* ***GERTRUDE*** >

GERTRUDE
One woe doth tread upon another's heel,
So fast they follow. —
Your sister's drowned, Laertes.
LAERTES
Drown'd? Oh, where?
GERTRUDE
There is a willow grows aslant a brook
That shows his hoar leaves in the glassy stream.
There with fantastic garlands did she make
Of crow-flowers, nettles, daisies, and long purples,
That liberal shepherds give a grosser name,
But our cold maids do 'dead men's fingers call them.
There, on the pendant boughs her coronet weeds
Clambering to hang, an envious sliver broke,
When down her weedy trophies and herself
Fell in the weeping brook.
Her clothes spread wide,
And mermaid-like a while they bore her up,
Which time she chanted snatches of old lauds
As one incapable of her own distress,
Or like a creature native and indued

EXPLANATION

Claudius wants assurance that his plan will work, a choice of a convenient time that suits them both and the appropriate method of use,

"Weigh what convenience both of time and means
May fit us"

Claudius is very thorough and skilled in his organisation because he ensured that he has a back up plan.

"Should have a back or second that might hold"

He has prepared a cup of poisoned drink that will kill Hamlet if he should escape Laertes' venomous attack.

"I'll have prepared him
A chalice for the nonce, whereon but sipping,
If he by chance escape your venom'd struck"

Enter ***GERTRUDE***

She is distraught and exclaims that one disaster after another is following them so fast. Ophelia is dead.

"One woe doth tread upon another's heel"

She fell and drowned in the 'weeping brook' while making garlands out of flowers. But while she was drowning, she was singing some hymns and acted as though she didn't realise the grave danger that she was in,

"As one incapable of her own distress,
Or like a creature native and indued"

GERTRUDE relates the sad news that Ophelia is drowned

GERTRUDE (*continues*)

Unto that element.
But long it could not be
Till that her garments, heavy with their drink,
Pulled the poor wretch from her melodious lay
To muddy death.

LAERTES

Alas, then she is drown'd.

GERTRUDE

Drown'd, drown'd.

LAERTES

Too much of water hast thou, poor Ophelia,
And therefore, I forbid my tears.
But yet
It is our trick.
Nature her custom holds,
Let shame say what it will.
When these are gone,
The woman will be out. —
Adieu, my lord.
I have a speech of fire
That fain would blaze,
But that this folly doubts it.

CLAUDIUS

Let's follow, Gertrude.
How much I had to do to calm his rage!
Now fear I this will give it start again.
Therefore let's follow.

< Exeunt >

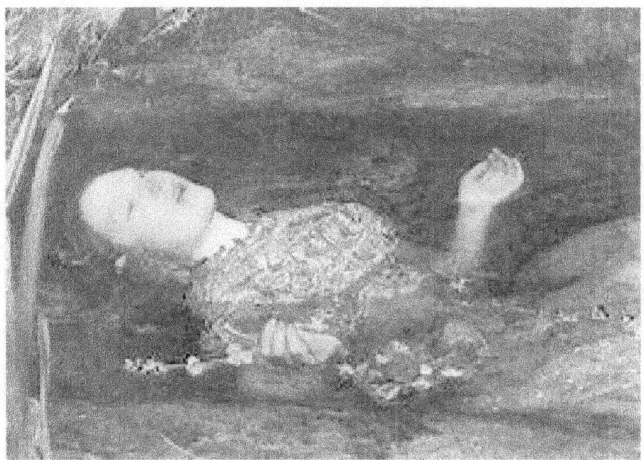

OPHELIA drowned by the weight of water,
"Till that her garments, heavy with their drink"

Laertes is so so distraught. This latest event will spur him on even more, to kill the architect of all this pain — Hamlet.

His determination knows no bounds when he says,

"When these are gone, the woman will be out"

He says that he has harsh words that he can speak but his sadness and his tears are drowning them,

"I have a speech of fire
That fain would blaze,
But that this folly doubts it."

Claudius' lies and hypocrisy is evident here. He is lying that he had to calm Laertes down, yet he was plotting and planning with him to kill Hamlet,

"How much I had to do to calm his rage!"

In Act 5 scene 1, the setting is the graveyard outside the walls of Elsinore castle, with a newly opened grave, the next day.

Enter a gravedigger and his companion discussing the circumstances surrounding Ophelia's death in the context of religious practice.

If she took her own life, then she should not be buried as a Christian as it is against God's law.

They go on to discuss their own profession compared with that of a mason, a shipwright, or a carpenter.

Exit the companion gravedigger while the gravedigger continues to dig and starts to sing.

Enter Hamlet and Horatio.

Now and then the gravedigger throws up a skull.

Hamlet considers the singing and treatment of the bones as disrespectful, and muses about the deceased previous professions.

Hamlet asks the gravedigger whose grave he digs. The reply is ambiguous, neither man nor woman but was a woman.

Hamlet then asks how long he has been a grave-maker to which the gravedigger replied since the young Hamlet was born but alas now the young Hamlet had been sent to England to recover his wits.

The gravedigger hands Hamlet the skull of Yorick, the court jester to Hamlet's father King hamlet. In responds, Hamlet begins his eulogy,

> *Alas, poor Yorick, I knew him, Horatio,*
> *a fellow of infinite jest, of most excellent fancy.*

Hamlet continues his muse on the buried remains of Alexander and of Julius Caesar concluding that even the famous are reduced to worm's meat and dust as are all creatures.

Enter Bearers with the corpse of Ophelia in an open coffin, followed by a Priest, her brother Laertes, the King Claudius, the Queen Gertrude, and Courtiers.

Hamlet recognises Laertes but when the Priest denies sanctification, realises that it is Ophelia in the coffin.

Laertes protests and leaps into the grave wishing to hold her in his arms once more while earth is piled on top.

Hamlet incensed by Laertes derogatory remarks about him, leaps into the grave, and a fight ensues between the two, which by command of the king is stopped by Courtiers.

Gertrude asks Hamlet the reason for his attack. Hamlet replies, his love for Ophelia.

The King tells Laertes, Hamlet is mad. Hamlet remarks in a dialogue that if Laertes desired to be buried with Ophelia, so did he.

The Queen rebukes her son Hamlet for his madness.

Exit Hamlet.

The King tells Horatio to wait upon Hamlet.

Exit Horatio.

To Laertes, the King tells him to be patience, as the matter of Ophelia's burial will be corrected, and a living monument erected.

To Gertrude, the King tells her to set some watch on her son.

Exit Claudius, Gertrude, Laertes, and Courtiers.

TEXT ACT 5 scene 1

A grave-yard, with a newly opened grave

< Enter a ***GRAVEDIGGER***
and the ***OTHER*** *gravedigger >*

GRAVEDIGGER
Is she to be buried in Christian burial,
When she wilfully seeks her own salvation?
OTHER
I tell thee she is.
Therefore make her grave straight.
The crowner hath sat on her
And finds it Christian burial.
GRAVEDIGGER
How can that be,
Unless she drowned herself in her own defense?
OTHER
Why, 'tis found so.
GRAVEDIGGER
It must be *se offendendo*.
It cannot be else.
For herelies the point:
If I drown myself wittingly, it argues an act.
And an act hath three branches—
It is to act, to do, to perform:
Argal, she drowned herself wittingly
OTHER
Nay, but hear you, Goodman Delver—
GRAVEDIGGER
Give me leave.
Here lies the water— good.
Here stands the man— good.
If the man go to this water and drown himself,
It is, will he nill he, he goes, mark you that.
But if the water come to him and drown him,
He drowns not himself.
Argal, he that is not guilty of his own death
Shortens not his own life.
OTHER
But is this law?
GRAVEDIGGER
Ay, marry, is 't. Crowner's quest law.
OTHER
Will you ha' the truth on 't?
If this had not been a gentlewoman,
She should have been buried out o' Christian burial.

EXPLANATION

They were discussing poor Ophelia's spiritual fate. Since she committed 'suicide' she is not entitled to a Christian burial. According to the Christian belief, suicide is not a Christian-like act.

"Is she to be buried in a Christian burial,
When she wilfully seeks her own salvation?"

The gravedigger is adamant that it was suicide, and that Ophelia should not be given a Christian burial.

The gravedigger clearly analyses Ophelia's drowning with some visual performance. He lays out the whole scenario that if a man goes to the water and drowns himself then he does it according to his own volition.

But if the water comes to him and drown him, then he doesn't drown himself. A man who is not guilty of his own death does not shorten his own life.

"Argal, he that is not guilty of his own death Shortens not his own life"

The other gravedigger got tired of his goading and remarked that if she wasn't rich then she would have been,

"If this had not been a gentlewoman,
She should have been buried out o' Christian burial"

The GRAVEDIGGER with OTHER digging Ophelia's grave

GRAVEDIGGER
Why, there thou say'st.
And the more pity that great folk
Should have countenance in this world to drown
Or hang themselves more than their even Christian.
Come, my spade.
There is no ancient gentleman
but gardeners, ditchers, and grave makers –
They hold up Adam's profession.

[He goes down into the open grave]

OTHER
Was he a gentleman?
GRAVEDIGGER
He was the first that ever bore arms.
OTHER
Why, he had none.
GRAVEDIGGER
What, art a heathen?
How dost thou understand the Scripture?
The Scripture says Adam digged.
Could he dig without arms?
I'll put another question to thee.
If thou answer'st me not to the purpose,
Confess thyself—
OTHER
Go to.
GRAVEDIGGER
What is he that builds stronger than either
The mason, the shipwright, or the carpenter?
OTHER
The gallows-maker,
For that frame out lives a thousand tenants.
GRAVEDIGGER
I like thy wit well, in good faith.
The gallows does well,
But how does it well?
It does well to those that do ill.
Now thou dost ill to say
The gallows is built stronger than the church.
Argal, the gallows may do well to thee.
To 't again, come.
OTHER
Who builds stronger than?
A mason, a shipwright, or a carpenter?

The gravedigger very bitterly states that the rich have the opportunity to drown or hang themselves more than us Christians.

"to drown
Or hang themselves more than their even Christian"

It is ironical that the gravediggers have a joke about the curse of Adam. After he sinned, God told Adam

"Cursed is the ground for your sake; in toil you shall eat of it"

It is rather symbolic of Ophelia's situation. She cannot be buried in consecrated grounds because she has sinned in the eyes of God.

GRAVEDIGGER poses a puzzle to his companion the OTHER, "What is he that builds stronger"

The Gravedigger says that,

"The gallows is built stronger than the church"

He means that the gallows is the more fitting punishment to those that do ill than that offered by the church – an eye for an eye – death for death.

The Gravedigger teases his companion the Other about,
"Who builds stronger than?
A mason, a shipwright, or a carpenter?"

The answer is of course, the 'grave-maker' as he offends nobody.

GRAVEDIGGER
Ay, tell me that, and unyoke.
OTHER
Marry, now I can tell.
GRAVEDIGGER
To 't.
OTHER
Mass, I cannot tell.
GRAVEDIGGER
Cudgel thy brains no more about it,
For your dull ass will not mend his pace with beating.
And when you are asked this question next,
Say 'A grave-maker'.
The houses that he makes last till doomsday.
Go, get thee to Yaughan.
Fetch me a stoup of liquor.

*< Exit **OTHER** >*

[Gravedigger continues digging]

[Digs and Sings]
In youth when I did love, did love,
Methought it was very sweet
To contract–o–the time, for–a–my behove,
Oh, methought, there–a–was nothing–a–meet.

*< Enter **HAMLET** and **HORATIO** >*

HAMLET
Has this fellow no feeling of his business?
He sings at grave-making.
HORATIO
Custom hath made it in him a property of easiness.
HAMLET
'Tis e'en so,
The hand of little employment
Hath the daintier sense.
GRAVEDIGGER
[sings]
But age with his stealing steps
Hath clawed me in his clutch,
And hath shipped me into the land
As if I had never been such.

[throws up a skull]

The Gravedigger and the Other jest with each other. The Gravedigger tells his companion not to think about it no more but when asked the question must reply,

"A grave-marker"

The OTHER being told by the GRAVEDIGGER to say "A grave-maker" **when asked the question who builds stronger?**

Hamlet hears the gravedigger sing and he is angry. Then as the gravedigger sings, he throws up a skull which horrifies Hamlet,

"Has this fellow no feeling of his business?
He sings at grave-making"

When Hamlet sees the skull, he is also angry at how indecently it was thrown.

GRAVEDIGGER, HORATIO with horses, and HAMLET exclaiming "He sings at grave-making"

Horatio remarks that the Gravedigger is so a customed to seeing skulls he is at ease with them.

"Custom hath made it in him a property of easiness"

HAMLET
That skull had a tongue in it and could sing once.
How the knave jowls it to the ground,
As if it were Cain's jawbone,
That did the first murder!
It might be the pate of a politician,
Which this ass now o'er-reaches,
One that would circumvent God,
Might it not?
HORATIO
It might, my lord.
HAMLET
Or of a courtier,
Which could say, "Good morrow, sweet lord!"
"How dost thou, good lord?"
This might be my Lord
Such-a-one that praised my Lord
Such-a-one's horse when he meant to beg it,
Might it not?
HORATIO
Ay, my lord.
HAMLET
Why, e'en so.
And now my Lady Worm's,
Chapless and knocked about
The mazard with a sexton's spade.
Here's fine revolution,
And we had the trick to see 't.
Did these bones cost no more the breeding
But to play at loggets with them?
Mine ache to think on't.
GRAVEDIGGER
[sings]
A pickaxe and a spade, a spade,
For and a shrouding sheet,
Oh, a pit of clay for to be made
For such a guest is meet.

[thro ws up another skull]

He says that it's faculties once worked and that it had a tongue in it and could sing once, just like the gravedigger,

"How the knave jowls it to the ground,
As if it were Cain's jawbone,
That did the first murder!"

Ironically, he uses the biblical imagery of Cain and Abel. Cain killed his brother Abel for his birth right and this can be attributed to Claudius' killing of his brother for the crown.

Hamlet further speculates that maybe he was a courtier who would greet you politely.

"Or of a courtier,
Which could say, "Good morrow, sweet lord!"

But irrespective, when in the grave, they are food for 'Lady Worms', and broken into pieces with a sexton's spade.

"And now my Lady Worm's,
Chapless and knocked about
The mazard with a sexton's spade"

Hamlet despairs to think that the bones are like bowling pins, scattered here and there, as if they are nothing with no history.

"But to play at loggets with them?
Mine ache to think on't."

HAMLET remarks "But to play at loggets with them? Mine ache to think on't"

HAMLET
There's another.
Why may not that be the skull of a lawyer?
Where be his quiddities now, his quillities,
His cases, his tenures, and his tricks?
Why does he suffer this rude knave now?
To knock him about the sconce with a dirty shovel
And will not tell him of his action of battery? Hum!
This fellow might be in 's time a great buyer of land,
With his statutes, his recognizances, his fines,
His double vouchers, his recoveries.
Is this the fine of his fines
And the recovery of his recoveries,
To have his fine pate full of fine dirt?
Will his vouchers vouch him
No more of his purchases,
And double ones too, than the length and breadth
Of a pair of indentures?
The very conveyances of his lands
Will hardly lie in this box,
And must the inheritor himself have no more, ha?

HORATIO
Not a jot more, my lord.

HAMLET
Is not parchment made of sheepskins?

HORATIO
Ay, my lord, and of calfskins too.

HAMLET
They are sheep and calves
Which seek out assurance in that.
I will speak to this fellow. —
Whose grave's this, sirrah?

GRAVEDIGGER
Mine, sir.
[sings]
Oh, a pit of clay for to be made
For such a guest is meet.

HAMLET
I think it be thine, indeed, for thou liest in 't.

GRAVEDIGGER
You lie out on 't, sir,
And therefore it is not yours.
For my part, I do not lie in 't,
And yet it is mine.

HAMLET
Thou dost lie in 't, to be in 't and say it is thine.
'Tis for the dead, not for the quick.
Therefore thou liest.

Hamlet surmises the possible trades of each skull he throws out of the grave.

"Why may not that be the skull of a lawyer?"

Hamlet and Horatio survey the graves.

Hamlet sees another skull and assumes that it may be the skull of a lawyer who is right up the social ladder but whose remains are now treated very disrespectfully by the Gravedigger. Hamlet asks the question,

"Why does he suffer this rude knave now?
To knock him about the sconce with a dirty shovel
And will not tell him of his action of battery?"

Hamlet surmises that perhaps,

"This fellow might be in 's time a great buyer of land"

Now, the deeds to his properties would barely fit into his grave.

"The very conveyances of his lands
Will hardly lie in this box"

Hamlet and the Gravedigger jest as to whose' grave it is. Because Hamlet is outside, and the Gravedigger inside, it is not Hamlet's.

"You lie out on 't, sir,
And therefore it is not yours.
For my part, I do not lie in 't,
And yet it is mine"

HAMLET jests with the GRAVEDIGGER as to whose' grave it is.

GRAVEDIGGER
'Tis a quick lie, sir.
'Twill away gain from me to you.
HAMLET
What man dost thou dig it for?
GRAVEDIGGER
For no man, sir.
HAMLET
What woman, then?
GRAVEDIGGER
For none, neither.
HAMLET
Who is to be buried in 't?
GRAVEDIGGER
One that was a woman, sir,
But, rest her soul, she's dead.
HAMLET
How absolute the knave is!
We must speak by the card,
Or equivocation will undo us.
By the Lord, Horatio,
these three years I have taken a note of it.
The age is grown so picked
That the toe of the peasant comes so near the heel
Of the courtier he galls his kibe.—
How long hast thou been a grave- maker?
GRAVEDIGGER
Of all the days i' the year,
I came to 't that day
That our last King Hamlet o'ercame Fortinbras.
HAMLET
How long is that since?
GRAVEDIGGER
Cannot you tell that?
Every fool can tell that.
It was the very day that young Hamlet was born,
He that is mad and sent into England.
HAMLET
Ay, marry, why was he sent into England?
GRAVEDIGGER
Why, because he was mad.
He shall recover his wits there,
Or, if he do not, it's no great matter there.
HAMLET
Why?
GRAVEDIGGER
'Twill not be seen in him there.
There the men are as mad as he.

Hamlet asks the Gravedigger who he digs for but is told neither a man nor woman. Instead,

"One that was a woman, sir,
But, rest her soul, she's dead"

Hamlet is not pleased by the Gravedigger's wordplay and remarks to Horatio'

"That the toe of the peasant comes so near the heel"
Of the courtier he galls his kibe"

In other words, the peasant comes so close to the courtier, he rubs (galls) his chilblain (kibe).

Hamlet jests with the gravedigger and then he enquires who he is digging the grave for. After much banter, he tells Hamlet that it is for a woman. He also tells Hamlet that he had worked as a gravedigger from the time he was born and when the late king Hamlet defeated Fortinbras,

"It was the day young Hamlet was born"

But he got mad and was sent off to England. Hamlet questions the gravedigger about himself because he is unaware that he is talking to Hamlet himself. He enquires further,

"Ay, marry why was he sent to England?"

Because he was crazy. He will recover from his madness there. If he doesn't, then it really doesn't matter because everyone is crazy there.

"Why, because he was mad.
He shall recover his wits there,
or, if he do not, it's no great matter there."

The GRAVEDIGGER does not realise he is talking with Hamlet

HAMLET
How came he mad?
GRAVEDIGGER
Very strangely, they say.
HAMLET
How "strangely"?
GRAVEDIGGER
Faith, e'en with losing his wits.
HAMLET
Upon what ground?
GRAVEDIGGER
Why, here in Denmark.
I have been sexton here, man and boy, thirty years.
HAMLET
How long will a man lie i' the earth ere he rot?
GRAVEDIGGER
Faith, if he be not rotten before he die—
As we havemany pocky corses nowadays
That will scarce hold the laying in—
He will last you some eight year or nine year.
A tanner will last you nine year.
HAMLET
Why he more than another?
GRAVEDIGGER
Why, sir, his hide is so tanned with his trade
That he will keep out water a great while,
And your water is a sore decayer
Of your whoreson dead body.
[indicates a skull]
Here's a skull now. This skull has
Lien in the earth three-and-twenty years.
HAMLET
Whose was it?
GRAVEDIGGER
A whoreson mad fellow's it was.
Whose do you think it was?
HAMLET
Nay, I know not.
GRAVEDIGGER
A pestilence on him for a mad rogue!
He poured a flagon of Rhenish on my head once.
This same skull,sir,
Was Yorick's skull, the king's jester
HAMLET
This?
GRAVEDIGGER
E'en that.

Hamlet asks him,

"How long will a man lie i' the earth ere he rot?"

The gravedigger gives a very smart and apt answer,

"Faith, if he be not rotten before he die —"

This response can well be attributed to Claudius' character which is rotten to the core before he dies, because of his devious deeds.

The Gravedigger explains that the condition of each skull is determined by exposure to water,

"And your water is a sore decayer"

The gravedigger points out Yorick's skull to Hamlet. He was the king's jester and Hamlet remembers him well. He used to carry him on his back.

HORATIO looks on as HAMLET holds in his hands the skull of Yorick, the deceased court jester to King Hamlet

HAMLET's eulogy to Yorick's skull

HAMLET
Let me see.
[takes the skull]
Alas, poor Yorick!
I knew him, Horatio,
A fellow of infinite jest, of most excellent fancy
He hath borne me on his back a thousand times,
And now, how abhorred in my imagination it is!
My gorge rises at it.
Here hung those lips
That I have kissed I know not how oft. —
Where be your gibes now? Your gambols?
Your songs? Your flashes of merriment
That were wont to set the table on a roar?
Not one now to mock your own grinning.
Quite chap-fallen?
Now get you to my lady's chamber and tell her,
Let her paint an inch thick,
To this favor she must come.
Make her laugh at that. —
Prithee, Horatio, tell me one thing.

HORATIO
What's that, my lord?

HAMLET
Dost thou think
Alexander looked o' this fashion i' th'earth?

HORATIO
E'en so.

HAMLET
And smelt so? Pah!
[puts down the skull]

HORATIO
E'en so, my lord.

HAMLET
To what base uses we may return, Horatio! Why may
not imagination trace the noble dust
of Alexander till he find it stopping a bunghole?

HORATIO
'Twere to consider too curiously, to consider so.

HAMLET
No, faith, not a jot.
But to follow him thither with modesty enough,
And likelihood to lead it, as thus:Alexander died,
Alexander was buried, Alexander return'th to dust,
The dust is earth, of earth we make loam —

EXPLANATION

He asks of Yorick,

"Where be your gibes now? Your gambols?
Your songs? Your flashes of merriment
That were wont to set the table on a roar?"

He asks Yorick if he won't be sad that he wouldn't be able to make anyone laugh anymore.

"Not one now to mock your own grinning.
Quite chap-fallen?"

He asks Yorick to go to his mother's room and tell her that no matter how much makeup she slathers she will, one day, end up in the grave just like him.

"Now get you to my lady's chamber and tell her,
Let her paint an inch thick,
To this favor she must come."

Hamlet ask if Alexander the Great looked like this skull. He says that when we die, we smell, and we are reduced to mere dust. He talks about 'noble dust' because Alexander the Great was reduced to dust although he was a great man. The reference to the biblical imagery,

"Ashes to ashes dust to dust."

Can be relevant here. God created man from dust and to dust they will return, irrespective of power and status, when they die.

Ironically Hamlet is very unwittingly foreshadowing his own royal death and he too will end up like Alexander the Great, irrespective of his status as prince.

"To what base uses we may return, Horatio! Why may not imagination trace the noble dust"

We witness Hamlet's strong sense of religious beliefs. He talks about man's creation by God. God took soil from the earth and created man and he said that man will return to the dust of the earth when he dies.

"Alexander return'th to dust,
The dust is earth"

TEXT ACT 5 scene 1

HAMLET (*continues*)
And why of that loam,
Whereto he was converted,
Might they not stop a beer barrel?
Imperious Caesar, dead and turned to clay,
Might stop a hole to keep the wind away.
Oh, that that earth, which kept the world in awe,
Should patch a wall t' expel the winter's flaw!
But soft, but soft a while.
Here comes the king,
The queen, the courtiers—

*< Enter King **CLAUDIUS**, Queen **GERTRUDE, LAERTES,** and the corpse of **OPHELIA** in an open coffin, with a **PRIEST** and other **LORDS'** Attendant >*

Who is this they follow,
And with such maimed rites?
This doth betoken
The corse they follow did with desp'rate hand
Fordo its own life.
'Twas of some estate.
Couch we a while and mark.

LAERTES
What ceremony else?

HAMLET
That is Laertes, a very noble youth, mark.

LAERTES
What ceremony else?

EXPLANATION

He says that when Alexander the Great died he was converted to soil.

"And why of that loam,
Whereto he was converted"

Hamlet sees the royal entourage arriving — the king, the queen, and the courtiers.

Hamlet notices the funeral procession with king and queen. He is curious as to whose procession they are following with such a plain and simple ceremony.

HORATIO listens as HAMLET asks, "Who is this they follow, And with such maimed rites?"

He guessed that it was someone who had committed suicide and who comes from a wealthy family.

"The corse they follow did with desp'rate hand
Fordo its own life"

Hamlet recognises Laertes, and remarks to Horatio,

"That is Laertes, a very noble youth, mark"

Shakespeare creates nail-baiting tension here. We are left in suspense about Hamlet's reaction when he discovers that the corpse is Ophelia's – his beloved.

Laertes is questioning the Priest as to what ceremony his sister is to receive. He is anxious that his sister Ophelia is buried with full Christian rites so that she may be entitled to be received in heaven.

PRIEST

Her obsequies have been as far enlarged
As we have warranty. Her death was doubtful,
And, but that great command o'ersways the order,
She should in ground unsanctified have lodg'd
Till the last trumpet.
For charitable prayers shards, flints,
And pebbles should be thrown on her.
Yet here she is allowed her virgin crants,
Her maiden strewments,
And the bringing home of bell and burial.

LAERTES

Must there no more be done?

PRIEST

No more be done.
We should profane the service of the dead
To sing a requiem and such rest to her
As to peace-parted souls.

LAERTES

Lay her i' th' earth,
And from her fair and unpolluted flesh
May violets spring!
I tell thee, churlish priest,
A minist'ring angel shall my sister be
When thou liest howling.

HAMLET

(*to Horatio*) What, the fair Ophelia?

GERTRUDE

[scatters flowers]

Sweets to the sweet.
Farewell!
I hoped thou shouldst have been my Hamlet's wife.
I thought thy bride-bed to have decked, sweet maid,
And not have strew'd thy grave.

LAERTES

Oh, treble woe
Fall ten times treble on that cursed head,
Whose wicked deed thy most ingenious sense
Depriv'd thee of! Hold off the earth awhile
Till I have caught her once more in mine arms.

[leaps into the grave]

Now pile your dust upon the quick and dead,
Till of this flat a mountain you have made,
T' o'ertop old Pelion or the skyish head
Of blue Olympus.

He hears the priest tell Laertes that Ophelia has been given the necessary Christian rites although her death was suspicious.

"Her obsequies have been as far enlarged
As we have warranty. Her death was doubtful."

The king gave orders to bury her here, she is dressed like a virgin with flowers strewn over her grave and the bell tolling for her.

"Yet here she is allowed her virgin chants,
Her maiden strewments,
And the bringing home of bell and burial."

Instead of,
"For charitable prayers shards, flints,
And pebbles should be thrown on her"

GERTRUDE says farewell to OPHELIA

Gertrude laments,
Farewell!
I hoped thou shouldst have been my Hamlet's wife.
I thought thy bride-bed to have decked, sweet maid,
And not have strew'd thy grave.

LAERTES exclaims over OPHELIA corpse. "Oh, treble woe"

HAMLET
(*comes forward*) What is he whose grief
Bears such an emphasis,
Whose phrase of sorrow
Conjures the wand'ring stars,
And makes them stand
Like wonder-wounded hearers?
This is I, Hamlet the Dane.

[leaps into the grave]

LAERTES
The devil take thy soul!

*[**HAMLET** and **LAERTES** grapple]*

HAMLET
Thou pray'st not well.
I prithee, take thy fingers from my throat,
For though I am not splenitive and rash,
Yet have I something in me dangerous,
Which let thy wisdom fear. Hold off thy hand.
CLAUDIUS
Pluck them asunder.
GERTRUDE
Hamlet, Hamlet!
ALL
Gentlemen—
HORATIO
(*to Hamlet*) Good my lord, be quiet.

< *Attendants part **HAMLET** and **LAERTES**, and they come up out of the grave* >

HAMLET
Why, I will fight with him upon this themeUntil
my eyelids will no longer wag.
GERTRUDE
O my son, what theme?
HAMLET
I loved Ophelia.
Forty thousand brothers
Could not with all their quantity of love
Make up my sum.
What wilt thou do for her?
CLAUDIUS
O, he is mad, Laertes.
GERTRUDE
For love of God, forbear him.

Hamlet is just as distraught as Laertes, and proclaims,

"What is he whose grief
Bears such an emphasis,
Whose phrase of sorrow
Conjures the wand'ring stars"

exclaiming

"This is I, Hamlet the Dane."

This is a direct challenge to Laertes' grief. Hamlet the Dane has a greater claim to grief than Laertes, even though Laertes is a blood relation and Hamlet is not.

Laertes is incensed, calling out,

"The devil take thy soul!"

HAMLET and LAERTES grapple

Claudius immediately instructs his attendants to, "Pluck them asunder"

CLAUDIUS declares "O, he is mad, Laertes"

HAMLET
'Swounds, show me what thou't do.
Woo't weep? Woo't fight?
Woo't fast? Woo't tear thyself?
Woo't drink up eisel, eat a crocodile?
I'll do't.
Dost thou come here to whine,
To outface me with leaping in her grave.
Be buried quick with her? — And so will I.
And if thou prate of mountains let them throw
Millions of acres on us, till our ground,
Singeing his pate against the burning zone,
Make Ossa like a wart!
Nay, an thou'lt mouth,
I'll rant as well as thou.

GERTRUDE
This is mere madness.
And thus, a while the fit will work on him.
Anon, as patient as the female dove
When that her golden couplets are disclos'd,
His silence will sit drooping.

HAMLET
Hear you, sir.
What is the reason that you use me thus?
I lov'd you ever. But it is no matter.
Let Hercules himself do what he may,
The cat will mew, and dog will have his day.

< *Exit **HAMLET*** >

CLAUDIUS
I pray thee, good Horatio, wait upon him.

< *Exit **HORATIO*** >

(*to Laertes*) Strengthen your patience
In our last night's speech.
We'll put the matter to the present push. —
Good Gertrude,
Set some watch over your son. —
This grave shall have a living monument.
An hour of quiet shortly shall we see.
Till then in patience our proceeding be.

< *Exeunt* >

HAMLET held back by Attendants with HORATIO looking on

LAERTES held back by Attendants

GERTRUDE tells her son HAMLET, "This is mere madness"

Claudius instructs Horatio to attend to Hamlet, and to Laertes,

"Strengthen your patience
In our last night's speech"

Their plot to kill Hamlet by poisoned sword, and poisoned wine, but make it appear accidental.

In Act 5 scene 2, the setting is inside the hall of Elsinore castle, the next day.

Enter Hamlet and Horatio.

Hamlet recounts how the night before the pirates captured him, not being able to sleep, he crept in the dark into Rosencrantz and Guildenstern's cabin and discovered letters signed by Claudius instructing the King of England to have Hamlet's head struck off with haste.

Hamlet hands to the sceptical Horatio the letters to read at his leisure. Hamlet proceeds to tell how he composed substitute letters in the flowery style of the originals instructing the King of England to put the bearers of the letters to sudden death. To authenticate the letters, he had used his father's signet, a model of the Danish seal.

Hamlet considers Rosencrantz and Guildenstern demise poetic justice and will repay in kind the evil done to him by Claudius who has killed his father, defiled his mother, and usurped the crown which should have been his.

Horatio reminds Hamlet that Claudius will soon discover the truth about happenings in England, but Hamlet tells him that although time is short, he will prevail.

Hamlet regrets his recent passion towards Laertes and will try and make amends.

Enter Osric, a Courtier, with news that the King expects Hamlet to accept a friendly duel with Laertes and has wagered six Barbary horses against six French swords, their assigns, and three liberal-conceited carriages, that Hamlet in a dozen passes can secure three hits at most. Hamlet accepts.

Exit Osric.

Enter a Lord enquiring if Hamlet needs more time to prepare, to which Hamlet replies, Nay. Exit the Lord.

Horatio implores Hamlet to withdraw if he feels there is treachery afoot, but Hamlet refuses saying he defies augury (fate).

Enter Attendants to set a table and seating; Trumpeters and Drummers; the King, the Queen, Laertes, Osric, Courtiers, and Attendants with foils and daggers.

Claudius puts Laertes' hand into Hamlet's in an act of friendly gesture. Hamlet asks Laertes' pardon who accepts stating he is not stirred to revenge in this bout but to honour, peace and love.

Osric brings forward some foils from which the two antagonists select and prepare to play (duel).

Enter Servants with flagons of wine.

First hit is declared in Hamlet's favour by Osric, the referee.

Claudius requests a stay, takes wine and drops a pearl (coated in poison) into the cup declaring this pearl is thine and inviting Hamlet to drink.

Hamlet declines saying he will play the next bout first.

Second hit is again declared in Hamlet's favour.

Gertrude rubs Hamlet's brow with her napkin.

Claudius tells Gertrude not to drink, but she asks his pardon and drinks from the poisoned cup, then offers it to her son Hamlet but he refuses. She wipes his brow again.

Now that Hamlet will not drink from the poison cup, Laertes tells Claudius he will hit him with the poison tip, but Claudius disagrees.

They play again in a third bout. Laertes wounds Hamlet with the poisoned foil, then in the scuffle, foils are exchanged, and Hamlet wounds Laertes with the poisoned foil.

The Queen falls: Horatio exclaims they both bleed; Laertes declares to Osric he is justly killed with his own treachery; Claudius falsely declares the Queen swoons to see the combatant's bleed; the Queen refutes this, exclaiming the drink is poisoned.

Gertrude dies. Hamlet cries villainy and orders the door to the hall to be locked.

Exit Osric.

Laertes himself dying, tells Hamlet he is also poisoned by the action of the foil, with not half an hour's life, and no medicine to cure it, and his mother the Queen by the poisoned cup.

Laertes blames Claudius.

Hamlet wounds Claudius calling him an incestuous, murderous, damn'd Dane, and gets him to drink from the poisoned cup so he may follow Gertrude.

Claudius dies.

Laertes asks Hamlet to exchange forgiveness with him. Laertes dies. Hamlet asks Horatio to tell his story.

Enter Osric to announce the arrival of young Fortinbras fresh from his conquest of Poland, and the Ambassadors of England.

Hamlet tells Horatio that young Fortinbras is to be the next King of Denmark. Hamlet dies. Horatio in sorrow proclaims:

> *Now cracks a noble heart. Good night, sweet prince,*
> *And flights of angels sing thee to thy rest.*

Enter Fortinbras, the English Ambassadors, and Soldiers with drums and colours.

Fortinbras exclaims O proud Death.

The First Ambassador proclaims the deaths of Rosencrantz and Guildenstern.

Horatio proclaims that all presents will hear of carnal, bloody, and unnatural acts, of accidental judgements, casual slaughters, of deaths put on by cunning and forced cause, and, in this upshot, purposes mistook fallen on the inventors' head.

Fortinbras with sorrow embraces his fortune, the right to wear the Crown of Denmark, and commands four captains to bear Hamlet like a soldier accompanied by music and the rite of war to the place of rest.

Exit the soldiers marching as they carry the bodies; after which a peal of ordnance is heard.

The hall of the castle

*< Enter **HAMLET** and **HORATIO** >*

HAMLET
So much for this, sir.
Now shall you see the other
You do remember all the circumstance?
HORATIO
Remember it, my lord?
HAMLET
Sir, in my heart there was a kind of fighting
That would not let me sleep. Methought, I lay
Worse than the mutines in the bilboes.
Rashly—
And praised be rashness for it: let us know
Our indiscretion sometimes serves us well
When our deep plots do pall,
And that should teach us
There's a divinity that shapes our ends,
Rough-hew them how we will—
HORATIO
That is most certain.
HAMLET
Up from my cabin,
My sea-gown scarf'd about me, in the dark
Grop'd I to find out them, had my desire,
Finger'd their packet, and in fine withdrew
To mine own room again, making so bold
(My fears forgetting manners) to unseal
Their grand commission, where I found, Horatio—
O royal knavery! —an exact command,
Larded with many several sorts of reasons
Importing Denmark's health, and England's too,
With—ho!— such bugs and goblins in my life,
That, on the supervise no leisure bated,
No, not to stay the grinding of the axe,
My head should be struck off.
HORATIO
Is 't possible?
HAMLET
[shows Horatio a document]
Here's the commission, read it at more leisure.
But wilt thou hear now how I did proceed?
HORATIO
I beseech you.

Hamlet has a serious chat with Horatio. He tells him of this strange feeling that would not allow him to sleep,

"Sir, in my heart, there was a kind of fighting
that would not let me sleep"

He says that there is Divine intervention that guides our actions even if we make mistakes,

"There's a divinity that shapes our ends"

Hamlet's Christian, religious conscience surfaces once more. He feels an ominous foreboding or some kind of premonition, because he acts on his instincts instantly, as though God is leading him.

He relays to Horatio the horror of finding out that the king was sending him to his death. He stole from his cabin in the dark and managed to get hold of his uncle's letter to the king of England. He took it to his room and read it. He was shocked to find a terrible mischief from the king. Outlined in the letter was precise instructions to kill him.

"O royal knavery! —an exact command"

For the well-being of Denmark and England to ensure that'

"My head should be struck off"

Horatio is shocked and Hamlet shows him the document.

"Here's the commission, read it at more leisure"

HAMLET discovers the letters condemning him to death inside Rosencrantz and Guildenstern cabin

HAMLET
Being thus benetted round with villainies—
Ere I could make a prologue to my brains,
They had begun the play— I sat me down,
Devis'd a new commission, wrote it fair.
I once did hold it, as our statists do,
A baseness to write fair, and labour'd much
How to forget that learning, but, sir, now
It did me yeoman's service.
Wilt thou know
Th' effect of what I wrote?

HORATIO
Ay, good my lord.

HAMLET
An earnest conjuration from the king,
As England was his faithful tributary,
As love between them like the palm might flourish,
As peace should stiff her wheaten garland wear
And stand a comma 'tween their amities,
And many such-like "as'es" of great charge,
That, on the view and knowing of these contents,
Without debatement further, more or less,
He should the bearers put to sudden death,
Not shriving time allow'd.

HORATIO
How was this sealed?

HAMLET
Why, even in that was heaven ordinant.
I had my father's signet in my purse,
Which was the model of that Danish seal
Folded the writ up in form of th' other,
Subscrib'd it, gave 't th' impression, plac'd it safely,
The changeling never known.
Now, the next day
Was our sea fight,
And what to this was sequent
Thou know'st already.

HORATIO
So Guildenstern and Rosencrantz go to 't.

Claudius' evil, hypocritical and deadly nature is exposed. He pretended to show love and displays of caring for Hamlet, like a father, yet this cruel antagonist is preparing to kill him.

Hamlet asks Horatio if he wants to hear what happened after that which he does. Hamlet says that being surrounded by villains and before he could make sense of things, they had started to act. He sat down and devised a new official document with different instructions,

"Devis'd a new commission, wrote it fair"

He wrote in good handwriting and very wittily wrote to the king giving him the King of Denmark's greetings. He uses a simile saying that he hopes that the love and friendship between the two countries will flourish,

"As love between them like the palm might flourish"

The development of the plot had taken an unusual twist and had reached an anti-climax.

The audience was nervous for the protagonist, Hamlet because they knew that his uncle was planning a deadly plot to kill him.

Now they can breathe a sigh of relief because Hamlet wrote that once the letter was read, the ones who are delivering it should be put to death immediately. The bearers should not be allowed any time with the priest for confession.

"He should the bearers put to sudden death,
Not shriving time allow'd"

ROSENCRANTZ and GUILDENSTERN about to be axed to death in England as ordered by Hamlet's substituted letters – their names instead of his

TEXT ACT 5 scene 2

HAMLET
Why, man, they did make love to this employment.
They are not near my conscience, their defeat
Does by their own insinuation grow.
'Tis dangerous when the baser nature comes
Between the pass and fell incensed points
Of mighty opposites.

HORATIO
Why, what a king is this!

HAMLET
Does it not, think thee, stand me now upon—
He that hath kill'd my king and whor'd my mother,
Popp'd in between th' election and my hopes,
Thrown out his angle for my proper life (And with
such coz'nage!)—
is 't not perfect conscience
To quit him with this arm.
And is 't not to be damn'd
To let this canker of our nature come
In further evil?

HORATIO
It must be shortly known to him from England
What is the issue of the business there?

HAMLET
It will be short. The interim's mine.
And a man's life's no more than to say "one."
But I am very sorry, good Horatio,
That to Laertes I forgot myself,
For by the image of my cause I see
The portraiture of his. I'll court his favours.
But sure, the bravery of his grief did put me
Into a tow'ring passion.

HORATIO
Peace. —
Who comes here?

EXPLANATION

The play is understood to be a revenge tragedy and here Hamlet took his revenge against the villains who planned and plotted to kill him. As the play climaxes the theme of revenge and retribution kicks in. Hamlet also unwittingly sought his revenge on Polonius for his active participation in helping his uncle to create mischief in his life.

Hamlet says that Rosencrantz and Guildenstern love this job and they deserve what's coming to them. He doesn't feel guilty,

"Why man they did make love to this employment.
They are not near my conscience"

Hamlet is determined more than ever to kill Claudius. Now he views things in a more philosophical manner.

His reasoning is vivid, and he seemed to be more confident and forthright after his experience in England.

He seemed to have lost that edgy, uncertain, and confused state that he was in.
He feels that it is his duty to take revenge on Claudius for the father who was killed, his mother who was whor'd, the thief who stole his crown and the murderer who set a trap to kill him.

"He that hath killed my king and whor'd my mother"

Hamlet uses the disease imagery that is prevalent in the play about Denmark being 'diseased.'
He accuses Claudius of being the disease that is corrupting the country with evil, and he wants it to stop and killing him will halt the disease.

"To let this canker of our nature come
In further evil?"

Hamlet now possess a very sound and sturdy mind. No more is he overcome with bitterness but is more psychologically and morally clued. He feels bad about his aggressive attitude towards Laertes and plans on making amends.

"But I am very sorry, good Horatio,
That to Laertes I forgot myself"

*< Enter young **OSRIC**, a courtier, hat in hand >*

OSRIC
Your lordship is right welcome back to Denmark.
HAMLET
I humbly thank you, sir.
(*Aside to Horatio*) Dost know this water-fly?
HORATIO
(*Aside to Hamlet*) No, my good lord.
HAMLET
(*Aside to Horatio*) Thy state is the more gracious,
For 'tis a vice to know him.
He hath much land, and fertile.
Let a beast be lord of beasts
And his crib shall stand at the king's mess.
'Tis a chough,
But, as I say,spacious in the possession of dirt.
OSRIC
Sweet lord, if your lordship were at leisure,
I should impart a thing to you from his Majesty.
HAMLET
I will receive it, sir, with all diligence of spirit.
Put your bonnet to his right use. 'Tis for the head.
OSRIC
I thank your lordship. It is very hot.
HAMLET
No, believe me, 'tis very cold.
The wind is northerly.
OSRIC
It is indifferent cold, my lord, indeed.
HAMLET
But yet methinks it is very sultry
and hot for my complexion.
OSRIC
Exceedingly, my lord. It is very sultry—as 'twere—
I cannot tell how.
My lord, his majesty bade me signify to you
That he has laid a great wager on your head.
Sir, this is the matter—
HAMLET
I beseech you, remember—
[indicates that OSRIC *should put on his hat]*

*Enter young **OSRIC***

Hamlet obviously doesn't like Osric and calls him a 'water-fly'.

He tells Horatio that he is lucky because it is unpleasant to know him, and he owns a lot of land.
"Thy state is the more gracious,
For 'tis a vice to know him."

HAMLET and HORATIO greet Osric below

Hamlet exchanges pleasantries with Osric, debating if Osric should put his bonnet upon his head. Hamlet suggests he should because
"No, believe me, 'tis very cold"

Osric, not wishing to be subservient, replies,
"It is indifferent cold, my lord, indeed"

And keeps his bonnet in his hands.

OSRIC keeps his bonnet in his hands against Hamlet's wish to have him put it on his head.

Osric announces to Hamlet that Claudius has,

"laid a great wager on your head"

OSRIC
Nay, good my lord, for mine ease, in good faith.
Sir, here is newly come to court Laertes,
Believe me, an absolute gentleman,
Full of most excellent differences,
Of very soft society and great showing.
Indeed, to speak feelingly of him,
He is the card or calendar of gentry,
For you shall find in him the continent
Of what part a gentleman would see.
HAMLET
Sir, his definement suffers no perdition in you,
Though I know to divide him inventorially
Would dizzy th' arithmetic of memory,
And yet but yaw neither, in respect of his quick sail.
But in the verity of extolment,
I take him to be a soul of great article,
And his infusion of such dearth and rareness as,
To make true diction of him,
His semblable is his mirror.
And who else would trace him?
His umbrage, nothing more.
OSRIC
Your lordship speaks most infallibly of him.
HAMLET
The concernancy, sir?
Why do we wrap the gentleman?
In our more rawer breath?
OSRIC
Sir?
HORATIO
(*Aside to Hamlet*)
Is 't not possible to understand in another tongue?
You will do 't, sir, really.
HAMLET
What imports the nomination of this gentleman?
OSRIC
Of Laertes?
HORATIO
(*Aside to Hamlet*) His purse is empty already.
All 's golden words are spent.
HAMLET
Of him, sir.
OSRIC
I know you are not ignorant—

Respectfully, Osric still refuses to put his bonnet on his head,

"Nay, good my lord, for mine ease, in good faith"

Osric, in veiled terms, speaks of an absolute gentleman,

"Full of most excellent differences"

Hamlet is baffled as he knows many fine gentlemen but cannot determine the one Osric speaks about. Instead of alluding to someone, Hamlet demands Osric name the gentlemen,

"The concernancy, sir?
Why do we wrap the gentleman?
In our more rawer breath?"

Perplexed, Horatio whispers to Hamlet,

"Is 't not possible to understand in another tongue?

HORATIO thinks Hamlet should speak to Osric in another language

Osric relents, and names Laertes as the unknown gentlemen. Aside, Horatio remarks to Hamlet,

"His purse is empty already.
All 's golden words are spent"

Osric, now comes to the point by first alerting Hamlet to the serious business at hand,

"I know you are not ignorant—"

HAMLET
I would you did, sir.
Yet in faith, if you did,
It would not much approve me.
Well, sir?
OSRIC
You are not ignorant of what excellence Laertes is—
HAMLET
I dare not confess that,
Lest I should compare with him in excellence,
But to know a man well were to know himself.
OSRIC
I mean, sir, for his weapon.
But in the imputation laid on him,
By them in his meed, he's unfellowed.
HAMLET
What's his weapon?
OSRIC
Rapier and dagger.
HAMLET
That's two of his weapons.
But well.
OSRIC
The king, sir,
Hath wagered with him six Barbary horses,
Against the which he has impawned, as I take it,
Six French rapiers and poniards with their assigns—
As girdle, hangers, and so.
Three of the carriages, in faith, are very dear to fancy,
very responsive to the hilts, most delicate carriages,
And of very liberal conceit.
HAMLET
What call you the carriages?
HORATIO
(*Aside to Hamlet*) I knew you must be edified
By the margin ere you had done.
OSRIC
The carriages, sir, are the hangers.
HAMLET
The phrase would be more germane to the matter
If we could carry cannon by our sides.
I would it might be hangers till then.
But, on six Barbary horses against six French swords,
Their assigns, and three liberal-conceited carriages—
That's the French bet against the Danish.
Why is this— "impawned," as you call it?

Hamlet now knows he is to duel with Laertes in an exhibition sword fight.

Hamlet acknowledges that Laertes is the better duellist,

"I dare not confess that,
Lest I should compare with him in excellence,
But to know a man well were to know himself"

Osric tells Hamlet, Laertes will use two weapons,

"Rapier and dagger"

Claudius has wagered in favour of Hamlet,

"six Barbary horses"

Against,

"Six French rapiers and poniards with their assigns—
As girdle, hangers, and so"

Hamlet is curious to know why such a wager.

"Why is this— "impawned," as you call it?"

HAMLET cannot understand why Claudius should wager such a large bet on the non-favourite such as himself,

OSRIC
The king, sir, hath laid
That in a dozen passes between yourself and him, He
shall not exceed you three hits.
He hath laid on twelve for nine,
And it would come to immediate trial
if your lordship would vouchsafe the answer.
HAMLET
How if I answer "No"?
OSRIC
I mean, my lord,
The opposition of your person in trial.
HAMLET
Sir, I will walk here in the hall.
If it please his Majesty,
'tis the breathing time of day with me.
Let the foils be brought, the gentleman willing,
And the king hold his purpose.
I will win for him, and I can.
If not, I will gain nothing
But my shame and the odd hits.
OSRIC
Shall I redeliver you e'en so?
HAMLET
To this effect, sir,
After what flourish your nature will.
OSRIC
I commend my duty to your lordship.
HAMLET
Yours, yours.
< *Exit* ***OSRIC*** >

He does well to commend it himself.
There are no tongues else for 's turn.
HORATIO
This lapwing runs away with the shell on his head.
HAMLET
He did comply, sir, with his dug before he sucked it.
Thus, has he— and many more of the same bevy
That I know the drossy age dotes on—
Only got the tune of the time
And outward habit of encounter,
A kind of yeasty collection,
Which carries them through and through
the most fanned and winnowed opinions.
And do but blow them to their trial,
The bubbles are out.

Osric explains the rules to win, but Hamlet asks

"How if I answer "No"?"

Osric wryly comments,

"I mean, my lord,
The opposition of your person in trial"

Hamlet says that he will go for a walk in the hall, and it is his exercise time whether the king is pleased or not. If the king thinks it's fine and if Laertes agrees then he will do it and win for the king,

"I will win for him, and I can.
If not, I will gain nothing
But my shame and the odd hits"

Hamlet's tone is curt and sarcastic in his dealings with Osric. This bitter tone was similarly used with his communication with Polonius, Rosencrantz, and Guildenstern because Hamlet is fully aware of how corrupt these stooges are for the king. Osric said that he will deliver Hamlet's message to the king.

"I commend my duty to your lordship."

Hamlet pokes fun at Osric and says that he blows his own trumpet because nobody else will do it for him.

"He does well to commend it himself.
There are no tongues else for 's turn."

Hamlet jokes that he admired his mother's nipple before he sucked it. Hamlet says that he's the same type of successful people that the corrupt age like the king loves and use.

"many more of the same bevy
That I know the drossy age dotes on—"

He only got the limited vocabulary and social graces to carry him through but if they are put to the test for real conversation and displays of wit, they will fail miserably.

"And do but blow them to their trial,
The bubbles are out."

*< Enter a **LORD** >*

LORD
My lord, his majesty commended him to you
By young Osric, who brings back to him that you
Attend him in the hall. He sends to know
If your pleasure hold to play with Laertes,
Or that you will take longer time.
HAMLET
I am constant to my purpose.
They follow the king's pleasure.
If his fitness speaks, mine is ready,
now or whensoever,
provided I be so able as now.
LORD
The king and queen and all are coming down.
HAMLET
In happy time.
LORD
The queen desires you
To use some gentle entertainment to Laertes
Before you fall to play.
HAMLET
She well instructs me.

*< Exit **LORD** >*

HORATIO
You will lose this wager, my lord.
HAMLET
I do not think so.
Since he went into France,
I have been in continual practice.
I shall win at the odds.
But thou wouldst not think
How ill all's here about my heart.
But it is no matter.
HORATIO
Nay, good my lord—
HAMLET
It is but foolery,
But it is such a kind of gain-giving
As would perhaps trouble a woman.

The lord says that Osric's message that Hamlet is keen to participate in the duel was delivered to the king and if he wants to do the duel now or wait.

"He sends to know
If your pleasure hold to play with Laertes"

The play has now reached its crescendo. There seems to be a flurry of activity and the pace has suddenly accelerated. The mood has also changed to a certain tenseness because of Hamlet's apprehension.

Hamlet decides to do the duel now and the Lord tells Hamlet that his mother wants him to be polite to Laertes before the fight.

"The queen desires you
To use some gentle entertainment to Laertes Before you fall to play."

Horatio is sceptical and uncomfortable with Hamlet's rash decision, and he warns him,

"You will lose this wager, my Lord"

Hamlet is very confident that he will win because he had been practicing constantly since Laertes' departure.

"Since he went into France,
I have been in continual practice,
I shall win at the odds."

Hamlet has a very eerie, foreboding feeling about his decision. It is probably the same ominous feeling he had when he discovered the letter in the ship ordering the king to kill him.

Shakespeare creates a lot of suspense and tension as the play is slowly reaching its final denouement.
We get nervous for Hamlet's situation because of Shakespeare's use of dramatic irony.

HORATIO
If your mind dislike anything, obey it.
I will forestall their repair hither
And say you are not fit.

HAMLET
Not a whit.
We defy augury.
There's a special providence
In the fall of a sparrow.
If it be now, 'tis not to come.
If it be not to come, it will be now.
If it be not now, yet it will come—
The readiness is all.
Since no man of aught he leaves knows,
What is 't to leave betimes? Let be.

*< Enter **ATTENDANTS** to set a table and seating; **TRUMPTERS** and **DRUMMERS**; the King **CLAUDIUS,** the Queen **GERTRUDE, LAERTES, OSRIC, COURTIERS**, and **ATTENDANTS** with foils and daggers >*

CLAUDIUS
Come, Hamlet, come,
And take this hand from me.
[puts Laertes' hand into Hamlet's]

HAMLET
(to Laertes) Give me your pardon, sir.
I've done you wrong.
But pardon 't, as you are a gentleman.
This presence knows,
And you must needs have heard,
How I am punish'd with sore distraction.
What I have done,
That might your nature, honour, and exception
Roughly awake, I here proclaim was madness.
Was 't Hamlet wrong'd Laertes?
Never Hamlet.
If Hamlet from himself be ta'en away,
And when he's not himself does wrong Laertes,
Then Hamlet does it not. Hamlet denies it.

Claudius, the architect of all evil is ready to pounce on innocent, unsuspecting Hamlet. There's a sense of pathos created her because Horatio urges Hamlet not to continue because he senses some danger.

"If your mind dislike anything, obey it."

Hamlet's religious beliefs surfaces once more. He says that God guides all things even the fall of the sparrow and what is to be, will be.

"There's a special providence
In the fall of a sparrow."

LEARTES, CLAUDIUS, HAMLET, GERTRUDE

This final scene prepares us for 'judgement day' or time for retribution. Hamlet is no longer grappling with his conscience. He is now convinced that his actions will be justified if he kills Claudius. He is not suffering a moral dilemma either because he is certain that the architect who was responsible for this juggernaut of evil, deserves to die.

Hamlet has also attained a level of social consciousness because he apologises to Laertes for doing him wrong. It's as though he is atoning for his sins for the judgement that he will face after death.

"Give me your pardon sir,
I've done you wrong."

HAMLET (*continues*)
Who does it, then?
His madness— If 't be so,
Hamlet is of the faction that is wrong'd.
His madness is poor Hamlet's enemy.
Sir, in this audience,
Let my disclaiming from a purpos'd evil
Free me so far in your most generous thoughtsThat I
have shot mine arrow o'er the house
And hurt my brother.

LAERTES
I am satisfied in nature,
Whose motive in this case should stir me most
To my revenge.
But in my terms of honour
I stand aloof, and will no reconcilement
Till by some elder masters, of known honour,
I have a voice and precedent of peace
To keep my name ungor'd.
But till that time
I do receive your offered love like love
And will not wrong it.

HAMLET
I embrace it freely,
And will this brother's wager frankly play. —
Give us the foils. Come on.

LAERTES
Come, one for me.

HAMLET
I'll be your foil, Laertes. In mine ignorance
Your skill shall, like a star i' th' darkest night,
Stick fiery off indeed.

LAERTES
You mock me, sir.

HAMLET
No, by this hand.

CLAUDIUS
Give them the foils, young Osric. —
[Osric brings forward some foils]
Cousin Hamlet,
You know the wager?

HAMLET
Very well, my lord.
Your Grace hath laid the odds o' th' weaker side.

He blames his state of insanity for insulting Laertes. Laertes says that he cannot forgive Hamlet for the death of his father and sister, but he accepts his token of love.

"I do receive your offered love like love
And will not wrong it."

Hamlet's unsuspecting and trusting nature is alarming here. Not only is he in the cruel jaws of danger from Claudius but deadly intent from Laertes as well. His exchange to Laertes here has a flow of friendship and camaraderie, unbeknown to him that Laertes is part of the king's treacherous plan to kill him. He thinks that this is a friendly match, so he is upbeat and carefree.

"I embrace it freely,
And will this brother's wager frankly play. — "

Claudius orders Osric to give them the swords and asks if he knows the bet. Hamlet tells Claudius,

HAMLET accepts his foil from OSRIC

Hamlet jests,

"I'll be your foil, Laertes"

But Laertes is in a different frame of mind, intent of mortally wounding Hamlet with his poisoned sword in the third bout.

Claudius is anxious to start the first bout so that Hamlet will drink the poisoned wine at the end of the bout to celebrate his win.

The question is: can Claudius kill Hamlet at the end of the first bout with the poisoned wine or will Laertes kill him with his poisoned sword in the third bout?

CLAUDIUS
I do not fear it. I have seen you both.
But since he is better'd, we have therefore odds.

LAERTES
[tests a rapier]
This is too heavy.
Let me see another.

HAMLET
[tests a rapier]
This likes me well.
These foils have all a length?

OSRIC
Ay, my good lord.

***HAMLET** and **LAERTES** prepare to fence*
*< Enter **SERVANTS** with flagons of wine >*

CLAUDIUS
Set me the stoups of wine upon that table.
If Hamlet give the first or second hit
Or quit in answer of the third exchange,
Let all the battlements their ordnance fire!
The king shall drink to Hamlet's better breath,
And in the cup an union shall he throw
Richer than that which four successive kings
In Denmark's crown have worn –
Give me the cups –
And let the kettle to the trumpet speak,
The trumpet to the cannoneer without,
The cannons to the heavens, the heavens to earth,
"Now the king drinks to Hamlet."
Come, begin. —
And you, the judges, bear a wary eye.

[*Trumpets sound*]

HAMLET
Come on, sir.

LAERTES
Come, my lord.

*< **HAMLET** and **LAERTES** fence >*

HAMLET
One.

LAERTES
No.

Claudius is beaming inside because his plan is working perfectly. He puts the goblets on the table and plans to toast if Hamlet wins by the third hit. He will also receive a military salute,

"The king shall drink to Hamlet's better breath"

Claudius is very confident that Hamlet is going to die. He acts very flamboyant and generous, and he drops a very expensive pearl into the cup.

"And in the cup an union shall he throw"

He summons the drums and the trumpets to play and the canons to fire and the canons must signal to heaven and heaven must signal to the earth that,

"Now the king drinks to Hamlet"

Claudius asks the judges to be vigilant and observe the hit when made.

"And you, the judges, bear a wary eye"

Trumpets sound

The first bout begin

HAMLET strikes and LAERRTES parries

HAMLET
Judgment?
OSRIC
A hit, a very palpable hit.
LAERTES
Well, again.
CLAUDIUS
Stay, give me drink. —
Hamlet, this pearl is thine.
Here's to thy health.

[Drums, trumpets sound, shot goes off
***CLAUDIUS** drops pearl into **HAMLET's** cup]*

Give him the cup.
HAMLET
I'll play this bout first.
Set it by a while.

[*An ATTENDANT sets cup on a table*]

Come.
[*They fence again*]

Another hit. What say you?

LAERTES
A touch, a touch, I do confess 't.

[*THEY rest*]

CLAUDIUS
Our son shall win.
GERTRUDE
He's fat, and scant of breath. —
Here, Hamlet, take my napkin, rub thy brows.
The queen carouses to thy fortune, Hamlet.

[*SHE gives **HAMLET** her napkin*
and picks up the cup with the pearl]
HAMLET
Good madam.
CLAUDIUS
Gertrude do not drink.
GERTRUDE
I will, my lord. I pray you, pardon me

[*SHE drinks and offers the cup to **HAMLET***]

Hamlet scores a hit. Claudius drops a pearl into the cup,
"Stay, give me drink. —
Hamlet, this pearl is thine.
Here's to thy health."

CLAUDIUS drop the poisoned pearl into the cup

He orders for the drink to be given to Hamlet. We are shocked at Claudius' hypocritical and ruthless character when he says that,
"Our son shall win"

Now he uses the pronoun, 'our' but earlier he said to Gertrude, (Act 5 scene 1 line 284)

"Good Gertrude, set some watch over your son."

Gertrude is very concerned about Hamlet, and she offers him her napkin to rub his brows.
She also wishes him good luck.

"Here Hamlet, take my napkin, rub thy brows.
The queen carouses to thy fortune, Hamlet."

She takes the cup to drink but Claudius tries to dissuade her.
"Gertrude do not drink"

CLAUDIUS
(*aside*) It is the poisoned cup. It is too late.
HAMLET
I dare not drink yet, madam – by and by
GERTRUDE
Come, let me wipe thy face.

[*SHE wipes* ***HAMLET'S*** *face*]

LAERTES
(*Aside to Claudius*) My lord, I'll hit him now.
CLAUDIUS
I do not think't.
LAERTES
(*aside*) And yet it is almost 'gainst my conscience.
HAMLET
Come, for the third, Laertes.
You do but dally.
I pray you, pass with your best violence.
I am afeard you make a wanton of me.
LAERTES
Say you so?
Come on.

[***HAMLET*** *and* ***LAERTES*** *fence, third bout*]

OSRIC
Nothing, neither way.
LAERTES
Have at you now!

[***LAERTES*** *wounds* ***HAMLET*** *in scuffling,*
They change rapiers.
HAMLET *wounds* ***LAERTES***]

CLAUDIUS
Part them!
They are incensed.
HAMLET
Nay, come, again.

[***HAMLET*** *wounds* ***LAERTES***]

Hamlet says,

"I dare not drink yet, Madam. By and by."

Gertrude is warming up towards her son. This display of warmth and love is very emotive because we know that she is about to die having drunk from the poisoned cup. The action reaches its peak and the pace is racing on. Too many incidents occur simultaneously.

HAMLET is wounded by LAERTES in the third bout

In retaliation for this illegal attack, there is a scuffle and Hamlet wound Laertes with the same poisoned sword.

LAERTES is wounded by HAMLET using the same poisoned sword

TEXT ACT 5 scene 2

[*The Queen **GERTRUDE** falls*]

OSRIC
Look to the queen there, ho!
HORATIO
They bleed on both sides. —
How is it, my lord?
OSRIC
How is 't, Laertes?
LAERTES
Why, as a woodcock to mine own springe, Osric.
I am justly kill'd with mine own treachery.
HAMLET
How does the queen?
CLAUDIUS
She swoons to see them bleed.
GERTRUDE
No, no, the drink, the drink! —
O my dear Hamlet!
The drink, the drink! I am poisoned.

[***GERTRUDE** dies*]

HAMLET
O villainy!
Ho, let the door be lock'd.

< *Exit **OSRIC*** >

Treachery! Seek it out.

EXPLANATION

Laertes wounds Hamlet in a scuffle and Hamlet wounds Laertes. The queen falls and Osric is worried,

"Look to the queen there, ho!"

*The Queen **GERTRUDE** falls*

Horatio is also concerned about Hamlet and Laertes says that he has been killed with his own treachery,

"Why as a woodcock to mine own springe, Osric.
I am justly kill'd with mine own treachery."

Justice has been done and even Laertes acknowledges it. He says that he was the architect of his own fate because of his treacherous behaviour towards Hamlet and now he deserves to die.

It's very moving and emotional when Hamlet, although wounded is concerned about his mother,

"How does the queen?"

Cold-hearted Claudius quickly lies that she fainted because she saw them bleed.

"She swoons to see them bleed.

But Gertrude blurts out the truth,

"No, no, the drink, the drink ! –
O my dear Hamlet!
The drink, the drink! I am poisoned."

Hamlet shouts, 'O villainy' and Laertes tells him that 'treachery' is here.

TEXT ACT 5 scene 2

LAERTES

It is here, Hamlet.
Hamlet, thou art slain.
No medicine in the world can do thee good.
In thee there is not half an hour of life.
The treacherous instrument is in thy hand,
Unbated and envenom'd.
The foul practice
Hath turned itself on me.
Lo, here I lie,
Never to rise again.
Thy mother's poison'd.
I can no more.
The king, the king's to blame.

HAMLET

The point envenomed too! –
Then, venom, to thy work.

[***HAMLET*** *wounds* ***CLAUDIUS***]

ALL

Treason! Treason!

CLAUDIUS

O, yet defend me, friends.
I am but hurt.

HAMLET

Here, thou incestuous, murderous, damn'd Dane,
Drink off this potion.
Is thy union here?
Follow my mother.

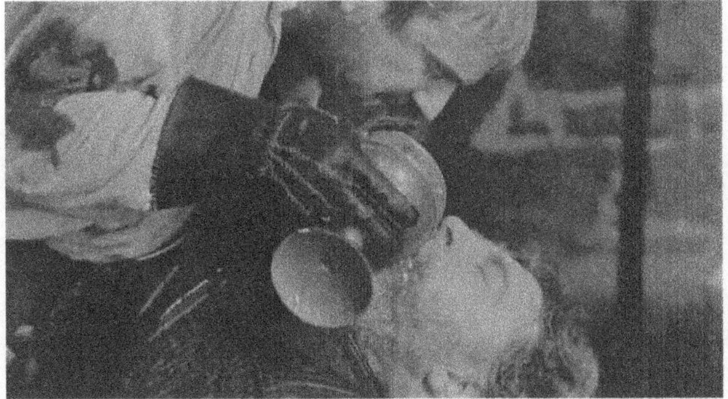

[***HAMLET*** *forces* ***CLAUDIUS*** *to drink the poisoned wine, and he dies*]

LAERTES

He is justly served.
It is a poison temper'd by himself.
Exchange forgiveness with me, noble Hamlet.
Mine and my father's death come not upon thee,
Nor thine on me.

[***LAERTES*** *dies*]

EXPLANATION

He reveals that Hamlet is slain and that no amount of medicine can keep him alive.

"Hamlet, thou art slain.
No medicine in the world can do thee good."

Laertes unfolds the king's moral corruption to Hamlet. The deadly weapon is in your hands – poisoned.

"The treacherous instrument is in thy hand, Unabated and envenom'd"

Laertes bemoaned the fact that he became the victim of his own treachery. He too seems to be seeking penance and getting prepared for the judgement that awaits him. He seeks both moral and religious pardon to exonerate himself.
Before he dies, he reveals that Claudius is responsible for these vile deeds,

"The king, the king's to blame"

Hamlet's main purpose was to rid Denmark of its moral disease. He was grappling with his conscience and even when the ghost goaded him to do it, his conscience got the better of him and he guiltily stalled any action towards it. One example is when Claudius was praying.

Laertes say that he got exactly what he deserves. He asks Hamlet for forgiveness, and he forgives Hamlet.

LAERTES mortally wounded by his own poisoned sword asks HAMLET to

"Exchange forgiveness with me, noble Hamlet.
Mine and my father's death come not upon thee,
Nor thine on me"

HAMLET
Heaven make thee free of it.
I follow thee. —
I am dead, Horatio. —
Wretched queen, adieu! —
You that look pale and tremble at this chance,
That are but mutes or audience to this act,
Had I but time— as this fell sergeant, Death,
Is strict in his arrest – O, I could tell you—
But let it be. — Horatio, I am dead.
Thou livest.
Report me and my cause aright
To the unsatisfied.

HORATIO
Never believe it.
I am more an antique Roman than a Dane.
Here's yet some liquor left.

[***HORATIO*** *lifts the poisoned cup*]

HAMLET
As thou'rt a man,
Give me the cup.
Let go! By heaven, I'll ha't.

[***HAMLET*** *takes the poisoned cup*]

O God, Horatio, what a wounded name,
Things standing thus unknown,
Shall live behind me!
If thou didst ever hold me in thy heart
Absent thee from felicity awhile,
And in this harsh world draw thy breath in pain
To tell my story.

[*Sounds of marching soldiers and a volley of shot*]

What warlike noise is this?

< *Enter* ***OSRIC*** >

Hamlet tells Laertes that God will forgive him. He bids farewell to the queen and to everyone else.

"Heaven make thee free of it"

Now Hamlet has achieved a moral and political certainty to rid Denmark of its disease by killing Claudius. In doing so he will restore Denmark to its former glory. Claudius now stands as the evil poison who corrupted his country. The list of Claudius' crimes is unending incest, murder, regicide etc. and Hamlet feels duty-bound to kill him to free Denmark from the chains of corruption.

In this tragic and climatic finale, Shakespeare created nail-biting tension and suspense as the tragic heroes and the revenge heroes very dramatically and meticulously carved out their ends. It was a race to encapsulate the economic, moral, social, and political norms into their worlds and in the end it all came crashing down. The term revenge tragedy can aptly be ascribed to this play and whether Claudius is a tragic hero is debatable.

Hamlet, however, has managed to achieve his uplifting of morality and religion albeit on the threshold of death, by killing Claudius.
The scene with the gravedigger and Hamlet's conversation was very apt. Hamlet was horrified at the treatment the gravedigger meted out to the skulls. Hamlet was shocked at the way he flung the sculls around with no dignity.

Hamlet 'sees' the skull of a lawyer, of Yorick – the clown and that of Alexander the Great and remarked that irrespective of our status and position in life, we all end up smelly and in the same way as the poor people. In death everyone is equal. This family saga consisted of so many irregularities, some flouting moral and religious rules for example, murder, treachery, incest, adultery and conspiracy and they all fought to the death to achieve it, but Shakespeare shows us that we all end up in the same way in death.

Hamlet dies and asks loyal Horatio to stay alive to tell his tale of woe to his people.

"And in this harsh world draw thy breath in pain
To tell my story"

OSRIC
Young Fortinbras,
With conquest come from Poland,
To th' ambassadors of England gives
This warlike volley.

HAMLET
O, I die, Horatio.
The potent poison quite o'er-crows my spirit.
I cannot live to hear the news from England.
But I do prophesy th' election lights
On Fortinbras.
He has my dying voice.
So tell him, with th' occurrents, more and less,
Which have solicited –
The rest is silence.

[***HAMLET*** *dies*]

HORATIO
Now cracks a noble heart. —
Good night, sweet prince,
And flights of angels sing thee to thy rest! —

< *Enter* ***FORTINBRAS*** *and the English* ***AMBASSADOR****, with drummer and Attendants and SOLDIERS* >

Why does the drum come hither?

FORTINBRAS
Where is this sight?

HORATIO
What is it ye would see?
If aught of woe or wonder,
cease your search.

FORTINBRAS
This quarry cries on havoc.
O proud death,
What feast is toward in thine eternal cell?
That thou so many princes at a shot
So bloodily hast struck?

AMBASSADOR
The sight is dismal,
And our affairs from England come too late.
The ears are senseless that should give us hearing,
To tell him his commandment is fulfilled,
That Rosencrantz and Guildenstern are dead.
Where should we have our thanks?

Osric says that Fortinbras has defeated Poland. Hamlet says that he is dying and he's sure that Fortinbras will win the war.

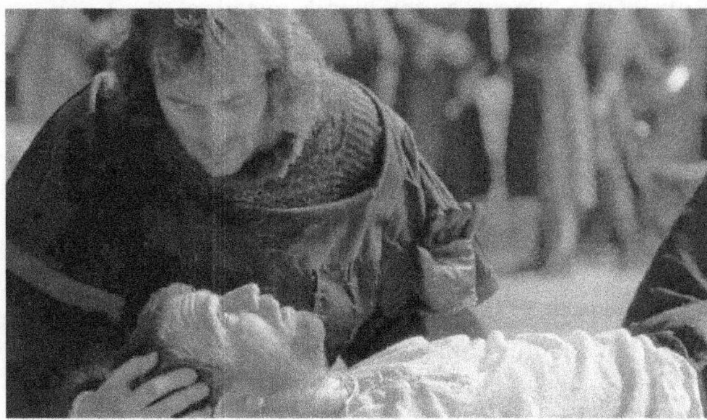

"O, I die Horatio.
The potent poison quite o'er-crows my spirit"

Horatio recites a passionate eulogy which sums up the tragic events leading to the death of the noblest of men,

"Now cracks a noble heart. —
Good night, sweet prince,
And flights of angels sing thee to thy rest! —"

Hamlet has taken revenge for the death of his father King Hamlet but at a terrible cost to himself and those most dear, his mother Gertrude and the woman he loved Ophelia.

Fortinbras is shocked at the carnage,

"This quarry cries on havoc.
O proud death,
What feast is toward in thine eternal cell?
That thou so many princes at a shot"

The Ambassador exclaims,

"The sight is dismal,
And our affairs from England come too late"

"That Rosencrantz and Guildenstern are dead"

The tragedy is at an end. Now only the hero need be saluted – This is I, Hamlet the Dane.

HORATIO
(*points to Claudius*) Not from his mouth,
Had it th' ability of life to thank you.
He never gave commandment for their death.
But since so jump upon this bloody question,
You from the Polack wars, and you from England,
Are here arriv'd,
Give order that these bodies
High on a stage be placed to the view,
And let me speak to th' yet-unknowing world
How these things came about.
So shall you hear
Of carnal, bloody, and unnatural acts,
Of accidental judgments, casual slaughters,
Of deaths put on by cunning and forced cause,And, in this upshot, purposes mistook
Fall'n on th' inventors' heads.
All this can I Truly deliver.
FORTINBRAS
Let us haste to hear it,
And call the noblest to the audience.
For me, with sorrow I embrace my fortune.
I have some rights of memory in this kingdom,
Which now to claim my vantage doth invite me.
HORATIO
Of that I shall have also cause to speak,
And from his mouth whose voice will draw on more.
But let this same be presently perform'd,
Even while men's minds are wild,
Lest more mischance
On plots and errors happen.
FORTINBRAS
Let four captains
Bear Hamlet like a soldier to the stage,
For he was likely, had he been put on,
To have prov'd most royally.
And, for his passage,
The soldiers' music and the rites of war
Speak loudly for him.
Take up the bodies.
Such a sight as this becomes the field,
But here shows much amiss.
Go, bid the soldiers shoot.

< Exeunt, soldiers marching, carrying the bodies, after which a peal of ordnance is shot off >

Horatio explains the machinations of the plot to Fortinbras.

"And let me speak to th' yet-unknowing world
How these things came about.
So shall you hear
Of carnal, bloody, and unnatural acts,
Of accidental judgments, casual slaughters,
Of deaths put on by cunning and forced cause,And, in this upshot, purposes mistook
Fall'n on th' inventors' heads.
All this can I Truly deliver."

Fortinbras is keen to spread the word so that his claim to the Danish throne can be legitimised,

"Let us haste to hear it,
And call the noblest to the audience.
For me, with sorrow I embrace my fortune"

Fortinbras, now soon be King of Denmark, pay tribute to Hamlet the most royal of Danes,

"Bear Hamlet like a soldier to the stage,
For he was likely, had he been put on,
To have prov'd most royally"

Prince Hamlet can now join his father King Hamlet, accompanied by fights of angels singing both to their rest.

Shakespeare has created a tragedy of horrific proportions but quenched by the nobliest of aspirations. Hamlet is the hero who defeated and serves justice on the villain Claudius, but at the cost of his own life and that of his mother Gertrude and his true love Ophelia. What a tragedy!

HAMLET

- He is the principal protagonist and a very complex character.
- Hamlet is drawn into a world of political intrigue, where unscrupulous ambitious relatives manipulate others for their own gain, trampling under foot anyone in their way.
- Hamlet feels betrayed by his mother Gertrude who he accuses of incestuous and immoral behaviour, and swift marriage to his father's brother Claudius.
- As soon as his father's spirit reveals Claudius' treachery, Hamlet changes his persona to one of revenge. To achieve his object, Hamlet creates a persona of madness to give himself time to find out the truth of the matter, not sure if the spirit is honest or not. Although still in love with Ophelia, Hamlet denies it, so should he fail, she will not be implicated.
- Hamlet is an opportunist, so when a troupe of players arrive, he gets them to adapt a play which will reveal Claudius' guilt by observing his reaction.
- The overriding conflict between his religious conscience and his duty to his dead father shapes his character.
- Hamlet is religious and decides not to take revenge when he observes Claudius praying.
- Hamlet is adept at outwitting Claudius and Polonius, but in his anger kills Polonius by mistake. He also foils Claudius' plot to have him executed by the King of England. Instead, using cunning, replacing Claudius' letters with that of his own, but this time ordering instead the execution of fellow students Rosencrantz and Guildenstern.
- His indecisiveness to act makes him feel like a coward but is inspired by Fortinbras' bravery.
- Hamlet is resourceful, convincing pirates to release him on parole, so he can return to Denmark and take revenge on Claudius.
- Hamlet is passionate, leaping into Ophelia's grave to prove his love.
- Hamlet is honourable, fulfilling his oath to his father's spirit.
- Hamlet is a true hero, never thinking about his own safety.
- Finally, he summoned up the courage to act according to his conscience and take revenge on Claudius, the usurper and murderer of his father.
- Young Fortinbras, pays tribute to Hamlet, instructs four captains to bear his body with full military honours, cannons firing, music playing as demanded by the rite of war.

CLAUDIUS

- Claudius is a usurper who murdered his brother Hamlet to gain the throne of Denmark. He is ambitious, covets wealth and power, and will remove any threat that reveals the truth about how he murdered his brother Hamlet to gain the throne.
- Claudius is decisive; ordering his ambassadors Voltemand and Cornelius to Norway to avert an invasion by young Fortinbras who instead, through their actions, diverts it to Poland.
- Claudius is not like Hamlet, he is an antihero, quick to take advantage of an opportunity favourable to himself, not others. He marries Gertrude the wife of the murdered king, to further legitimise his claim to the throne.
- Claudius is manipulative. Saying they will be rewarded; he gets schoolfellows Rosencrantz and Guildenstern to entertain and find out the reasons for Hamlet's sullen mood.
- Claudius is ruthless and makes use of other people's grievances to eliminate opponents. He makes use of Laertes' desire to take revenge for the deaths of his father Polonius and his sister Ophelia, to eliminate in a duel, Hamlet who is now aware of his guilt.
- Claudius is a betrayer. He warned Gertrude not to drink the wine, but did not physically stop her, or tell her why. He deliberately allowed Gertrude to drink, knowing that Laertes would soon mortally wound Hamlet with the poisoned rapier, thus both would die, leaving neither mother nor son alive to contest his actions.
- Claudius is a deceiver, never revealing the truth unless it is to his advantage. He deceived Laertes into taking revenge on Hamlet. Dying, Laertes says Claudius is justly served as he is the instigator of their deaths.
- He flouted the sacred rule laid down in 'The Divine Right of Kings' where in the 1600's kings were seen as being chosen by God to represent him on Earth, so an attack on a king would be a violation against God. Consequently, if his subjects had known, Claudius' murder of his older brother Hamlet to usurp the throne would have been seen as a violation of God's law.
- He is the epitome of villainy, yet he has the ability to keep cool and reason out any situation to suit his purpose. For example, his plots to kill the troublesome Hamlet.

VOLTEMAND AND CORNELIUS

Voltemand and Cornelius are the Danish Ambassadors to Norway, sent by Claudius to deliver diplomatic letters to the King of Norway instructing him to suppress his nephew's ambition to take back lands lost by his father to King Hamlet, and thus avert war. Norway is a vassal state of Denmark, as is England (fictional history). They return with news that the King of Norway has instructed his nephew young Fortinbras instead to attack the Polacks but seeks permission to pass through Denmark to get to Poland.

GERTRUDE

- Gertrude is the obedient queen who fulfils her royal duties but has created controversy by marrying Claudius, the brother of her deceased husband King Hamlet.
- Gertrude is unopinionated, never questioning unless it is to further assist Claudius.
- Gertrude is selfless, always helping those in distress like Ophelia, and her son Hamlet. Yet she becomes Hamlet's target. He continuously accuses her of sexual promiscuity, describing her marital bed as 'rank sweat of an enseam'd bed, Stewed in corruption'.
- She is even seen as 'lustful' by the ghost who accuses her of being 'seemingly virtuous'. Yet she does not defend her actions.
- Despite her knowledge that her hasty marriage to Claudius has caused concern to Hamlet which led to his erratic behaviour, she offered no apology or even justified her actions to ease her son's pain.
- She fits the stereotype of the typical Elizabethan woman of that era who were very docile and had 'no voice'. Hence her few utterances and short speeches because women had to be subservient to men.
- Her forthright command to Polonius to stop playacting shows that she can be assertive when the occasion arises. Even to the very end when she desperately tried to save her son's life by warning him of the poisoned cup of drink. We can assume that she eventually tried to make amends to Hamlet albeit too late. Her show of affection when she wiped his brow is also endearing.
- She is completely in compliance with Claudius' actions, saying 'I shall obey you', and she very readily defends him especially when Laertes returns with rioters, demanding to know where his father Polonius is. She tells Laertes that he is targeting the wrong person for Polonius' death, but not revealing that it is her son who has done the deed. Her loyalty is still to protect Claudius as well as her son.
- In the very pivotal closet scene, we tend to empathise with her because she becomes aware that Claudius had killed her husband. For the first time she feels a sense of guilt and shame. She utters, 'Thou turn'st mine eyes into my very soul, And there I see such black and grained spots'. Even the ghost witnesses her agony and warns Hamlet not to distress her. We can also assume that she, in some ways, redeemed herself to the ghost and unwittingly sought his forgiveness with this reaction.

OSRIC

Osric is a young and absurd courtier sent by Claudius to invite Hamlet to the duel with Laertes, and later to act as referee in the duel between Hamlet and Laertes.

POLONIUS

- Father of Ophelia and Laertes and courtier to King Claudius.
- Polonius is an opportunist, seeking to advance his position and that of his family at court. He sees an opening when his daughter Ophelia is courted by Hamlet. He is a skilled operator but is foiled by Hamlet's plan to take revenge on Claudius for the murder of his father.
- He uses Ophelia as bait but accepts Claudius' conclusions of Hamlet's madness as a ruse, and seeking to provide evidence, is inadvertently killed by Hamlet.
- He schemes a plan for Ophelia and Hamlet to meet in order to detect the reason for Hamlet's insanity, insisting to Claudius and Gertrude that his behaviour stems from rejected love by his daughter Ophelia.
- His character is developed through his interaction with his family, Claudius, Gertrude, and Hamlet.
- He uses his daughter as a pawn, and he manipulates both her mind and her sexuality to carry favour with Claudius and Gertrude. He even controls her emotions forbidding her to welcome any attention from Hamlet.
- We can conclude that Polonius' overbearing attitude towards his children contributed to his and their untimely demise.
- He is headstrong and stubborn, insisting 'I have found the very cause of Hamlet's lunacy'.
- He is the master of his own concoctions, and his self-importance and 'superior knowledge' are the very ingredients that caused his downfall.
- He spies on Hamlet, his son Laertes, and Hamlet and Ophelia together. And ironically, it was that very distorted scheme of his that led to his death when he was unwittingly killed by Hamlet's sword
- His undying loyalty to the deceptive and vile Claudius was the major cause of his downfall. He, just like Claudius was unscrupulous and deceitful in his dealings with Hamlet becoming an enemy, and hamlet belittling him, calling him a 'fishmonger'. He was bent on getting Claudius' approval at any cost. "I assure my good liege I hold my duty as I hold my soul, Both to my God and to my gracious king".

YOUNG FORTINBRAS

Young Fortinbras is a man of action much admired by Hamlet, but with more determination in completing his mission, as shown by defeating the Polacks. He recognises Hamlet's dilemma and the reason for his revenge, and declares that he would have proved to be most royal, but now must claim his rights to the throne of Denmark as no one is left

OPHELIA

- Ophelia is a young inexperienced woman who believes in true love but is betrayed by her first true love Hamlet.
- She is subservient to her father but used by him for political gain.
- She does not understand the real worth even when explained by Hamlet who tries to protect her innocent by telling her virtue is best guarded in a nunnery.
- Ophelia is associated to purity and innocence which she must maintain until married. The constant reference to flowers enhances her beauty and virtue like the purity of nature.
- She appears childlike and naïve, and this led to her becoming the victim of manipulation and greed.
- She is dominated wholly by her father and her brother - body and soul. He even controls her sexuality treating it as a commodity. She is forced by her father to forsake her love for Hamlet which she obediently agrees to, "No, my good lord. But as you did command, I did repel his fetters and denied His access to me".
- She cannot even think for herself and make her own decisions, "I do not know, my Lord, what I should think".
- When her father dies, the impact is too great because she depended on him to survive. Hence leading to her state of insanity and death.
- She also became the target of Hamlet's abuse and she cried in shock that he is mad.
- She had the strength of mind to handle it despite the pressure from her father, brother, and Claudius to be a pawn in their games against Hamlet, to find out why is mad.
- She was bold enough to withstand all the emotional pain because she loved Hamlet but was forced to reject him by her father Polonius.
- She is the sweetest and alluring character in the play and her beauty and innocence intrigues us.

ROSENCRANTZ AND GUILDENSTERN

- Rosencrantz and Guildenstern are schoolfellows of Hamlet and have known each other from a young age.
- Temptation and advancement have interjected, and so ever the opportunists, they work to their advantage not Hamlet's. However, Hamlet is much shrewder, and tricks them to admitting it is Claudius and Gertrude they work for.
- Hamlet writes new letters ordering the execution of Rosencrantz and Guildenstern on their arrival in England, thus thwarting Claudius' plan to do the same to him. He authenticates the letters by use of his signet ring.
- Hamlet dies before the English ambassadors arrive to confirm their execution.

LAERTES

- Laertes is brother of Ophelia, older and wiser. He is the male heir, widely travelled, and is expected to uphold the family honour. The murder of his father Polonius demanded he take revenge.
- Laertes and Hamlet are on the same mission – to seek revenge. Shakespeare has carefully created a structure and dynamic with them.
- We can juxtapose the way in which they differ in status, at opposite ends of the spectrum in society, and the manner in which they sought revenge - Hamlet in a more subdued, calm fashion as opposed to Laertes' boisterous, threatening manner.
- Hamlet grapples with his moral and religious conscience whereas Laertes stated that he was unconcerned about these issues and was bent on seeking immediate revenge. His behaviour is completely opposite to Hamlet's because he is impulsive and erratic.
- His action is swift when he learns about his father's death. He raises hell, demanding justice, and revenge. He gathers a crowd of followers and invades Elsinore castle, threatening to kill the culprit who killed his father. He was pacified by Claudius because he is more action than reasoning. His impulsiveness contributed to his death because during his fit of passion he was manipulated by Claudius, and he became a pawn in his deadly game to kill Hamlet.
- Laertes is used as a foil to Hamlet because Shakespeare gave them the same problem but they both reacted completely differently to seek revenge. Sadly, both paid dearly with their lives in the end.

HORATIO

- Unlike Rosencrantz and Guildenstern, Horatio remains faithful and loyal to Hamlet right to the very end.
- Hamlet trusted him wholly and said that although Horatio did not have money, he was the most admirable, and Hamlet trusted him with his secrets like his experience on the ship when Claudius plotted to kill him and the appearance of the ghost.
- When the ghost arrives, Horatio is worried about Hamlet's safety and warns that "What if it tempts you toward the flood, my lord, or to the dreadful summit of the cliff".
- Horatio also promises Hamlet that he will keep the appearance of the ghost a secret.
- He even agrees to Hamlet's request to observe Claudius' reaction to the play.
- He also tries to dissuade Hamlet from participating in the forthcoming duel with Laertes, fearing that it was a excuse to kill Hamlet by foul means.
- In the end he is heartbroken at Hamlet's death, and he promises to tell Hamlet's story.
- He concludes very emotionally, "Now cracks a noble heart. Good night, sweet prince, and flights of angels sing thee to thy rest".

THE GHOST

- The Ghost claims to be the spirit of Hamlet's father King Hamlet and sets Hamlet on a quest to avenge his father's foul and most unnatural murder. The perpetrator, the younger brother Claudius who poured poison into his older brother's ear as he lay sleeping in the orchard. The motive may have been his incestuous relationship with queen Gertrude who he married shortly after the funeral of his brother Hamlet, or his ambition to become king and wield power and gain wealth. The Ghost claims his revenge is based on both: his ambition for kingship, and his corruption of virtue by incestuous means. But strangely, once avenged, this would permit him to exit from purgatory and enter heaven. The case of two wrong don't make a right, seems to be absence.
- Early on, Hamlet is not convinced that the ghost is genuine, but when he devises a plan to prove it one way or the other, he finds the ghost spoke the truth. Claudius suddenly exited from the revised play when the Player Lucianus poured poison into the Player King's ear, just as Claudius did to King Hamlet in real life.
- In contrast to Horatio, Marcellus, Barnardo, and Francisco, who could see but not hear the ghost, Gertrude could neither see nor hear it, and remarks Alas he's mad. Hamlet could both see and hear the ghost. Hamlet is the only one who has ever spoken to it.

SUPERNATURAL

Shakespeare uses the supernatural in the form of a ghost, to catalyse the plot. People in Shakespeare's time believed in superstition. Religion did not explain unnatural events except to assign them as an act of God or the work of the devil. For those found in league with the devil, punishment took the form of torture, ducting stools, pillory, or burning at the stake. The ghost is the catalyst that sets Hamlet on the road to avenge its murder.

- Although Hamlet is stunned by the Ghost's resemblance to his father in Act 1 scene 4, it is not until Act 1 scene 5, the Ghost declares itself as Hamlet's father's spirit.
- The Ghost demands that Hamlet, "Revenge his foul and most unnatural murder", accusing his younger brother Claudius, Hamlet's uncle, of usurping the crown by murder, motivated by lust for power and lust for Queen Gertrude whom he married in haste two months after the murdered king's death.
- The Ghost in its monologue provides Hamlet with powerful motivation to take revenge on his uncle Claudius, the usurper of his father's crown, and seducer of Queen Gertrude his mother.
- Hamlet is convinced of the Ghost's truthfulness, declaring to Horatio in Act 1 scene 5, "It is an honest ghost". However, by Act 2 scene 2, Hamlet in a soliloquy, expresses doubt as to the Ghost's true intent, "May be a devil, and the devil hath power t' assume a pleasing shape".
- In Act 3 scene 2, the Ghost is vindicated as Hamlet observes Claudius' guilt when he suddenly stops the play on seeing the poison poured into the Player King's ear. Hamlet declares, "O good Horatio, I'll take the ghost's word for a thousand pound".
- In Act 3 scene 4, in the Ghost's last visitation, it rebukes Hamlet for his tirade against his mother Gertrude, revealing a humanised trait to its character.
- Shakespeare uses the character of the Ghost as an instrument to [1] instigate revenge against the vile Claudius [2] use Hamlet as the tool for revenge [3] moderate Hamlet's tirade against his mother Queen Gertrude.
- Hamlet's quest is initially driven by the ghost and heaven, as revealed in Act 3 scene 4, when Hamlet tells Gertrude, "That I must be their scourge and minister". However, by Act 5 scene 1, his quest had changed to one of grief, as he declares his love for Ophelia.

The ghost is a powerful image used by Shakespeare to mirror human flaws: temptation, revenge, and inconsistency. In Act 1 scene 5, the Ghost tells Hamlet not to be tempted by deceit perpetrated by Claudius,

> "But virtue, s it never will be mov'd
> Though lewdness court it in a shape of heaven"

REVENGE

The main theme of Shakespeare's Hamlet is Revenge and how it plays out. Based on honour and religion, revenge is pursued by Hamlet for his father's murder, and by Laertes for his sister's madness and subsequent death. The instigator of revenge is the ghost who demands of Hamlet, in Act 1 scene 5, "Revenge his foul and most unnatural murder".

- The object of this revenge is Hamlet's uncle Claudius, who the Ghost vilifies. In Act 1 scene 5, the Ghost tells Hamlet, "The serpent that did sting thy father's life, now wears his crown".
- The Ghost further seeks revenge for the incestuous marriage of its wife Gertrude to its brother Claudius, "So to seduce! – won to his shameful, the will of my most seeming-virtuous queen".
- Hamlet is at first determined to pursue his mission to avenge his father's murder by stealth in the form of feigning madness, but then doubts the truth as told by the ghost, Act 2 scene 2, "The spirit that I have seen may be a devil hath power".
- Later in Act2 scene 2, Hamlet, in his soliloquy, intends to resolve this doubt by observing the reaction of Claudius to a play with modification, "The play's the thing wherein I'll catch the conscience of the king".
- In Act 3 scene 3, Gertrude summons Hamlet to her chamber to discover his motives behind the play. On route, Hamlet passes Claudius kneeling in prayer but decides not to take revenge, fearing that he would contravene the laws of heaven, making Claudius a martyr instead, "Am I then reveng'd to take him in the purging of his soul".
- In Gertrude's chamber, Hamlet kills Polonius by stabbing through an arras, thinking it is Claudius. Hamlet regrets Polonius' death but feels he is a tool of heaven, "I do repent: but heaven hath pleas'd it so".
- In Act 4 scene 4, on the road to England, having learnt of Prince Fortinbras dedication to his task, Hamlet in his soliloquy, questions his own inactivity in not completing his mission of revenge, "How all occasions do inform against me, and spur my dull revenge".
- In Act 5 scene 2, Hamlet tells Horatio how he had taken revenge on his traitorous schoolfellows Rosencrantz and Guildenstern by writing theirs names instead of his, in letters from Claudius to the King of England, demanding the immediate execution by decapitation, justifying his actions, "Why, man, they did make love to this employment".
- Unknown to Hamlet, in Act 4 scene 7, Claudius on learning of Hamlets return, and determined to remove him permanently after the failure to have him executed by the King of England, schemes with Laertes to kill him in a duel of honour.
- In Act 5 scene 2, the tragic consequence is that Hamlet is revenged, mortally wounding Claudius with Laertes' poisoned rapier, and then forcing Claudius to drink from the poisoned cup in revenge for the poisoning of Gertrude.
- Hamlet did not want to take revenge on Laertes, but Laertes struck him with an unbated rapier tipped with poison, without warning, causing Hamlet to take Laertes' rapier and do the same to him.

- Shakespeare creates a melee of revenge and unintentional killing in the final scene.

Revenge is bittersweet. Hamlet fulfils the oath made to the Ghost but suffers his own death and that of Gertrude his mother, and Ophelia his beloved.

Similar for Laertes, revenge is bittersweet. Laertes fulfils his revenge for Hamlet's killing of Polonius his father, and dishonouring Ophelia his sister, but asks Hamlet's forgiveness just before he dies, realising it is Claudius who is at fault,

> "Exchange forgiveness with me, noble Hamlet
> Mine and my father's death come not upon thee,
> Nor thine on me"

MADNESS

The theme of Madness is a ploy used by Shakespeare to make the character of Hamlet survivable, otherwise in reality Claudius would have had to charge Hamlet with treason early-on in the play. Shakespeare also makes use of madness to justify the demise of Ophelia, and the revenge of Laertes towards Hamlet.

- Act 1 scene 5, Hamlet makes plain to Horatio and Marcellus his intent to feign madness, "hereafter shall think meet to put an antic disposition on _" but warns Horatio and Marcellus to never speak or acknowledge any dealings with him, "at such time seeing me, never shall, that you know aught of me – this do swear".
- Act 2 scene 2, Claudius having sent for Rosencrantz and Guildenstern, seeks their opinion on Hamlet's transformation, and elicit their services in determining the truth of Hamlet's madness.
- Ophelia tells her father Polonius about Hamlet's wild behaviour indicative of madness. Polonius is keen to make Claudius aware of Hamlet's love for Ophelia.
- Polonius, the king's advisor, is not so sure, convinced that his daughter Ophelia is the cause of Hamlet's madness, as proved by a love *letter* written by Hamlet to Ophelia. Polonius is keen to prove his theory, so proposes that he and Claudius should hide behind an arras then listen to the conservation between Hamlet and Ophelia, "Be you and I behind an arras then, mark the encounter. If he love her not".
- Enter Hamlet, reading a book, Polonius seizes the opportunity to walk and talks with him, but elicits no true reason to Hamlet's madness. Hamlet recognises Polonius' intent to determine the cause of his madness, and remarks, "These tedious old fools".
- Enter Rosencrantz and Guildenstern to try to elicit the nature of Hamlet's madness, but he gets them to confess to their duplicity by asking, "Were you not sent for?".

- Hamlet now knows that Claudius is still unsure about Hamlet's state of mind, and so he must continue the pretence for survival. The players arrive, and Hamlet hatches a plot to expose Claudius' guilt, getting the players to perform *'The Murder of Gonzago'* with additions to make Claudius reveal his guilt.
- At the start of Act 3 scene 1, Rosencrantz and Guildenstern can offer Claudius and Gertrude no definitive answer as to Hamlet's madness, but he did show a kind of joy to the recently arrived players, ordering them to perform in front of their majesties tonight.
- Still determined to resolve the true nature of Hamlet's madness, Claudius arranges for Polonius and himself to overhear a brief encounter between Hamlet and Ophelia. Hamlet enters completes his soliloquy on life, love, death, and indecision (To be or Not to be etc). Even to Ophelia, Hamlet's strategy is one of madness: denying he gave any remembrances; questioning her honesty; declaring he did love her once, but not now; directing her to a nunnery to avoid marriage and the sin of childbirth, else marry a fool who would not consider her a monster as a wise man would do. Ophelia is shocked, and remark, "Heavenly powers, restore him".
- Hamlet rants how a woman glamourises herself to entice man and plead ignorance, driving man mad, "and make your wantonness your ignorance. Go to, I'll no more on't, it hath made me mad". Hamlet continues his rant, "I say we will have no more marriage. Those that are married already – all but one – shall live". The phrase '- all but one -' alludes to the forthcoming revenge killing of Claudius, thus freeing Gertrude from marriage.
- Claudius tells Polonius he is not convinced by what he has heard, "Love? His affections do not that way tend". Polonius responds by telling Claudius, that Hamlet's grief sprung from neglected love, and recommends Hamlet be send to England or be confined somewhere. Claudius remarks, "Madness in great ones must be not unwatch'd go".
- In Act 3 scene 2, just before the play starts, Claudius asks Hamlet how he fares but receives a cryptic response, "Excellent, I'faith, of the chameleon's dish. I eat the air, promise-crammed. You cannot feed capons so". Claudius is baffled, but Hamlet is implying he is like a chameleon eating at Claudius' empty promises that would not even feed a capon (castrated chicken). Hamlet jests in a nonsensical way with Ophelia to keep up the pretence of madness.
- Polonius informs Claudius of Hamlet's compliance to visit his mother, and confirms he will hide behind the arras, to assess Hamlet's intent. Hamlet's madness causes Claudius to resort to prayer, seeking forgiveness for his sin of murder.
- In Act 3 scene 4, Gertrude is so frightened by Hamlet's behaviour she thinks he is mad and remarks, "Thou wilt not murder me?". She now knows the true reason for Hamlet's madness, hatred of her marriage to Claudius. In his rage, Hamlet stabs through the arras, killing Polonius, but he justifies it as, "I do repent; but heaven hath pleas'd it so".

- The murder of Polonius triggers the madness of Ophelia, the daughter of Polonius, and makes Laertes, the son of Polonius, intent on revenge.
- In Act 4 scene 1, when asked about Hamlet, Gertrude tells Claudius, "Mad as the sea and wind when both contend".
- In Act 4 scene 2, Hamlet continues his act of madness when questioned by Rosencrantz, not revealing where he has hidden the body of Polonius.
- In Act 4 scene 3, Hamlet continues his act of madness when questioned by Claudius, but eventually revealing, in a cryptic message, where to find the body. Claudius decides madness or not, Hamlet is too dangerous to be allowed to live, and therefore is to be sent to England with his schoolfellows Rosencrantz and Guildenstern. Unbeknown to Hamlet, his schoolfellows have letters to order his execution on arrival in England.
- In Act 4 scene 5, Ophelia wanders aimlessly, showing madness in her actions. A gentleman tells Gertrude, she "speaks thinks in doubt that carry but half sense. Her speech is nothing". Enter Ophelia who replies to Gertrude in cryptic words and song focused on grief. Claudius asks Horatio to, "Follow her close; give her good watch, I pray you". Later, Laertes bursts into the council chamber demanding to know where his father Polonius is, only to be told he is dead but not by Claudius' hand. Laertes is shocked when Ophelia appears and remarks, "A document in madness: thoughts and remembrance fitted". Laertes is intent of revenge not just for the death of his father but the madness of his sister.

The theme of madness is in two forms: that contrived by Hamlet to survive and achieve revenge; and that due to natural grief experienced by Ophelia at the loss of her father Polonius and loss of love by Hamlet.

POLITICS

The theme of Politics is the undercurrent that creates the main theme of revenge and used by Shakespeare to justify the reality of the play where opportunists like Claudius usurp to achieve their political ambitions. Polonius is also an opportunist, scheming to advance his position with the King and that of his family, with opportunities like the engagement of his daughter Ophelia to the next in line to the throne Prince Hamlet.

In the play, (**note:** this is Shakespeare's own fictional history) Denmark has achieved her ambition of making Norway and England vassal states, and now it is a question of internal strife. Who rules? In Denmark, it is King Claudius who succeeded his brother King Hamlet by dubious means, hence Hamlet's quest for revenge.

It was the late King Hamlet who slew King Fortinbras of Norway. There is tension as Denmark fears that the dead king's son Prince Fortinbras might invade. To the East, Norway is against Poland, and may invade. To the West, Paris in France and Wittenberg in Germany are places where Danish student are schooled. Elsinore is a royal castle on the bleak east coast of Denmark.

- In Act 1 scene 1, Marcellus is keen to know why Denmark is casting brazen cannon, importing implements of war, and building ships even on a Sunday. Horatio explains to repel any incursion by young Prince Fortinbras to secure food, "For food and diet to some enterprise", and reclaim land lost by his father King Fortinbras who was defeated by the now deceased King Hamlet.
- At the start of **Act 1 scene 2**, Claudius in a monologue to the Danish court, prologues the course of events which legitimises his reign, and in verbal irony, and political necessity to gain support for future action against young Fortinbras who now tries to reclaim land lost by this father, and gained by King Hamlet.
- Claudius instructs Cornelius and Voltemand, his Ambassadors to Norway, to deliver a letter to Old Norway, brother of King Norway who Hamlet's father slew in battle, and uncle to young Fortinbras.
- Claudius is politically astute, granting permission for Polonius' son, Laertes, to return to Paris in France to continue his schooling, but not Hamlet to his schooling in Wittenberg in Germany. Gertrude his mother and Claudius his uncle, have noticed Hamlet still mourns his father two months on passing.
- Claudius tells Hamlet of his political importance, "You are the most immediate to our throne". Hamlet had no choice but to accept their decision to stay in Denmark.
- In Act 1 scene 3, Polonius reveals his political astuteness when he tells his son Laertes, "Give every man thy ear, but few thy voice". And then when speaking about Hamlet's love, warns his daughter Ophelia, "Do not believe his vows; for they are brokers".
- In Act 1 scene 4, even the supernatural can cause political comment. Marcellus remarks to Horatio, "Something is rotten in the state of Denmark".
- In Act 2 scene 1 & scene 2, Polonius uses internal politics to help advance his position by using Hamlet affections for his daughter Ophelia as a lever.
- In Act 4 scene 5, Laertes (seditious political intrigue) storms into the council chamber with his rebel band shouting, "Laertes shall be king, Laertes king". Claudius agrees to accept Laertes' demands the punishment and burial of the assailant
- At the end of **Act 5 scene 2**, young Fortinbras (international political intrigue) arrives with his army having subdued the Polacks, to find the Danish royal family decimated, and himself proclaimed the new king of Denmark.

Shakespeare creates a political dichotomy. Old Hamlet is an idealist whereas his brother Claudius is a pragmatist who resorts to regicide to secure the highest prize in the kingdom.

There are only two women in Hamlet: Gertrude the wife of Claudius the king and Ophelia, the daughter of Polonius, advisor to the King. Shakespeare creates different roles for each. Gertrude is supportive of Claudius and unopinionated. Ophelia is different, much younger, not married, nor acquainted with royal protocol, and emotionally immature.

- In Act 1 scene 2, where Claudius asks Hamlet, "how it is that clouds still hang on him", to which he replies, "not so, I am too much in the sun". Gertrude acts as a mediator, "Good Hamlet, cast thy nighted colour off, and let thine eye look like a friend on Denmark"
- Gertrude shows her motherly qualities, "Let not thy mother lose her prayers, Hamlet".
- In Act 2 scene 2, Gertrude, in support of her husband Claudius, tells Rosencrantz and Guildenstern, "Your visitation shall receive such thanks".
- In Act 2 scene 2, in a **ground-breaking**, watershed moment very early on in the play, in response to Claudius claim that Polonius had found the cause of Hamlet's lunacy. Gertrude exhibiting a women's intuition, reveals the true reason, "His father's death and our o'er-hasty marriage".
- In Act 3 scene 1, on meeting Ophelia, Gertrude shows her affinity with other women, wishing her success in returning Hamlet to his previous way of life, "Of Hamlet's wildness; so shall I hope your virtues, will bring him to his wonted way again".
- In Act 3 scene 2, in a motherly, protective role, Gertrude invites Hamlet to sit by her to watch the play, "Come hither, my dear Hamlet, sit by me". But instead, he lays at Ophelia's feet, still acting in an odd manner. Hamlet is distancing himself from his mother, to be in a better position to view Claudius and Gertrude's reaction to the murder scene where the poisoner pours poison into the player king's ear.
- Hamlet asks Gertrude how she likes the *dumb-show*. Gertrude replies in an indignant fashion, "The lady doth protest too much, methinks", referring to the player Queen.
- In Act 3 scene 4, Gertrude is waiting for Hamlet to arrive at her chambers to convey the king's displeasure at the play. As agreed with Claudius and Gertrude, Polonius hides behind the arras, to make sense of Hamlet's state of mind. Gertrude accuses Hamlet of an idle tongue; he accuses her of a wicked tongue. Gertrude is shocked when Hamlet then tells her that she is the queen, her husband's brother's wife, and would it was not so, she is his mother. Gertrude's thoughts on Hamlet's madness are confirmed – his hatred for her marriage to Claudius.
- Next, Hamlet orders her to sit and not move. Feeling threatened, Gertrude asks, "What wilt thou do? Thou wilt not murder me? Help, Ho!". In response Polonius exclaims 'What ho! Help!', causing Hamlet to thrust his rapier through the arras at the unknown voice, in the hope it is Claudius the king, only to find he has killed Polonius the father of Ophelia the girl he had a crush on. Gertrude declares Hamlet mad.

- Hamlet admits he wished it had been Claudius he killed and proceeds to rant about the merits of his father, Gertrude's previous husband, to that of his brother Claudius; and the immoral actions of Gertrude in marrying Claudius just two months since his brother's death. Gertrude pleads to Hamlet, "O speak to me no more, these words like daggers enter in my ear". Not until the Ghost appears, who is invisible to Gertrude, reminding Hamlet that his anger should be vented on Claudius not his former queen, does Hamlet relent. To placate Hamlet, Gertrude asks him what she should do. **Hamlet forbids her to enter the king's bed just in case she reveals his fake madness which she now knows**. Finally, Hamlet tells Gertrude he does not trust Rosencrantz and Guildenstern and intends to turn their plot against them.
- In Act 4 scene 1, Gertrude does not tell Claudius about **Hamlet's fake madness**, but instead claims, "Mad as the sea and wind when both contend which is the mightier".
- In Act 4 scene 5, Gertrude is informed of Ophelia's distress over the death of her father Polonius. Gertrude, is the only witness to the killing, offers sympathy to Ophelia. Gertrude defends Claudius from Laertes' wrath by telling him, "But not by him".
- At the end of Act 4 scene 7, Gertrude tells Claudius and Laertes the sad death of Ophelia by drowning while sitting on a branch of a willow tree which broke, thrusting her in a weeping brook, where her garments heavy with water dragged her under to her death
- In Act 5 scene 1, scattering flowers onto Ophelia's open coffin, Gertrude says a sorrowful farewell, "Sweets to the sweet. Farewell. I hop'd thou shouldst have been my Hamlet's wife".
- In Act 5 scene 2, in the duel, Hamlet scores a second hit against Laertes. To celebrate Gertrude picks up the cup, unaware it is poisoned. Claudius, realising the danger, tells her not to drink. Gertrude replies she will, and drinks before offering the cup to her son Hamlet who refuses, wishing to stay focused on the next bout. In the third bout, Gertrude collapses cries out, "O my dear Hamlet! The drink, the drink! I am poison'd".

Shakespeare creates tension between Gertrude and Hamlet - mother and son. Hamlet is convinced that Gertrude married Claudius to legitimise their incestuous relationship. The counterpoint is Hamlet's love for Ophelia.

Gertrude is dutiful and supportive to Claudius even revealing the true reason for Hamlet's madness in Act 2 scene 2, - her hasty re-marriage so soon after Hamlet's father's death, and not Polonius' idea of feverish love for his daughter Ophelia. Claudius remains unsure, but after the killing of Polonius and Hamlet's verbal rage against her, in Act 3 scene 4, Gertrude better understands her son and his quest for revenge. In Act 4 scene 1, Gertrude fails to reveal to Claudius her son's intent, describing him as 'Mad as the sea and wind when both contend which is the mightier'. Gertrude's last gasp, at the end of Act 5 scene 2, is to warn her son Hamlet not to drink the poisoned wine, thus alerting Hamlet to her husband's treachery. Hamlet takes his revenge by wounding Claudius with the poisoned tipped rapier and forcing the dying Claudius to drink from the poisoned cup.

Ophelia is a tool used by her father Polonius to advance his and his family's position in court. Unfortunately, Hamlet although in love with Ophelia defers his courtship to pursue his clandestine mission of revenge. Unfortunately, this meant faking madness which leads to dire consequences. Polonius uses Hamlet's madness to make out that the madness is caused by infatuated love. Ophelia is confused and cannot understand why Hamlet denies his love letters. She feels rejected. The death of her father in Act 3 scene 4, causes such grief, that she becomes inward bound, induces madness inside. Eventually, in Act 4 scene 7, news reaches Gertrude of her tragic death. Whether she decided not to survive or was not in her power is unknown.

- In Act 1 scene 3, Ophelia makes her entrance, and receives some brotherly advice. Laertes tells her, perhaps Hamlet love you now, but his high status may dictate otherwise, therefore she must keep her virtue. Ophelia thanks him for good advice but reminds him not to be a pastor who preachers but does not put into practice.
- Next, her father Polonius arrives and tells her he has been told and cautioned about her many liaisons with Hamlet and wishes to know the truth! Ophelia replies, "He hath, my lord, of late made many tenders of his affection to me".
- Polonius is dismissive and exclaims she speaks like a green girl and asks if she believes Hamlet's declarations (tenders). Ophelia is submissive and replies, "I do not know, my lord, what I should think". Polonius tells her she is foolish as a baby to take Hamlet's declarations as true and in effect declared her father a fool. Ophelia retorts, "My lord, he hath importun'd me with love in honourable fashion". Polonius objects at the word fashion, but Ophelia determined to show Hamlet's worth, replies, "And hath given countenance to his speech, my lord, with almost all the holy vows of heaven". Polonius concludes by telling Ophelia that despite promises, young men easily fall out of love, and she should spend less time with Hamlet. In deference, Ophelia agrees to obey.
- In Act 2 scene 1, Polonius asks Ophelia what's the matter, to be told by her that while sewing in her closet Hamlet had enter her room in a dishevelled state, grabbed her wrist, stood back at arm's length, waving his head up and down three times, sighing piteously and profoundly, then let me go keeping his eyes on me the whole time as he left. Polonius replies, "Come, go with me, I will go seek the king. This is the very ecstasy of love". Polonius asks Ophelia if she had used hard words towards Hamlet that may have provoked his action. Ophelia replies, "I did repel his letters and denied His access to me".
- In Act 3 scene 1, Ophelia is instructed by Polonius with the king and queen's approval, to walk alone and read a prayer book. Hamlet enters having just finished his soliloquy on 'To be or not to be'. They exchange greetings, but when Ophelia tries return his mementos (remembrances), Hamlet denies they are his. Ophelia protests he did. Hamlet then questions her honesty and fairness and claims her honesty should not be dictated by her beauty. Ophelia replies, "Could beauty, my lord, have better commerce than with honesty". Hamlet retorts that beauty will sooner transform honesty into ill-repute than honesty into beauty, and therefore he loved her once.

- Next, Ophelia replies, "Indeed, my lord, you made me believe so". Hamlet tells her that there is no virtue in his stock, therefore he never loved her, but used her. Ophelia indignant, exclaims, "I was the more deceived". Hamlet berates womanhood and marriage, reiterating that Ophelia should get herself to a nunnery. Ophelia, in a soliloquy, laments Hamlet's affliction, "O, what a noble mind is here o'erthrown!".
- In Act 3 scene 2, Ophelia enters accompanied by Claudius, Gertrude and others to attend the play, unknown to them, modified by Hamlet, on the '*Murder of Gonzago*'. Gertrude asks Hamlet to come hither and sit by her, but he turns to Ophelia and lies down at her feet, frolics with her, but she maintains her virtue. She asks him about the play, and he replies, mischief. He responds to all her questions in a sensible manner, and just before the Player Lucianus enters on stage, he answers Ophelia's final question to him by saying, "the croaking raven doth bellow for revenge".
- In Act 4 scene 5, Ophelia enters asking where the beauteous Majesty of Denmark is. Gertrude who has been told by the Gentleman that she is distressed over her father's death, says 'How now, Ophelia'. Ophelia breaks into *song*

Essentially, Ophelia is saying to Gertrude her previous virtuous husband King Hamlet is dead and gone as is my father Polonius. Essentially, both murdered by villians.

Ophelia tells Gertrude to pay attention once again, and again breaks into *song*.

Essentially, Ophelia is saying to Gertrude her previous virtuous (white shroud and white snow) husband King Hamlet she did not properly mourn but instead married his brother. Essentially, she is not virtuous like her previous husband.

Neither Gertrude nor Claudius who has just arrived, comprehend Ophelia's true meaning.

Claudius asks Ophelia about her well-being. She replies by allegory of a baker's daughter turned into an owl for providing short measure; by declaring that God will decide our fate.
Ophelia does not want to talk about her father Polonius but breaks into *song*.

Essentially, Ophelia is saying to Gertrude and Claudius she is trapped in a patriarchal society where women are expected to obey father and brother or men of high rank, in all matters, and are discarded in love. Essentially, Hamlet discarded her.

Ophelia is saying to Gertrude and Claudius that like Hamlet, men take the sexual favours from women, promising marriage but then renege. Essentially, Hamlet promised marriage to Ophelia but then reneged. Ophelia exits leaving all saddened by her state of mind.

Shakespeare in writing Hamlet centres the story around four men (Claudius, Polonius, Laertes, Hamlet) and two women (Gertrude and Ophelia). Whereas Claudius and Polonius are motivated by ambition, Hamlet and Laertes are not. Gertrude and Ophelia are pawns in a chess game. They have no say or control over events except to suffer the consequences of living in a patriarchal society.

In contrast, Gertrude is viewed by Hamlet as an unworthy mother with moral issues, re-marrying too soon after her first husband's death, not realising that the person she married, King Hamlet's brother Claudius, was his murderer. Her action is pragmatic, to secure a future for herself and her son Hamlet. Although, Hamlet fails to understand this. Gertrude's last action before she dies is to warn Hamlet that the cup is poisoned, but it is too late because she does not realise that her son is already mortally wounded by Laertes' poisoned tipped rapier.

In contrast, Ophelia is viewed by Hamlet as a love interest who like him is young but below his station in life. She is overawed and truly believes Hamlet desires to marry her, having spent much time with him and received many gifts from him. Ophelia is cautioned by her father Polonius not to expect marriage, as young men of rank like Hamlet frequently fall in and out of love and are obligated to marry those chosen for them. Instead, Polonius uses Ophelia as a political tool to advance his position at court. The death of her father Polonius by Hamlet the man she loves, causes her much distress and bewilderment. In response, she walks in a trance singing cryptic verse, handing out flowers, and demure salutations. All agree, she has lost her mind, but perhaps in reality she has rejected the world around her and is at a loss as to what to do. Gertrude announces Ophelia's tragic end by drowning.

It maybe that Hamlet, knowing what he must do to avenge his father's death, sought to protect Ophelia, by not having her implicated. She would have seen through his charade of madness and might have disclosed all. At her funeral, he expressed much grief, jumping into her open grave and struggling with her brother Laertes, and declaring his love for Ophelia to the funeral cartage, Act 5 scene 1,

> "I lov'd Ophelia. Forty thousand brothers
> Could not with all their quantity of love
> Make up my sum. What wilt thou do for her?"

Both women are essential to the plot: Gertrude representing women in society with power and influence in their lives and Ophelia representing those without such opportunities – however, all subservient to men. Without the two women, the machinations required to make the plot work in an entertaining and realistic way would not exist. The Elizabethan's made it one of their most popular plays because of this.

EXAM STYLE QUESTIONS

QUESTION 1: HAMLET – ESSAY QUESTION

Gertrude and Ophelia's passivity makes them vulnerable to exploitation and manipulation.

Critically discuss the extent to which you agree with the above statement.

Your response should take the form of a well-constructed essay of 400–450 words
(2–2½ pages). **[25 Marks]**

QUESTION 2: HAMLET – CONTEXTUAL QUESTION

Read the extracts below (Act 2 scene 2) and then answer the questions that follow.

GUILDENSTERN
But we both obey, And here give up ourselves in the full bent, To lay our service freely at your feet To be commanded.
CLAUDIUS
Thanks Rosencrantz, and gentle Guildenstern.
GERTRUDE
Thanks Guildenstern, and gentle Rosencrantz, And I beseech you instantly to visit My too much changéd son. Go some of you And bring these gentlemen where Hamlet is.
GUILDENSTERN
Heavens make our presence and our practices Pleasant and helpful to him!
GERTRUDE
Ay, amen!

Rosencrantz and Guildenstern off. Enter Polonius. He speaks apart with the king.

POLONIUS
The ambassadors from Norway, my good lord, Are joyfully returned.
CLAUDIUS
Thou still hast been the father of good news.
POLONIUS
Have I, my lord? Assure you, my good liege, I hold my duty as I hold my soul,
Both to my God and to my gracious king, And I do think, or else this brain of mine Hunts not the trail of policy so sure As it hath used to do, that I have found The very cause of Hamlet's lunacy.
CLAUDIUS
O speak of that! That do I long to hear.
POLONIUS
Give first admittance to th'ambassadors. My news shall be the fruit to that great feast.

CLAUDIUS
Thyself do grace to them, and bring them in.

Polonius off

He tells me, my dear Gertrude, he hath found The head and source of all your son's distemper.

● ● ●

[Re-enter Polonius]

POLONIUS
You know sometimes he walks four hours together Here in the lobby.
GERTRUDE
So he does, indeed.
POLONIUS
At such a time I'll loose my daughter to him. Be you and I behind an arras then. Mark the encounter.

Q2.1 Refer to lines 1–4: 'But we both ...To be commanded.' Explain what has prompted Claudius and Gertrude to send for Rosencrantz and Guildenstern. **[3 Marks]**
Q2.2 Refer to line 8: 'My too much changéd son.' Account for the change that has come upon Hamlet. **[3 Marks]**
Q2.3 Refer to lines 18–20: 'Assure you, ... my gracious king'. Discuss how this statement is typical of Polonius's character. **[3 Marks]**
Q2.4 Refer to line 36: 'At such a time I'll loose my daughter to him.' Based on your knowledge of the play as a whole, comment on the role Ophelia plays in influencing Hamlet's attitude toward women. **[3 Marks]**
Q2.5 Refer to lines 10–11: 'Heavens make our ... helpful to him!' Comment on the irony of Guildenstern's words in the above lines. **[3 Marks]**

QUESTION 3: HAMLET – CONTEXTUAL QUESTION

Read the extracts below (Act 3 scene 3) and then answer the questions that follow.

CLAUDIUS
O, my offence is rank, it smells to heaven; It hath the primal eldest curse upon't, A brother's murder! Pray can I not, Though inclination be as sharp as will. My stronger guilt defeats my strong intent.

● ● ●

Enter Hamlet and pauses, seeing the King

HAMLET (Approaches the entry to the lobby)
Now might I do it pat, now he is a-praying – And now I'll do't (He draws his sword) and so he goes to heaven, And so am I revenged. That would be scanned. A villain kills my father, and for that I his sole son do this same villain send To heaven. Why, this is bait and salary, not revenge. He took my father grossly, full of bread, With all his crimes broad blown, as flush as May, And how his audit stands who knows save heaven? But in our circumstance and course of thought, 'Tis heavy with him. And am I then revenged To take him in the purging of his soul, When he is fit and seasoned for his passage? No.

He sheathes his sword

Up, sword, and know thou a more horrid hent, When he is drunk asleep, or in his rage, Or in th'incestuous pleasure of his bed, At game, a-swearing, or about some act That has no relish of salvation in't, Then trip him that his heels may kick at heaven, And that his soul may be as damned and black As hell whereto it goes. My mother stays. This physic but prolongs thy sickly days.

Off

CLAUDIUS (Rises)
My words fly up, my thoughts remain below. Words without thoughts never to heaven go.

Q3.1 Refer to line 3: 'Pray can I not'. Account for Claudius's inability to pray for forgiveness. **[3 Marks]**
Q3.2 Refer to Hamlet's words and the stage directions in lines 7–9: '(Approaches the entry ... draws his sword)'. If you were the director of a production of Hamlet, how would you instruct the actor to deliver these lines? Pay specific attention to body language and tone. Motivate your instructions. **[3 Marks]**
Q3.3 Hamlet's hesitation in taking revenge is a sign of cowardice. Critically comment on the extent to which you agree with this statement. **[4 Marks]**

QUESTION 4: HAMLET – ESSAY QUESTION

Hamlet's behaviour throughout the play has unintended consequences. Critically discuss the extent to which you agree with the above statement. Your response should take the form of a well-constructed essay of 400–450 words (2–2½ pages). **[25 Marks]**

QUESTION 5: HAMLET – CONTEXTUAL QUESTION

Read the extracts below (Act 1 scene 2) and then answer the questions that follow.

CLAUDIUS
But now, my cousin Hamlet, and my son–
HAMLET
A little more than kin, and less than kind.
CLAUDIUS
How is it that the clouds still hang on you?
HAMLET
Not so, my lord, I am too much i'th' sun.
GERTRUDE
Good Hamlet, cast thy nightly colour off, And let thine eye look like a friend on Denmark. Do not for ever with thy vailèd lids Seek for thy noble father in the dust. Thou know'st 'tis common–all that lives must die, Passing through nature to eternity.
HAMLET
Ay, madam, it is common.
GERTRUDE
If it be,
Why seems it so particular with thee?
HAMLET
Seems, madam? Nay, it is. I know not 'seems'. 'Tis not alone my inky cloak, good mother, Nor customary suits of solemn black, Nor windy suspiration of forced breath No, nor the fruitful river in the eye Nor the dejected haviour of the visage, Together with all forms, moods, shows of grief That can denote me truly. These indeed 'seem',
For they are actions that a man might play; But I have that within which passeth show– These but the trappings and the suits of woe.
CLAUDIUS
'Tis sweet and commendable in your nature, Hamlet, To give these mourning duties to your father; But you must know your father lost a father; That father lost, lost his; and the survivor bound In filial obligation for some term To do obsequious sorrow. But to persever In obstinate condolement is a course Of impious stubbornness, 'tis unmanly grief, It shows a will most incorrect to heaven, A heart unfortified, a mind impatient, An understanding simple and unschooled.

Q5.1 Refer to line 2: 'A little more than kin, and less than kind.' Account for Hamlet's reaction to Claudius's greeting. **[3 Marks]**
Q5.2 Refer to lines 5–10: 'Good Hamlet, cast ... nature to eternity.' Suggest what motivates Gertrude to utter these words in the above lines. **[3 Marks]**
Q5.3 Refer to lines 30–32: 'But to persever ... 'tis unmanly grief'. In the light of later events, comment on whether Claudius is being sincere. **[3 Marks]**
Q5.4 Refer to line 33: 'It shows a will most incorrect to heaven'. Discuss the irony in this line in the context of the play. **[3 Marks]**

QUESTION 6: HAMLET – CONTEXTUAL QUESTION

Read the extracts below (Act 3 scene 2) and then answer the questions that follow.

HAMLET (to GERTRUDE)
Madam, how like you this play?
GERTRUDE
The lady protests too much, methinks.
HAMLET
O, but she'll keep her word.
CLAUDIUS
Have you heard the argument? Is there no offence in't?
HAMLET
No, no, they do but jest, poison in jest. No offence i'th' world.
CLAUDIUS
What do you call the play?
HAMLET
The Mousetrap. Marry, how? Tropically. This play is the image of a murder done in Vienna. Gonzago is the Duke's name, his wife Baptista. You shall see anon. 'Tis a knavish piece of work; but what o' that? Your majesty, and we that have free souls, it touches us not. Let the galled jade wince, our withers are unwrung.

Enter PLAYER LUCIANUS

This is one Lucianus, nephew to the King.

HAMLET (To LUCIANUS)
Begin, murderer. Pox, leave thy damnable faces and begin. Come: 'the croaking raven doth bellow for revenge'.
PLAYER LUCIANUS
Thoughts black, hands apt, drugs fit, and time agreeing, Confederate season, else no creature seeing; Thou mixture rank of midnight weeds collected, With Hecate's ban thrice blasted, thrice infected, Thy natural magic and dire property On wholesome life usurp immediately.

He pours the poison in the PLAYER KING'S ear

HAMLET
He poisons him i'th' garden for's estate. His name's Gonzago. The story is extant, and writ in choice Italian. You shall see anon how the murderer gets the love of Gonzago's wife. **OPHELIA**
The King rises.

HAMLET
What, frighted with false fire?
GERTRUDE (to CLAUDIUS)
How fares my lord?
POLONIUS
Give o'er the play.
CLAUDIUS
Give me some light. Away.

Q6.1 Refer to lines 4–5: 'Have you heard ... no/offence in't?' Account for Claudius's question. **[3 Marks]**
Q6.2 Discuss the significance of Hamlet's choice of play, The Mousetrap (line 9). **[3 Marks]**
Q6.3 Refer to lines 17–20: '(To LUCIANUS)/Begin, murderer. ... bellow for/ revenge.' If you were the director of a production of Hamlet, how would you instruct the actor to deliver these lines? Pay specific attention to body language and tone. Motivate your instructions. **[3 Marks]**
Q6.4 Hamlet resorts to deception to serve his own interests. Do you agree with this statement? Justify your response. **[4 Marks]**

QUESTION 7: HAMLET – ESSAY QUESTION

Hamlet is responsible for his own tragic fate.
Assess the validity of this statement.
Your response should take the form of a well-constructed essay of 400–450 words (2–2½ pages). **[25 Marks]**

QUESTION 8: HAMLET – CONTEXTUAL QUESTION

Read the extracts below (Act 1 scene 5) and then answer the questions that follow.

HORATIO
Not I, my lord, by heaven.
MARCELLUS
Nor I, my lord.
HAMLET
How say you then, would heart of man once think it? But you'll be secret
HORATIO AND MARCELLUS
Ay, by heaven, my lord.

HAMLET
There's ne'er a villain dwelling in all Denmark But he's an arrant knave.
HORATIO
There needs no ghost, my lord, come from the grave To tell us this.
HAMLET
Why, right, you are i'th' right, And so without more circumstance at all I hold it fit that we shake hands and part, You as your business and desires shall point you – For every man has business and desire, Such as it is – and for mine own poor part, Look you, I'll go pray.

HORATIO
O day and night, but this is wondrous strange!
HAMLET
And therefore as a stranger give it welcome. There are more things in heaven and earth, Horatio, Than are dreamt of in our philosophy. But come, Here as before, never, so help you mercy, How strange or odd soe'er I bear myself – As I perchance hereafter shall think meet To put an antic disposition on – That you at such time seeing me never shall, With arms encumbered thus, or this headshake, Or by pronouncing of some doubtful phrase As 'Well, we know' or 'We could an if we would', Or 'If we list to speak', or 'There be, an if they might', Or such ambiguous giving out, to note That you know aught of me – this not to do, So grace and mercy at your most need help you, Swear.

Q8.1 Refer to line 5: 'But you'll be secret?' Account for Hamlet's concern with secrecy at this point in the play. **[3 Marks]**
Q8.2 Explain the Ghost's motive in approaching Hamlet. **[3 Marks]**
Q8.3 Refer to lines 17–18: '– and for mine own poor part,'/'Look you, I'll go pray.' Discuss the extent to which it would be justifiable for the audience to pity Hamlet at this point in the play. **[3 Marks]**
Q8.4 Refer to line 26: 'To put an antic disposition on –'. Critically comment on Hamlet's decision to pretend to be mad. **[3 Marks]**

QUESTION 9: HAMLET – CONTEXTUAL QUESTION

Read the extracts below (Act 3 scene 4) and then answer the questions that follow.

Enter GERTRUDE and POLONIUS
POLONIUS
He will come straight. Look you lay home to him. Tell him his pranks have been too broad to bear with, And that your grace hath screened and stood between Much heat and him. I'll silence me e'en here. Pray you be round with him.

HAMLET (offstage)
Mother, mother, mother!
GERTRUDE
I'll warrant you. Fear me not. Withdraw; I hear him coming.

POLONIUS hides behind the arras. Enter HAMLET

HAMLET
Now, mother, what's the matter?
GERTRUDE
Hamlet, thou hast thy father much offended.
HAMLET
Mother, you have my father much offended.
GERTRUDE
Come, come, you answer with an idle tongue.
HAMLET
Go, go, you question with a wicked tongue.
GERTRUDE
Why, how now, Hamlet?
HAMLET
What's the matter now?
GERTRUDE
Have you forgot me?
HAMLET
No, by the rood, not so. You are the Queen, your husband's brother's wife. But – would you were not so – you are my mother.
GERTRUDE
Nay, then, I'll set those to you that can speak.
HAMLET
Come, come, and sit you down. You shall not budge. You go not till I set you up a glass Where you may see the inmost part of you.
GERTRUDE
What wilt thou do? Thou wilt not murder me? Help, help, ho!
POLONIUS (behind the arras)
What ho! Help, help, help!
HAMLET
How now, a rat? Dead for a ducat, dead.

He thrusts his sword through the arras

POLONIUS
O, I am slain!
GERTRUDE (to HAMLET)
O me, what hast thou done?
HAMLET
Nay, I know not. Is it the King?
GERTRUDE
O, what a rash and bloody deed is this!
HAMLET
A bloody deed – almost as bad, good mother, As kill a king and marry with his brother.

Q9.1 Refer to lines 4–5: 'And that your grace ...'/'Much heat and him.' Suggest how Gertrude's later actions will validate this statement. **[3 Marks]**
Q9.2 Refer to line 12: 'Hamlet, thou hast thy father much offended.' Comment on the irony of Gertrude's words. **[3 Marks]**
Q9.3 Refer to lines 23–26: 'Come, come, and ...'/'part of you.' If you were the director of a production of Hamlet, how would you instruct the actor to deliver these lines? Justify your instructions with reference to both body language and tone. **[3 Marks]**
Q9.4 Using this extract as a starting point and drawing on your knowledge of the play as a whole, critically comment on the nature of betrayal as presented in the play. **[4 Marks]**

QUESTION 10: HAMLET – ESSAY QUESTION

The problem of making moral choices is a significant issue in the play.
Critically assess the validity of this statement.
Your response should take the form of a well-constructed essay of 400–450 words (2–2½ pages). **[25 Marks]**

QUESTION 11: HAMLET – CONTEXTUAL QUESTION

Read the extracts below (Act 3 scene 1) and then answer the questions that follow.

HAMLET
Get thee to a nunnery. Why wouldst thou be a breeder of sinners? I am myself indifferent honest, but yet I could accuse me of such things that it were better my mother had not borne me. I am very proud, revengeful, ambitious, with more offences at my beck than I have thoughts to put them in, imagination to give them shape, or time to act them in. What should such fellows as I do crawling between heaven and earth? We are arrant knaves, all. Believe none of us. Go thy ways to a nunnery. Where's your father?

OPHELIA
At home, my lord.
HAMLET
Let the doors be shut upon him, that he may play the fool nowhere but in's own house. Farewell.
OPHELIA
O help him, you sweet heavens!
HAMLET
If thou dost marry, I'll give thee this plague for thy dowry: be thou as chaste as ice, as pure as snow, thou shalt not escape calumny. Get thee to a nunnery, go, farewell. Or if thou wilt needs marry, marry a fool; for wise men know well enough what monsters you make of them. To a nunnery, go, and quickly, too. Farewell.
OPHELIA
O heavenly powers, restore him!

Q11.1 Account for Hamlet's feelings toward Ophelia at this stage of the play. (2)
Q11.2 Refer to lines 3–4: 'that it were better/my mother had not borne me.' How does this statement reflect Hamlet's state of mind? **[2 Marks]**
Q11.3 Refer to line 11: 'At home, my lord.' Suggest a reason for Hamlet's annoyance at Ophelia's response. **[2 Marks]**
Q11.4 Discuss how the play demonstrates that Ophelia is subject to patriarchal (male) domination in her home. **[2 Marks]**
Q11.5 Comment on the extent to which it would be justifiable to attribute Ophelia's suicide to Hamlet. **[3 Marks]**

QUESTION 12: HAMLET – CONTEXTUAL QUESTION

Read the extracts below (Act 4 scene 7) and then answer the questions that follow.

CLAUDIUS
Now must your conscience my acquittance seal, And you must put me in your heart for friend, Sith you have heard, and with a knowing ear, That he which hath your noble father slain Pursued my life.
LAERTES
It well appears. But tell me Why you proceeded not against these feats, So crimeful and so capital in nature, As by your safety, wisdom, all things else, You mainly were stirred up.

CLAUDIUS
O, for two special reasons, Which may to you perhaps seem much unsinewed, And yet to me they're strong. The Queen his mother Lives almost by his looks; and for myself – My virtue or my plague, be it either which – She's so conjunctive to my life and soul That, as the star moves not but in his sphere, I could not but by her. The other motive Why to a public count I might not go Is the great love the general gender bear him, Who, dipping all his faults in their affection, Would, like the spring that turneth wood to stone, Convert his guilts to graces; so that my arrows, Too slightly timbered for so loud a wind, Would have reverted to my bow again, And not where I had aimed them.
LAERTES
And so have I a noble father lost, A sister driven into desperate terms, Who has, if praises may go back again, Stood challenger, on mount, of all the age For her perfections. But my revenge will come.
CLAUDIUS
Break not your sleeps for that. You must not think That we are made of stuff so flat and dull That we can let our beard be shook with danger, And think it pastime. You shortly shall hear more. I loved your father, and we love ourself. And that, I hope, will teach you to imagine –

Q12.1 Refer to line 14: 'Lives almost by his looks'. Explain how Gertrude's final act will clearly indicate her love for Hamlet. **[3 Marks]**
Q12.2 Refer to line 2: 'And you must put me in your heart for friend'. Discuss the irony in this line. **[3 Marks]**
Q12.3 Refer to lines 27–31: 'And so have ... revenge will come.' If you were the director of a production of Hamlet, describe how you would direct the actor playing Laertes to deliver these lines. Justify your answer with reference to both body language and tone **[3 Marks]**
Q12.4 Claudius is a villain without any redeeming qualities. Using your knowledge of the play as a whole, critically discuss the extent to which you agree with this statement.
[4 Marks]

Q1 *There are two sides to Claudius - the cowardly, treacherous villain; and the tormented sinner who longs for redemption, is benevolent and loves his queen.*

Discuss these two aspects of Claudius's character, showing which, in your opinion, is more dominant.

Q2 *The predicaments that Hamlet faces are those that have always confronted mankind: the desire to take revenge; rejected love; parent /child conflicts.*

Do you agree?

Q3 *Claudius is a weak king, ruled by passion and ambition. Gertrude is a foolish woman, insensitive to the effect of her actions. They are both to blame for the corrupt kingdom in which Hamlet finds himself.*

Do you agree with this assessment?

Q4 *Had there been no women whom he loved, Hamlet would have coped perfectly well with the situation in Denmark.*

Do you agree?

Q5 *Polonius is not a major character in the sense that Hamlet and Claudius are: yet he is apparently a leading figure in the court, he is directly or indirectly involved in much of the main action, and his accidental murder at Hamlet's hands is certainly a 'major' event of considerable significance and dramatic import.*

What is your view of Polonius' role in the play? Refer in particular to the dramatic importance of his death.

Q6 *"O God, Horatio, what a wounded name,*
Things standing thus unknown, shall I leave behind me!
If thou didst ever hold me in thy heart,
Absent thee from felicity awhile,
And in this harsh world draw thy breath in pain
To tell my story."

Imagine that you are Horatio and that you have been invited to write an account of your dealings with Hamlet, giving your interpretation of "his story". Decide what sort of name (reputation) you wish to have left behind for Hamlet - and then tell his story accordingly.

Q7 *Hamlet asks of his father's ghost in Act 3 Scene 4:*

"Do you not come your tardy son to chide,
That, lapsed in time and passion, lets go by
The important acting of your dread command?"

To what extent do you agree with Hamlet's assessment of himself at this stage of the play? Pay particular attention to the highlighted words.

Q8 *Some readers believe Hamlet procrastinates after the Ghost's direct statements, " Revenge his foul and most unnatural murder," and "The serpent that did sting thy father's life/Now wears his crown." Others say he immediately puts his plans in action.*

What is your view? Argue in support of your opinion, showing your understanding of Hamlet's procrastination or action throughout the play.

Q9 *Hamlet's behaviour throughout the play has consequences (for Denmark and for the people with whom he mixes) which he would not have expected or planned.*

Discuss.

Q10 *"Therefore, since brevity is the soul of wit,*
And tediousness the limbs and outward flourishes,
I will be brief. Your noble son is mad.
Mad call I it; for to define true madness,
What is it but to bed nothing else but mad?" (Polonius)

There have been many discussions about whether or not Hamlet was mad. Polonius was convinced he knew the answer. Hamlet declared that he was only mad occasionally and Fortinbras and Horatio do not raise the issue. Even Laertes, who was mad with anger as a result of his father's murder and Ophelia's insanity, does not dismiss Hamlet as a madman. With whom do you side? Why?

Q11 *Hamlet is no "sweet prince". In pursuit of his revenge, he becomes increasingly ruthless, callous and cruel.*

In the light of the above statement examine Hamlet's relationships with the other characters in the play and decide whether or not you agree with the comment.

Q12 *Daughter, sister, lover - in all these relationships Ophelia simply accepts the fact that she is being dominated.*

Do you agree?

Q13 *A man of spontaneous action rather than one who is given to contriving and plotting.*

How acceptable do you find this comment on Hamlet's character? Discuss with reference to the incidents in the play.

Q14 What different aspects of Hamlet's character are brought out by his dealings with TWO of the following:

(i) Horatio
(ii) (ii) Ophelia
(iii) (iii) Rosencrantz and Guildenstern

Q15 *Hamlet is placed by Fate in a position where his noble qualities are made ineffective by his fatal indecision.*

Discuss the character of Hamlet in the light of this comment, illustrating your answer from the play itself.

Q16 *In Hamlet Shakespeare explores the relationships between various children and their parents. He looks at the influence a parent has on a child and the value of parental guidance.*

Discuss this aspect of the play taking into account Polonius and his children and Hamlet and his parents. (Your answer should concentrate more on Hamlet than on Polonius.)

Q17 Write an essay in which you discuss what the play has to say about political power and the use and abuse of such power.

Q18 *In the course of the play, Hamlet grows up.*

Do you agree completely, partly, or not at all? Explain your opinion.

Q19 *'Although Hamlet sometimes disappoints loved ones, tells lies, and even murders, we are still able to sympathise with him.'*

Discuss this statement in an essay of about 1½ pages, showing clearly whether you believe this to be true.

Q20 *There are many contrasts in the play, Hamlet. For example: there is honesty but also dishonesty, faithfulness and infidelity, love and hatred, honour and dishonour, revenge and forgiveness. This suggests that nothing was simple, nothing was easy.*
And for the three hours of the play we, the audience, find ourselves constantly swept from one opinion to the opposite. Sometimes we agree with what is happening on stage, at other times we find it disgusting.
This is why it is difficult to decide exactly what kind of person Hamlet is.

Discuss.

Q21 *A 'foil' is anything that by contrast of some kind makes more apparent the quality or qualities of something else.*
Three of Hamlet's foils are young men who, like Hamlet, have, or imagine they have, good cause for revenge. They are Laertes, Fortinbras and Pyrrhus (the young Greer warrior in the play-extract spoken by Hamlet and the First Player).

If you compare and contrast Hamlet with each of these characters, how does it affect your understanding of him? Deal with these three foils one by one.

Q22 *There are only two female characters in Hamlet: Gertrude and Ophelia. What are these two? Innocent dupes? Manipulated victims of a patriarchal (male-dominated) society? Cunning self-seekers who at least partly deserve their fates? All of the above? None of the above? Is it even valid to discuss them in the same breath?*

What do you think?

Q23 *"Confused, bewildered and frightened"*
"Conniving, cunning and in full control"

Consider and discuss the character of Hamlet in the light of these two extremes.

Q24 *"There are many subjects in Hamlet. There is politics, force opposed to morality. There is the tragedy of love as well as family drama. There is everything you want, including deep psychological analysis, a bloody story, a duel, and general slaughter."*

Select one of the issues raised by Kott in the above statement and, referring to the play, show how this play has taken on universal appeal and value.

Q25 *"Bear Hamlet, like a soldier, to the stage;*
For he was likely, had he been put on,
To have proved most royal: and for his passage,
The soldier's music and the rite of war
Speak loudly for him."

Fortinbras believes that if Hamlet had been faced with the responsibility of kingship, he would have been a fine king, and orders that Hamlet be accorded the funeral honours of a royal warrior.

Do you agree with this viewpoint? Discuss the idea, referring to this and other passages in the play.

Q26 *"Hamlet, the man, represents a type of individual greatness that is not bound by time or space. He and his philosophising are as real and as topical today as they must have been in Shakespeare's time."*

Discuss this statement with reference to the text.

Q27 "There is a divinity which shapes our ends,
Rough-hew them how we will."

Hamlet utters these words in Act V scene 2 on his return to Denmark. A subtle change seems to have come over him; in what way is the above quotation indicative of this change? From your knowledge of the play as a whole, would you say that this philosophy is vindicated?

Q28 Why does Hamlet procrastinate in carrying out the ghost's instructions? Is Hamlet a coward or a hero? When Hamlet finally does kill Claudius, is it not perhaps the best time to have done so?

Q29 Consider aspects of *Hamlet, Prince of Denmark* that make this play a tragedy.

(Besides the structure of the play, think of Hamlet's isolation - he also rises far above the other characters in the play - his betrayal, his wasted potential, his being a "victim of circumstances", et al.)

Q30 *In many ways Hamlet is an anachronism in the play ... He represents a "new" type of independent thinking; a rational, intellectual approach to moral problems more in keeping with a much later age of intellectual enlightenment; he needs to justify his actions to himself - he has a moral conscience; and it is this sense of personal integrity that accounts for his hatred of deception.*

Discuss.

Q31 To what extent, do you think, is Shakespeare presenting Hamlet as a type of ideal man?

(Your answer must include an assessment of Hamlet's procrastination. Does this vindicate the theory of Hamlet as an ideal or is it a flaw in his character?)

AUTHOR

Evelyn Samuel was born in South Africa, educated at the University of Durban-Westville, gaining a BA in English, Speech and Drama. She then went on to gain a Higher Education Diploma at the University of South Africa, and then onto the UK where her knowledge and skills were applied in educating students to achieve top grades in English Language and Literature up to A-level. Evelyn gained her Qualified Teacher Status in 2006, but in her pursuit to explore new horizons, continued her education gaining Diplomas in teaching English as a Foreign Language' to International Students, 'Writing Stories for Children', and most recently, gaining a Diploma in 'Travel Journalism'. Apart from teaching and writing, Evelyn's interests include travel to exotic places, cycling, dance, cuisine, and exploring new horizons.

To date, Evelyn has written many Study Guides to help student achieve top grades. Check-out the info below.

www.EveSuperEasyBooks.com
EveSuperEasyBooks@gmail.com

STUDY GUIDE

Evelyn provides an in depth **SUPER SUPER EASY** interpretation of Shakespeare's HAMLET, a popular poignant revenge tragedy, first performed circa 1601. This guide is a must for those students determined to achieve a top grade in English Literature at any level from Key Stage 3 to GCSE to A-level.

STORY LINE

Political intrigue, lust, and avarice by a usurper combinate in a carnage of death in the final scene of the tragedy.

The ghost claiming to be the spirit of Hamlet's death father seeks revenge for his murder by his brother Claudius who has now usurped the throne of Denmark. It expects Hamlet to enact this revenge.

Unsure if the ghost is genuine in its accusations, Hamlet embarks on a strategy of feigning madness. The marriage of his mother Gertrude to Claudius so soon after his father death, makes Hamlet suspicious his father was murdered for power and lust.

To convince all that he is mad, Hamlet rejects Ophelia's love, and seeks to find the truth. Claudius reveals his guilt when Hamlet instructs a band of players to enact the murder of his father.

Ophelia's father Polonius is inadvertently killed by Hamlet, which causes her to become mad and drown. Hamlet is exiled to England but by a quirk of fate discovers letters ordering his immediate execution by the King of England. Hamlet changes the contents of the letters, ordering his school fellows Rosencrantz and Guildenstern to be executed instead.

Ophelia's brother Laertes is manipulated by Claudius to take revenge on Hamlet by devious methods of poisoned sword and poisoned wine in an exhibition sword duel. The final outcome is the death of Gertrude the queen, Laertes, and the villainous Claudius the king. With no heirs, young Fortinbras lays claim to the throne of Denmark. The ghost is avenged but Hamlet is no more.

www.ingramcontent.com/pod-product-compliance
Lightning Source LLC
Chambersburg PA
CBHW080907190726
48294CB00008B/1998